500

Strangest Racing Stories

500
Strangest Racing Stories

Graham Sharpe

A Racing Post company

DEDICATION

TO: The Bish; Mikey M; Golak, Hushie and Lawro: the five strangest and best racing companions a chap could ever hope for. Not forgetting the strangest racing WAGS – Sheila; Barbie; Shirl; Trish and Elaine – winners every one.

Published in 2007 by Highdown,
an imprint of Raceform Ltd
Compton, Newbury, Berkshire, RG20 6NL

A catalogue record for this book is available from the British Library.

ISBN 978-1-905156-34-4

Cover designed by Tracey Scarlett
Interiors designed by Adrian Morrish

Printed in Great Britain by William Clowes Ltd, Beccles, Suffolk

STRANGELY ENOUGH ...

I am not aware that legendary Sixties hell-raiser and rock singer Jim Morrison, leader of The Doors, ever sat on, or bet on, a horse. He did, though, write an epic and strange track entitled 'Horse Latitudes' about 18th century sailors chucking horses over the side of boats and, more importantly, a big hit single called 'People Are Strange'. I recall thinking when I first heard the lyrics of this song just how accurate they were: 'People are strange when you're a stranger, faces look ugly when you're alone'.

In so many walks of life 'strange' equals interesting – more interesting than 'normal', so much more interesting, in fact, that whenever like-minded people gather to talk about their hobbies, their work, their lives, it is invariably the element of strange which creates the biggest stir in their discussions and conversations.

People are strange, and they love to hear about strange, and, being the author of the biography of the strangest politician ever, the late Screaming Lord Sutch, I love to write about strange, which is how this investigation into the strangest elements of horse racing has come to be compiled.

I have never been able to resist stories of strange and unlikely racecourse and racing events. I have experienced many at first hand, and anyone who has ever been racing anywhere will invariably experience something strange whilst doing so – it is one of the unwritten laws of the Universe and one which racing has exploited so successfully over the years. When you enter a racecourse you leave the world of normal behind at the turnstile or gate.

Racing's lengthy history and worldwide appeal provides rich pickings for connoisseurs of the strange and I reckon this book can justifiably claim to be the strangest volume yet written about its strange and wonderful subject. And whereas Jim Morrison's 'People Are Strange' included the couplet, 'When you're strange, no one remembers your name' that is far from the case in horse racing. Not only have the names of the strange been recorded and remembered – they can now be properly and deservedly celebrated.

I have delved into the darkest recesses of racing to uncover stratas of strange which otherwise would have been lost and forgotten; scoured almost forgotten chapters of long out of print volumes; and chased up the truth behind apocryphal yarns, long lost legends and mythical lore.

Many people may be aware of some of these strands of strangeness from centuries of material – I guarantee that no one will know or have come across them all. Except me, that is and, as many who know me will tell you, they don't come much stranger than me, betting without John McCririck, of course. Which I take as a compliment.

Join me in the strangest trip through the world of horse racing you are ever likely to undergo – until the next time you go racing, that is.

Graham Sharpe

1. GLAND NATIONAL?

When the fertility of racehorse-turned-stallion Rabelais began to wane at the mature age of 28, his owners opted for an unprecedented course of action in order to prolong his breeding career.

Standing at Maisons Laffitte in France, Rabelais was handed over for treatment to a Professor Voronoff, whose revolutionary technique involved acquiring another horse – one which was 'perfectly useless for racing and of no value as a stallion', and carrying out an operation whereby 'parts of this animal's reproductive glands were grafted on to Rabelais'.

Stunned members of the Thoroughbred Breeders' Association were the first people from the outside world to hear about this equine Frankenstein-style exercise at their 1928 Annual General Meeting.

They were told that although the operation itself had proved successful, Rabelais had died several days later, ostensibly from the effects of chloroform during the operation – what you might, and I stress, might term a genital anaesthetic, then!

Addressing the AGM, Mr G H Drummond explained that 'the operation implanted in the subject some of the vital qualities of the inferior animal' and warned that 'this would be a most dangerous practice if imported to England.'

As long-standing member, Mr Drummond further observed, 'An animal, after being gland grafted, is not the same animal as it was before.'

Evidence was furnished to the AGM that similar operations had been performed upon Belgian stallion Ayala, and Ard Patrick in Germany – with similar, ultimately fatal consequences. It was also suggested that operations planting the ovary of one mare on another, had taken place.

Horrified, members of the Association duly voted on the motion moved by Mr George Lambton 'that this Association strongly disapproves of the practice of gland grafting.'

Carried unanimously.

2. MIST OUT

'It ain't right. I know I ain't did it' was the despairing comment, blurted out in a Southern drawl by American jockey Sylvester Carmouche, as he was convicted of perhaps the most audacious fraud perpetrated during a horse race. Carmouche hit on his brainwave as the runners lined up at Delta Downs racecourse in Louisiana in January 1990. They came under orders in swirling fog as Carmouche eased his mount, Landing Officer, a 23/1 outsider, to the rear of the field, allowing the remaining runners to head off into the mist as he gradually dropped behind the tailenders, dawdling along in the fog until the others returned for their second circuit.

At which point Carmouche galvanised his fresh mount to dash ahead of the pack, hurtling home 25 lengths clear of the tiring field.

No one was deceived for long and the Louisiana Racing Commission suspended him for ten years – then, to add insult to injury, Carmouche was taken to trial by State Prosecutors for the attempted theft of $90 – the difference between the $140 he would have been paid had his victory been, er, conventional – and the usual $50 riding fee.

He was convicted and ordered to spend 30 days in jail, despite his protestations that he hadn't been spotted in the race because he had 'kept to the far side of the course'.

He wasn't mist.

**The whole field got lost in fog once – at Derby on November 13, 1889, when the track's Foston Plate was declared void after the runners became disorientated and ended up running behind a cricket pavilion.

**In the late 1860s, racing writer Alexander Scott was at a race meeting at West Drayton where 'a very heavy mist hung over the course, making it impossible to see more than 70 yards or so.' He watched a novice hurdle in which one of the runners fell on the first circuit – 'he trotted behind a haystack at the edge of the course. When the other runners came round for the last circuit, I was staggered to see our fallen horseman jump in behind and, being on a fresh horse, he won easily in the end.'

**In 1947 Eddie Dempsey rode Caughoo to a 100/1 shock Grand National triumph. The Irish jockey was accused some time later by runner-up rider Daniel McCann of taking a short cut through fog from the fence before Becher's Brook to the one after Valentine's. The pair came to blows and the dispute ended in court where McCann's allegations were thrown out.

3. WE ARE JUST A LITTLE AMUSED

When the Queen's horse Enharmonic won a race at Spain's homely little San Sebastian racecourse (a Basque region track where, on my last visit they announced the start of races with a blast of the William Tell Overture) in August 1993 the Royal financiers looked forward to the injection of £53,000 of foreign currency from the prize money.

By Christmas-time those officials began to chase the money up, a little concerned at the non arrival of the missing wads of pesetas, only to discover that their Spanish counterparts declared that, for tax purposes, they needed proof of Her Majesty's nationality.

Baffled English mandarins eventually satisfied the recalcitrant senors, who handed over the dosh, with the Queen's racing manager, Lord Carnarvon, observing with a droll straight face, 'It appears the Spanish authorities wanted proof that the Queen is British. It is really quite amusing.'

**In July 2006 it was revealed that Sheikh Mohammed, one of the wealthiest men in the world, had been refused an owner's licence in Japan, which would have enabled him to have runners in their top events – for financial reasons.

'The reason given was that they questioned Darley Japan's financial ability to have horses in training' reported the Sheikh's bloodstock adviser, John Ferguson.

Cynics speculated that the decision might have had more to do with parochial protectionism.

4. JAILBIRD

The 1929 Derby winner Trigo's mother, five-time winner Athasi had, another claim to fame being one of the few racehorses, perhaps the only one, unless you know better, ever to be jailed.

Changing hands in Ireland to corn merchant Mr William Burnett, after the death of her original purchaser, his brother D W Barnett, she was being escorted to her new owner by a groom who decided to prepare himself for the trek by taking a dram or two – and was subsequently arrested for being 'drunk in charge of a mare', the pair of them being locked up as a result.

5. BACKING A WINNER AFTER THE RACE HAS BEEN WON

In April 1999 punters at Newbury were freely permitted to back a horse which had already won the race he was contesting.

The Knayton Claiming Stakes at Thirsk was won by 15/8 favourite Diamond Promise and the result clearly shown on TV screens at Newbury where racegoers waiting to bet on the next race there were told that they could not do so until the Thirsk race had finished.

Pointing out that it had already done so and that they knew what had won, tote staff insisted that their computers were indicating that this was not the case.

'Are you telling me that the tote is still open (for Thirsk) and if I wanted I could have a bet?' one woman racegoer asked, and was told she could. 'So I had £10 on Diamond Promise' she said, 'I mentioned to a friend they were accepting bets on a race already run and it rippled round the room. Another table picked up about £160.'

The Tote later admitted to paying out some £2,000 from 25 bets. 'I have to say an error was made' commented chief executive, John Heaton.

They said it couldn't happen again – and it probably hasn't, but in May 2006, Kempton winner Resolve, which should have paid a dividend of £3.60, was shown as paying £22.50. 'Some lucky punters were able to take advantage of the situation,' confirmed Tote spokesman Paul Petrie.

6. WHEN IS A TATTENHAM A TOTTENHAM?

Everyone knows that the runners in the world's most famous race, the Epsom Derby, run round the racing world's most famous bend – Tattenham Corner. But should they? Not according to the Bloodstock Breeders' Review for 1929 which revealed, 'From old documents it appears that, about the time of the Stuarts, a member of the Tottenham family brought a tract of land in the parish of Banstead, which remained in the possession of the family for many years, and which came to a point at the spot where the present five-furlong course joins the Derby course, abutting on the road from Epsom to Walton. The corner at the point of this land became known as 'Tottenhams's Corner' which was corrupted to

'Tattenham's Corner'. It is thus incorrect to talk of horses coming 'round Tattenham Corner' as the corner is on the opposite side of the course.'

And it is a virtually unknown fact that in 1876 plans were put in train which might well have changed the course for ever.

Epsom's Clerk of the Course, a man named Dorling, came up with a scheme which involved 'diverting the Derby track in order to avoid paying a rental of £1,000 a year to Mr Carew, then lord of the manor at Epsom,' divulged racing figure George Hodgman, a prominent bookmaker, owner and trainer of the day.

'If he could have saved so substantial a sum, and not made worse an already bad track, well and good. But anyone familiar with the course and anyone who had seen the fresh staking-out must have immediately recognised that the safety of and fairness to competitors were being sacrificed to motives of economy.'

Hodgman was so concerned that he called in the assistance of the turf's most influential administrator of the day, Admiral Rous, asking him to look closely at Dorling's dealings – 'The Admiral coincided with me to the letter, and he requested the Messrs Weatherby to write to Mr Dorling, instructing him that on no consideration was he to interfere with the Derby track.'

7. GRAVE MATTERS

When racing fan Derek Plunton of Winchester died in May 1998 his family took out an advertisement in the local paper, requesting 'no flowers or donations' but suggesting that mourners should back Derek's 2000 Guineas tip, King of Kings – which duly obliged at 7/2.

• In May 1989 Truro man Alan Rix died aged 62 and was cremated in a coffin containing betting slips and a copy of the *Sporting Life*, before his ashes were scattered at Newton Abbot racecourse.

• Scottish racing man, Bill Brown knew he was dying and asked his vicar, the Reverend Rob White to ask mourners at his 1988 funeral to back Wolverhampton runner Grey General – which was a 4/1 winner.

• And way back in 1801 another tip from beyond the grave paid off when Cox, trainer of

Derby hope, Eleanor, died before the race was run, with his final words being: 'Depend on it, that Eleanor is a Hell of a mare'. She won the Classic.

8. LIFE'S A BEACH

The conditions of entry for fillies entered in the 8.30 race at Hollywood Park Racetrack on Friday, July 14, 2006, were a little on the unusual side – 'Girls of all ages and races may apply. Must look great in a bikini. Must also have a great personality, fun spirit, and be able to run a little bit'.

Yes, the runners for the first annual Bikini Mile – race distance quarter of a mile – were '14 hot girls in bikinis'.

The girls were paraded before the race, wearing numbered armbands and running shoes as well as their bikinis, and were given a trumpet fanfare. They were then led out on to the track and to the starting gate before the stalls opened and the runners, battling for a first prize of $500, sprinted for the line.

Sadly, although there is photographic evidence of the race, no record seems to have been kept of the names of the placed runners, despite my efforts to obtain them from the track itself.

9. AND YOU THOUGHT McCRIRICK WAS BAD ENOUGH!

Racegoers in the 19th century could find themselves rubbing shoulders with some odd characters.

Racing writer 'Thormanby' wrote of the 'old time eccentrics' of the turf in his 1913 book, *Sporting Stories* in which he told of 'Donkey Jemmy' who 'used to wear a yellow wig and made a living braying like a donkey. Sixpence a bray was his charge,' Thormanby wrote. 'Many old Turfites will remember a thin, middle-aged man who used to appear in woman's attire with ribbons in his hair, a faded yellow fan in one hand, and a green and pink parasol in the other, who began a dialogue commencing with 'Well, Lady Jane, how are the flowers today?'

Then there was the 'list-seller', Matthias Elderton, better known as Jerry, 'who made fun for the lookers-on during the intervals of racing – with a wig and cocked hat on his head, and an old ragged uniform, sometimes naval, sometimes military, his fingers covered with brass rings, the neck of a bottle picked up from some luncheon-party stuck in his eye, he would strut up to some grandee, tap him on the shoulder, and with the affectation of an aristocratic drawl, say "How de do, my lord, how's her ladyship, and the little honourables?"'

Jerry was not above accosting Royalty, it seems, and held out his hand to the Prince Regent which, perhaps unwisely, 'the Prince did not disdain to shake.'

Jerry met a messy end during the 1848 Goodwood meeting. Standing on a coach playing the crowd, the horses shied and upset the cart throwing Jerry beneath it from where 'he was picked up in a fearfully crushed condition.'

10. BUTT YOU MUST BE F***ING JOKING, SO KISS MY A**E!

Racing was rocked, and opinions starkly divided, as three unusually high profile jockey-related disciplinary cases hit the sport in July 2006.

On Sunday, July 23 – ironically, only a few days after the World Cup Final had ended in controversy as French star Zinedine Zidane was sent off for head-butting an opponent – jockey Paul O'Neill was seen on the Attheraces TV channel head butting his mount City Affair at Stratford, after the horse had played up on its way to the start of a novice hurdle race, unseating O'Neill in the process.

Zidane's defence had been that his opponent had provoked him by insulting him. Some reports said that the Frenchman had been called 'son of a terrorist whore' by his Italian opponent. It seems unlikely that City Affair had made any such comment to O'Neill.

The pictures were picked up by news agencies and shown around the world, causing uproar and outrage even though it soon became obvious that the horse was not injured.

There was huge criticism of O'Neill's eventual punishment of a single day's suspension, justified by the authorities because the horse had not been hurt.

Dr Peter Webber defended their verdict – 'The outcome of his action was insignificant. The horse felt virtually nothing and certainly wasn't injured.'

Sportswriter Mick Dennis summed up the wider implications of the O'Neill case which seemed to have been overlooked but which would reverberate with potential racegoers. 'It was an act of violence against the horse. Would you take your family to see horses head-butted?'

On Thursday, July 27, jockey Paul Doe was suspended for ten days for persistently swearing at Newmarket stewards – reportedly calling one of them, Capt Adrian Pratt, 'a f***ing pig' – after being initially suspended for two days and fined £275 for a careless riding offence. The disciplinary panel declared it 'about as bad a case of abusive behaviour as can be imagined.'

'For some reason I snapped and went crazy' admitted Doe, later.

Those comparing Doe's punishment with O'Neill's wondered how significant the outcome of Doe's actions were. The stewards would have felt virtually nothing and certainly weren't injured.

On Saturday, July 29, Belgian superstar jockey Christophe Soumillon landed his first ever win at Ascot in some twenty attempts, several of which had resulted in criticism of his riding. Soumillon partnered Hurricane Run to victory in a thrilling finish to the King George VI and Queen Elizabeth Diamond Stakes. 'Understandably overcome with emotion, the Belgian placed his left hand over his heart', described *Racing Post* reporter Lee Mottershead, 'before guiding the index finger of that hand towards his derriere. With the digit in position, it was then directed into the interior of the posterior before being licked by his tongue, after which the end of the tongue was seen protruding for some moments.'

In his defence it was suggested by some apologists that this was an acceptable gesture 'within polite French society'.

To many of us it looked like an unmistakable invitation to onlookers and critics to 'kiss my arse'.

The jockey was banned for six days for excessive use of the whip during the race. But no action was taken over his gestures.

11. EARLIEST HANDS-DROPPER?

Punters hate nothing as much as a jockey who has a race won, only to switch off, drop his hands, and get caught on the line.

The history of such incidents is probably virtually as old as racing itself, but perhaps the earliest high profile example took place at Goodwood in the 1835 King's Guineas, a race in which betting in-running was also taking place!

Only two of the five declared runners had gone to post and Rockingham, winner of a Cup race the previous day, was the red hot 1/5 favourite.

All went as expected as Rockingham drew a dozen lengths clear of Lucifer whose jockey, Twitchett, had even been called upon by connections to ease off – at which point one spectator laid a companion odds of 800/1 about the apparently beaten horse.

Rockingham's jockey, Robinson, began to ease his mount to canter past the post, having won for a second time in 24 hours.

However, says a contemporary report of the race, 'The rider of Lucifer, instead of pulling up as ordered, kept his horse going, so that when Rockingham reached the stand, there was not half the distance between the two that there was at the distance-post; and Twitchett at this moment making a desperate rush, completely took Robinson by surprise within a few yards of the winning post, and before the latter could get his horse into action, had won the race by two lengths to the utter astonishment of every person on the course.

'To show how forlorn the chances of Lucifer's winning appeared at the distance-post, we may state that a bet of £100 to half-a-crown was actually laid on Rockingham at the stand.'

12. BOOTS WAS MADE FOR FALLING

Adelaide jumps jockey Les Boots was undoubtedly the world's worst jump jockey with a career record of 39 starts and 41 falls.

The discrepancy is accounted for by two falls in a single race, after remounting – followed by a third when he fell from the stretcher carrying him to the medical room!

Born in 1915, it was said that whenever he was racing over jumps his wife packed his pyjamas with his kit as he would probably be spending the night in hospital.

Boots turned to the flat with little more success – never finishing placed in any race. He retired in 1947 without a winner to his name and lived on until 1987.

13. I OBJECT – TO MYSELF!

Jockey Tony Charlton on Metal Oiseau was furious after the neck and neck photo finish with Gallant Effort at Fontwell in February 1993.

Believing himself to have been hampered or interfered with he immediately slapped in an objection to the 'winner' – only to discover that the photo-finish had shown him to be the winner.

He quickly withdrew the objection.

An equally dubious objection was made in April 1993 when Barry Leavy, who had fallen from Local Customer before the final fence at Sandon point to point, objected to winner Mount Argos – then wondered why the stewards declined the opportunity of awarding the race to a riderless horse.

14. DON'T HANG AROUND THERE, LADS

Okay, so there have been a few complaints about the viewing at the newly refurbished Ascot racecourse, but at least racegoers don't have to worry about multiple cadavers swinging gently in the breeze interrupting their view of the action.

Back on August,16, 1731, the organisers of the race meeting at York's brand new Knavesmire course had to plan for the fact that three robbers – knaves, indeed – Joseph Askwith, and brothers Richard and John Freeman – were due to be hanged there that morning, prior to the start of racing.

With co-operation all round, time was found to hang the villains – despite all three proclaiming their innocence with their very dying breaths – allowing the crowd to get a good look at their duly lifeless corpses, and then get them cut down in order to enable racegoers to get an uninterrupted view of Lord Lonsdale's Monkey winning both heats of the 100 guineas King's Plate.

Eight years later, notorious highwayman Dick Turpin was put to death at Knavesmire, prior to the race meeting at which the King's Plate was won by Smallhopes.

No wonder the course quickly gained a reputation for not hanging around.

Northampton racecourse also hosted public hangings, between 1715 and 1818.

15. BOOKIES' FAVOURITE HORSE

Ribofilio was the ultimate talking horse, racing his way into the affections of bookmakers everywhere when starting favourite for FOUR Classics in 1969 – the English 2000 Guineas; Derby; St Leger, plus the Irish Derby – and losing the lot.

He finished his career in the St Simon Stakes, that October, starting as favourite – and losing.

16. HORSE TRIED AND CONVICTED

Minoru won the Derby in 1909. He was the first horse to win the Classic in the colours of a Royal owner, belonging to King Edward VII.

The horse was later sold to Russia, where he was reported to have vanished during the Revolution. One report said that he and the 1913 Derby winner Aboyeur were harnessed to a cart and driven from Moscow to a place called Novorossiysk and thence sent to Serbia.

However, in his 1968 autobiography *Racing With The Gods* , Marcus Marsh, trainer and son of Minoru's trainer Richard Marsh, revealed another fate for the late King's pride and joy – 'Poor Minoru, a horse so gentle that as children we had been allowed to walk freely into his box, had been sold to the Czar and subsequently executed as a royalist in the revolution, an act so senseless that it defies description.'

Other reports enlarged on this story, suggesting that the horse had been 'tried' by court martial 'for crimes against the proletariat' and, inevitably, found guilty and 'summarily beheaded.'

Perhaps it was as well that the horse's Royal owner did not live to hear of this fate – although had he have lived beyond 1910, perhaps Minoru might not have met such a grisly, bizarre end.

King Edward VII died on the night of May 6, 1910, shortly after his Witch of Air had won at Kempton – indeed his last words, to son, King George V, were reported to be a comment on the horse's victory.

17. 'JAIL TRAINERS FOR NON-TRIERS'

Racing can sometimes be an insular sport, unaware of the image it can have amongst 'outsiders'.

Outsiders like, for example, former *The Sun* editor, Kelvin Mackenzie, who, in his column in that paper on August 10, 2006, called for the jailing of trainers and owners.

Mackenzie was fulminating against Sir Michael Stoute after his record fine under the non-triers rule.

Pointing out that his jockey was banned, Mackenzie asked, 'Why didn't they ban Stoute for a similar period?'

Then he really hit his stride in one of the most damning attacks ever made on the sport – 'Racing is a racket. Everyday punters put their hard-earned £20 on horses they believe have a chance. In many cases – as with Florimund (Stoute's horse) – they are being ripped off. The trainer knows it has no chance. The owner knows it has no chance. The jockey knows it has no chance.

'It's so bad that the only honest people at the track are the bookmakers.' ranted Mackenzie – a man who, as I know from personal experience, rather enjoys a wager from time to time.

'We need a criminal law for non-trying that means trainers and owners will end up behind bars and the sport will at least be cleaned up' he added, after alleging that he had witnessed what he considered to be 'blatant examples of non-trying' at Lingfield recently.

Just a few days earlier, racing had also been savaged in a *Sunday Times* column by Rod Liddle in which he pondered the one-day ban awarded to jockey Paul O'Neill who had head-butted his horse – 'If your objection to O'Neill was motivated by a concern for animal welfare, then there are one or two priorities to be sorted out,' he declared, having made reference to 'the 5000 'retired' horses sent to the abattoir each year, the thousands of colts put down because they didn't quite make the grade, the hundreds of horses killed or maimed going over fences.'

Not everyone likes us, you know.

18. ARGY BARGY

It was 1990, and Argentinian punter Victor Rosales felt the time was right to change the course of his life. And he knew just how to do it. He withdrew his life savings of some £10,000 and headed off to the races in Buenos Aires to stick the lot on 12/1 shot Broncaro.

Rosales watched as the three year old came out of the stalls, watched as the horse struggled to match strides with his opponents. Watched as it finished stone last. Watched the horse come back in from the course, pulled out a revolver, and shot the horse dead.

19. LOSING STREAK

Running at Fontwell in May 1995, Boxing Match acquired a unique form book entry – 'Weakening when hit streaker, pulled up'.

29-year-old Stephen Brighton had disrobed and run onto the course – straight into the path of Boxing Match and jockey Rodney Farrant.

20. WHAT A BRUM DO – THEY WENT RACING, AND A WAR BROKE OUT

A race meeting took place at Aston Park in Birmingham on Monday, March 26, 1855, which ended up looking more like a military re-enactment enthusiasts' day out.

Over 16,000 racegoers headed to the course for the steeplechase card, and the omens were had when gangs of men objected to the admission fee of one penny, and broke down the barrier rails. Once in they proceeded to stage regular fights amongst themselves.

The local *Birmingham Mercury* later commented on the 'many sham sailors' present, 'each deploring the loss of an arm or leg, such members, it was observed, being closely strapped or bandaged in such a manner as to excite the commiseration of passers-by.' Oh well, must have made a pleasant change from being 'offered' lucky heather.

The racing action itself was fairly routine, opening up with a 3m hcp chase won by the odds-on favourite, before an exciting three way tussle for the Birmingham Grand Annual

Chase, followed by a walkover in the third, then a chase in which the top weight was 14st 3lbs, carried into third place.

Prior to the last there was so much violence amongst the crowd that the three amateurs scheduled to ride all refused to leave the weighing room and were replaced by three tougher professionals.

But it was only when the card had been completed that the real fun began as a mob amused itself by ripping up racecourse rails and fence posts after which, reported the *Mercury*, 'several thousand of the spectators, including the riff-raff of the town, were seized with a sort of military ardour, so they determined to indulge themselves with a mock fight in imitation of the heroic efforts which have lately transpired in the Crimea' – as you do!

The mob now made off to a patch of open ground where they took sides – 'allies (7,000 strong) and Russians (4,000)' – and proceeded to act out the recently fought Battle of the Alma.

'Bludgeons and sticks of considerable length were brought into requisition as weapons and those who formed the Russian ranks were driven into the gardens. Several encounters took place in which much personal injury was done. Two lads had their eyes cut out, and others were much bruised and wounded about the head'.

The violence went on into the night and three men were later jailed. It was the first and last time that racing was ever staged at Aston Park. As the *Birmingham Journal* explained: 'The disorderly and disgraceful conduct of a large number of Birmingham worthies, expressively denominated "roughs" at our steeple chases, held at Aston last year induced the managers of this annual sport to fix upon the vicinity of Knowle for the celebration of the good old English pastime for the year 1856.'

21. WOP'S IT ALL ABOUT, LUCA?

Italian trainer Luca Cumani is now such an Anglophile that he says: 'I've been in England too long and I enjoy it too much to leave. It's the only place to train'.

But he is well aware that his Italian roots are the derivation of his long-held nickname, The Wop – a reference to less politically correct days when it was acceptable to call a man of his background such a thing.

He has also been known as 'Filthy', as in 'Filthy lucre', but is so fond of the original nickname that he decided to acquire a car number-plate to celebrate it.

'It's only in a certain section of the press that I've been known as Filthy. I'm known as The Wop and I prefer that,' he told the *Racing Post*'s Peter Thomas. 'It's true, I'm a wop. I even wanted to get personalised numberplates, WOP 1, but apparently you're not allowed to have it.'

22. WAS JAMES DEAN THE FIRST DOPER?

In 1930, shortly before he died in the October of that year, a vet from Bishop Auckland, Captain J (Jimmy) G Deans, MRCVS, wrote to newspapers *The Yorkshire Post* and *The Sportsman*, boasting that he had pioneered the doping of racehorses in Britain, albeit before it was made illegal in 1904.

Deans, born at Hawick declared, 'As the first veterinary surgeon in England to attempt the hypodermic injection of a stimulant into a racehorse before running, I confidently assert that it is possible to treat a horse by this method, not once, but many times, without any detrimental effect, either immediately or in future.'

Doping, which had been going on for some while, brought in via some unscrupulous American sources, was only outlawed when the eminently respectable trainer, George Lambton deliberately and having told the Jockey Club of his actions, doped his horses in certain races, thus demonstrating the advantage doped horses could receive, when the great majority of those he treated won races they could not otherwise have been expected to win: 'I obtained six dopes from a well-known veterinary surgeon. Their effect on a horse was astonishing. I used five of them and had four winners and a second. None of the horses had shown any form throughout the year.'

Deans, who owned a number of horses himself, and was well known in northern turf circles years before Lambton's dramatic demonstration, offered his trainer clients 'speedy balls'. He 'rather prided himself on having doped horses before ever the Americans came over here and started wholesale doping,' recalled northern trainer John McGuigan in his 1946 autobiography, recalling Deans' claims that 'he could alter the form of horses for the better from 14lbs to 21lbs.'

A graphic description of what it was like to ride a horse 'treated' by Deans, was supplied by jockey Harry Taylor – good enough to ride his mount Buffalo Bill into 3rd place in the 1901 Grand National.

Taylor wrote, 'I believe I was the first jockey in England to ride a doped horse over fences at a race meeting.' This is likely to have been towards the end of the 1890s, although the precise date is difficult to pin down.

The horse, Sporran, 'doped by that well-known veterinary surgeon, J G Deans of Bishop Auckland', was running at Cartmel on a Whit Monday.

Taylor went to the track the day before. 'When I arrived I found Sporran so lame that I could not even trot him, let alone give him the steady gallop I had intended. I got a wire off to (owner) Mr Rogerson, informing him that it would be impossible for Sporran to run. In due course a reply came, 'Am sending Deans, have horse ready to run'.

'So, on the Monday morning Sporran walked over from Grange to Cartmel, quite the lamest horse I ever saw sent to a racecourse to run. I weighed out in Mr Rogerson's colours and just as I was about to mount, Mr Deans came along, gave my horse a dope with a hyperdermic (sic) syringe in the shoulder.

'Now, ordinarily, Sporran was a quiet and docile horse, but when I was thrown into the saddle he pricked his ears, then got on to his toes and, when we were through the paddock gate, all sign of lameness was gone.

'A horse called Lord Percy, ridden by Fred Hassall was favourite, his friend Mr Massey Harper riding something else to give as much help as he could to Fred.

'Cartmel course is three times round for two miles, and by the time the flag dropped my mount was a maniac. Coming round the second turn the first time the others had me wedged in on the rails with one leg over them. I fully expected going over every minute, or bringing my old pal Bob Harper down.

'Sporran was absolutely uncontrollable and was galloping between Sillybody's (Bob's mount's) hind legs. The second time we got round to the same place Sporran, not seeing an opening, made one with a mad dive between the rails and the favourite. Fred Hassall yelled out some pretty strong compliments about my riding, but I couldn't stop to listen for Sporran went on and won as he liked – the difficulty being to pull him up.

'By the time I had weighed in, Sporran was dead lame again but won on each of the two subsequent occasions on which he was doctored.'

23. EGGED ON TO BE SUPERSTITIOUS

Perhaps the earliest superstition to be connected with racing, a sport with plenty to choose from, is that outlined in a 1695 publication called *Camden's Britannia*, which declares: 'Where the owner of a horse eats eggs he must be very careful to eat an even number, otherwise they endanger their horses. Jockeys are not at all to eat eggs, and whatever horseman does it, he must wash his hands immediately after.'

24. HARD TO SWALLOW

As jockey Josh Gifford, riding Timber, cruised past rival Tim Brookshaw on Joss Merlin in the Bromford Novices Hurdle at Birmingham on November 14, 1961, he had the race so much at his mercy that he turned round to grin at his defeated rival.

What happened next, though, literally wiped the smile off his face – and cost him the race, because Gifford's false teeth became dislodged and slipped to the back of his throat, threatening to choke him. Joss Merlin swept past to win as Gifford coughed and spluttered desperately. Gifford always ensured he rode without the teeth in after that.

25. YOU STUPID **NT, EASTERBY

'It's an old Yorkshire expression that means 'silly bugger'' claimed trainer Mick Easterby after using a four letter, taboo word during a live Channel 4 TV interview which most people who heard it believed to mean something rather different from that.

Viewers rang in to complain about the interview in May 2006, with C4 presenter and racing writer Alistair Down, who also attempted to defend the veteran handler: 'Sorry if some of you found his language a bit broad. He is a bit of a colourful character and I'm sure no offence was intended.' But it seemed to have been taken, as C4 later issued a formal apology.

Some observers were surprised at the attitude of the Horseracing Regulatory Authority who commented, 'We didn't even think about bringing any sort of disrepute charge against him,' particularly as jockey Tony Dobbin was banned for four days for using the same word against Hexham's clerk of the course the previous May.

26. BOOKING FOR CHANNON

Mick Channon obviously knew all about getting booked during his days as a Southampton and England footballer, and when he teamed up with writer Peter Batt for Mick Channon: The Authorised Biography, published by Highdown in 2004, I was interested to hear him being interviewed about the book on Radio 5 Live's Drive show by presenter Peter Allen.

Mick sounded a little grumpy as he was being quizzed about parts of the book and then stunned both the interviewer and most of those listening by confessing that he hadn't read it.

27. STAR PERFORMER

Fergus Shanahan, deputy editor of *The Sun*, told me of the time he was called upon to make a trophy presentation at Sandown Park.

'Having been well refreshed earlier, I was a bit thirsty by the time I got up to the podium and asked this waiter, dressed in a black suit, to nip off and get me a glass of water. I was taken aback when he said "No", so I asked why, and he said, "I'm Alvin Stardust."'

28. NO ORDINARY WAGER

'At the Ordinary (a celebratory meal) at Oswestry Races this week,' reported the *Shrewsbury Chronicle* in 1808, 'a gentleman, well known in the sporting world, undertook for the trifling (pun possibly intended, as you will see) sum of 7/- to eat three quarts of Custard in the short space of two minutes, which he performed with apparent ease in 16 seconds under the given time.

'The same gentleman offered to lay a considerable sum that he eats double the quantity in the above mentioned time, and which it is expected will be determined at the ensuing Wrexham races.'

I have been unable to discover whether he managed the feat.

29. BLAYDON RIOTS

Everyone has heard the folk-song 'The Blaydon Races', composed in 1862 to commemorate the second year of the race meeting at the track, four miles from Newcastle, by music hall entertainer George Ridley, a purveyor of 'drolleries' and singer of 'comic and sentimental' songs according to the local media of the day.

In his late twenties when he wrote the song, Ridley, known as Geordy, would survive only another two years before dying of tuberculosis.

The song will last forever with its seven verses capturing the excitement and colour of a trip to the races:

'O lads, ye shud only seen us gannin'
We pass'd the foaks upon the road just as they wor stannin'
Thor wes lots o' lads and lasses there, all wi' smiling faces
Gawn along the Scotswood Road, to see the Blaydon Races.'

But what few today are aware of is that the meeting itself ended half a century later in a riotous fashion which might well have inspired another verse or two had Geordy been alive to see it.

Two years into the Great War, the Ministry of Munitions had given special dispensation for the races to be held on Saturday, September 2, 1916, and attended by their workers. They soon wished they hadn't.

It all kicked off after a heavily backed favourite, Anxious Moments, passed the post in front to the delight of the crowd, only for the bookies to be tipped off that the jockey had carried far less than his allocated weight.

Not surprisingly, they refused to pay out and the stewards duly disqualified the horse, awarding the race to runner-up Jeanie.

'But the backers of Anxious Moments, not knowing quite what had happened, at once stormed the weighing room and displayed such a menacing attitude that the stewards again consulted — and declared the race void,' reported the *Newcastle Chronicle*.

This appeased no one. Now there were two sets of punters not getting paid out.

'The scene became wilder, and after stone throwing, the mob took possession of the weighing room, smashed the scales and windows, and did as much damage to the appointments of the course as possible.'

An eyewitness, ex-miner John Fox said, 'There was some twisting with the horses, that's what caused the trouble. The crowd destroyed the stands and set them on fire.'

One bookie was reported to have jumped into the Tyne 'to escape the angry hordes.'

Bookie Joe Barnett was there. He remembered, 'In the weighing room the riot started. The weighing scale came right through the window. Bottles were thrown through every other window. The bar was smashed up. And they finished by wrecking and setting fire to the stand.'

That was the end of the Blaydon Races – apart from a brief centenary revival, attended by an extraordinary 250,000 on June 9, 1962.

30. CALAMITY FOR JANE

Racecourse judge Jane Stickels,56, had become a figure of fun and abuse, widely known as 'Calamity Jane' long before she was finally relieved of her duties in the summer of 2006.

And, many would say, with some justification, after consistently giving the wrong results to races, costing the bookmaking industry and punters millions of pounds.

Ms Stickels first hit the headlines in 1994 when she corrected her result of a dead-heat between Absalom's Lady and Large Action, at Kempton Park, making the former the outright winner.

In 1997 she was criticised by Sir Michael Stoute when she did the opposite – calling a winner instead of a dead-heat in Goodwood's Prestige Stakes in which Stoute believed his Alignment was inseparable from winner Midnight Line.

In 1999 on June 19, she wrongly identified a fourth placed horse in a 16 runner handicap and was featured in the BBC consumer programme Watchdog after she blamed 'a slip of the pen' for promoting sixth placed Statajack rather than awarding the place to Fourdaned. Three weeks later, on July 8 she mistakenly announced Full Flow the short head-winner of Newmarket's Superlative Stakes, only to reverse that decision and make Thady the winner.

She was then suspended and re-trained, returning to the job and even becoming involved in the training of new judges. On March 6, 2006 there was uproar again when Ms Stickels announced 9/4 favourite, Welsh Dragon as the winner of the 4.30 at Lingfield – only it wasn't. The 14/1 shot Miss Dagger had crossed the line in front.

Course commentator, Simon Holt, was so convinced that Ms Stickels had got it wrong that he entered the judge's box to ask whether she was certain she was right.

Ms Stickels examined the photo again, announced over the course PA system that there might be an alteration in the result, and then announced the amended result with Miss Dagger placed first.

By then, though, bookies had paid out to punters who had supported the heavily backed favourite – 'This buffoon has cost the industry £7 million. I paid out £6,000 on what turned out to be a loser. Her eyesight can't be trusted,' raged on-course bookie, Barry Dennis and although other bookmaker sources down-played that amount, there is no doubt they had been hard hit. Some bookies even paid out on both 'winners'.

John McCririck called for her to be sacked, 'This error is inexcusable.'

The owners of the real winner were also disgusted. They received £2,388 prize money, but were unable to collect a similar amount in betting winnings.

However, Ms Stickels will also be remembered for another piece of racing history, according to the BBC's website, which declared in April 2003: 'Pub quiz contestants please take note ... the words "They're under starter's orders ... and they're off" are no more. They were said for the last time at Plumpton on 31 March by the judge Jane Stickels. They were axed at the request of racing broadcaster Attheraces, which wanted to save valuable seconds for commentators. Now the words "They're racing" and "Away they go" will be the convention.'

The site insisted this was not an April Fool spoof.

31. NON TRIER? RUN THE RACE AGAIN!

Non triers have always been a controversial element of racing, with officials finding it almost impossible to prove with certainty when such a thing has happened.

But in 1875 the stewards at Windsor came up with an inventive solution, Racing man Alexander Scott was at the track to back a horse he had been tipped, Nougat, partnered by jockey Bobby Wyatt. 'I had backed Nougat on the advice of Jacob Baylis, the owner, and when the horse was beaten, hurried away to catch the train to town,' he later recalled.

But he had left too quickly, 'Next day when I met Jacob on his accustomed pitch in Tattersalls, he at once remarked, "Mr Scott, if you had stayed a little longer you would have seen another race for your money. Not being satisfied with the running of my horse Nougat, Sir George Chetwynd (the steward) ordered both horses – Carlos, the winner of the race, and Nougat – to be raced over the same distance again with different jockeys up, but carrying the same weights – and Nougat won very easily."'

Scott was adamant that 'this is the only occasion in my experience that the Stewards saw fit to put horses together again after racing in order to check the earlier running.

What they thought of the Nougat case was reflected in the suspension of Bobby Wyatt for two years.'

Wyatt, a well known owner and trainer as well as jockey, clearly learned little from this punishment. In 1883 he rode a horse, Brilliancy, which finished well down the field at Sandown only to reappear the next day and scoot up after being so heavily backed that 'the layers were so full up that they refused to make an offer against Wyatt's mount.'

The Stewards disqualified Brilliancy, not only for that race, 'but for all races she had previously won when carrying the colours of her owner,' a Mr Radmall, who was ordered to pay back all the stakes of the races in question.

Radmall was warned off – as was Wyatt, whose career was finished, as 'the whole business completely unhinged his mind.'

32. McCOY DID THE BUSINESS

When Tony McCoy and his mount Family Business parted company in a novice chase at Southwell in January 2002 one shrewd operator on Betfair saw the opportunity of pinching a few quid from mug punters by offering 999/1 about McCoy and Family Business winning the race.

Two mugs fell for it and risked £2 each as they watched the unseated jockey optimistically remounting the horse.

Astonishingly, one by one the other runners came to grief, leaving McCoy and Family Business to pick their way through the wreckage of the race to win it – winning two pounds short of two grand each for those so-called mug punters and costing the smarty pants layer four quid light of four thousand pounds.

You would have thought that may have acted as a cautionary tale for exchange users. But as the 2006 Cheltenham Festival opened a horse called Noland looked out of contention in the very first race and once again 999/1 was chalked up against his chances. One punter chucked in £20 at that price – and was almost £20,000 better off when Noland found a second wind and charged up the Cheltenham hill to just put his head in front of Straw Bear, ridden by Tony McCoy, as they flashed past the post.

33. SO HOW DO YOU SPELL HORSE RACING, HORSERACING, HORSE-RACING, (HORSE)RACING ?

There is absolutely no uniform agreement on how to spell the generic name for the sport of racing horses.

Some say it should be Horse Racing. Into that category, presumably comes Gerald Hammond, Reader in English at the University of Manchester, who you might expect to be in a position to give us the conclusive ruling. After all, he wrote *A Book of Words: Horse Racing* which, in 1992, emerged to enlighten us about the derivation and usage of hundreds of words used in racing.

And as the title of his book opted for Horse Racing, it is fair to assume that he believes that is how it should be spelled, er, spelt.

Well, until you look inside and see on the opening page, 'Horse-racing; a book of words' and you read the entry in the book for 'horse' in which he says 'Horse-racing's first attestation is in 1654' and makes no mention of the other two versions.

He clearly doesn't know.

And nor do Wray Vamplew and Joyce Kay, who wrote 2005's *Encyclopaedia of British Horseracing*.

In fact, as early in the book as the introduction, they ask 'is it horseracing, horse-racing or horse racing?' before confessing they haven't a clue – 'There is no standard version but this book has opted for horseracing, as in the British Horseracing Board'.

Fair enough. And they also have the support of the HRA – the Horseracing Regulatory Authority.

One of the earliest books to use the name of the sport in its title is 1863's *'Horse-Racing: Its History'*, but perhaps the author was not entirely sure, because he declines to be identified anywhere in the work.

However, when, in 1740, the Government was introducing legislation about racing it put forward 'an act to restrain and prevent the excessive increase of horse races.'

As for (Horse)Racing, well, I invented that one myself.

So, quite clearly noone really knows. Now then, let's look at racehorses, race horses, race-horses … , no, let's not!

34. CRUMLIN CRAICDOWN

Given the legendary love of racing and the craic shown by the Irish over hundreds of years, it is bizarre to discover that the sport was banned by law in and around Dublin for some 40 years, after a meeting at nearby Crumlin was heavy-handedly and literally stopped in its tracks.

The Crumlin races had been attracting criticism for some years when, in 1789, the pressure on them was stepped up by an article in the *Freeman's Journal*, declaring that they would 'occasion the idleness of the lower orders of working manufacturers, the calling of industrious thousands of artificers from their occupations, to attend where dissipation, club-law and tumult only exist'.

I think it is a fair bet this was a publication bigger with the bosses than the working classes.

There were other jibes at the sports, contemporary outrage at the 'horrible riots, fractured skulls and broken limbs which have particularly distinguished several former races at Crumlin' and a call for 'a total stop' to them.

There was some hope for the meeting, in that local magistrates had acted as stewards there, but when folk – 'a multitude' – began to gather for the 1790 runnings, the horses were saddled, jockeys mounted – only for the military to arrive with a 'strong force of cavalry and infantry', headed by a Mr Justice Wilson, determined to stop the meeting from going ahead – which was duly achieved.

And by May 1791 a bill was introduced – 'Wheras much idleness, drunkenness and riot have for some years past been occasioned by the frequency of horse races in the neighbourhood of the City of Dublin, for remedying whereof be it enacted ... that it shall not be lawful for any person to cause any horse, mare or gelding to run for any public prize whatever within nine miles of His Majesty's Castle of Dublin.'

The bill, enabling racehorses to be confiscated and sold, remained in force until the 1830s.

35. FRANKING THE FORM

Trainer Frank Hayes persuaded the owner of his outsider, Sweet Kiss, to allow him to ride the horse for its Belmont Park, New York, race in February 1923.

The 35-year-old conjured a career best display from the horse which romped home at 20/1. Delighted by the victory, connections went over to congratulate Hayes, only for him to slump over in the saddle, dead from a coronary.

36. NEVER SAY DIE

American jockey Ralph Neves was thrown from his horse during a race at Bay Meadows, California in May 1936. It was a terrible fall, compounded when the horse came down on top of the stricken jockey.

Spectators and jockeys alike rushed to free the trapped rider but doctors at the track could not find any pulse or heartbeat, and declared him dead.

Neves was wrapped in a sheet and taken by ambulance on a short drive to the nearby hospital where his body was placed in a cold-storage room prior to collection by the funeral director.

Some half an hour later, Neves stirred and returned to consciousness, finding himself in a cold, dark room. Disorientated, he grabbed a sheet and wandered out of the hospital, un-noticed by medics.

Neves somehow made his way back to the track where he caused something of a sensation amongst the racegoers still mourning his demise.

He made a full recovery, rode the very next day and ended up top rider at the track that season.

37. CHUFFED TO BITS TO BE SPONSORED

The first ever commercial sponsorship of an Irish race took place on June 26, 1844 when, at Bellewston, the Dublin and Drogheda Railway Company added 25 sovereigns to a handicap sweepstakes of 5 sovereigns. Perhaps they believed it would impress trainers.

38. SOMETHING FISHY ABOUT THAT BOOKIE

Mid-19th century bookmaker 'Big' Bill Fisher liked to make sure punters were aware of his presence at the races, particularly on big days.

So, on Derby day 1882 he turned up at Epsom and took his pitch on the downs, living up to his surname by placing in front of his pitch an aquarium with real live fish in it. Completing the effect he leaned fishing rods and tackle against the aquarium.

Duly impressed with this piscatorial panache the cash flowed in, much of it for Shotover, the 11/2 second favourite, which romped home by three quarters of a length, whereupon it became obvious that the angler-bookie had been reeling in the punters – because he promptly fled the course, leaving the winning backers staring helplessly at the aquarium and fishing tackle.

Fisher was never caught on course again.

Another nautical theme brightened up the Epsom scene a year or so later, and also brought the punters flocking round when, remembered by racing writer Alexander Scott, 'two enterprising bookmakers drove up to the course in a large lifeboat mounted on four wheels, and, dressed in the uniform of midshipmen of the Navy, betted with the crowds that swarmed around to admire the turn-out with its four spanking grey horses.'

The bookies called themselves 'Our Boys' and served up champagne to their best clients – nor did they sail off after the race.

And you thought Barry Dennis was the last word in bookie flamboyance! I can't, somehow, imagine Dennis being so delighted at a winning result that he would christen one of his children accordingly. But in 1877 leading bookie of the day, Dick Dunn, cleaned up when a horse named Cradle won the Royal Hunt Cup at 100/15. So delighted was he that he rushed to Maple's store to purchase a 50 guinea cradle for his newborn son, who he promptly christened Richard Cradle Dunn in a similar style to that in which top jockey of the time, Tom Cannon won the Somersetshire Stakes on Mornington and christened his son that very name. It was a successful ploy as Mornington Cannon became a Derby-winning rider.

39. WEIGHED IN, OUT!

Jockey W Evans almost starved himself to do the 7st 9lbs he had to carry in the 1907 Melbourne Cup on Apologue. It was a tough, tiring race and Evans was exhausted after getting the horse home in first place.

The *Brisbane Courier* described what happened – 'As Evans rode back to scale, he was cheered as only a Cup crowd can cheer a winner. Evans tried to acknowledge the compliment by lifting his hand to his cap, but it was noticed that he was deathly pale. It was with some difficulty that he ungirthed his horse, and as he mounted the steps to weigh-in, he was seen to stagger and fall in a dead faint. One of the officials lifted him on to the scale, and he was weighed in an unconscious state, amidst intense excitement.'

Evans came round an hour later.

40. THE GHOST TRAINER

'I should not be in this book as like several other women I am only a ghost, unrecognised, without responsibility, but the fact remains that I train the horses and the mistakes and failures are mine, ditto the rare triumphs. One day, perhaps the powers that be will grow up and recognise it is possible for a woman to train a horse.'

In 1961, when she wrote these words as her entry to the annual *Directory of the Turf*, the who's who of the racing world, Mrs Florence Nagle was training horses but because it was not permitted for women to be trainers, she had to pretend that she was not and that her head lad was actually doing the training.

Mrs Nagle was finally able to sweep away the ludicrous restraint on her sex when she took her case to the Court of Appeal and in July 1966, Lord Justice Denning declared: 'If she is to carry on her trade without stooping to subterfuge she has to have a training licence.'

Thus were the Jockey Club forced to recognise female trainers. And a couple of years later, in the 1970 *Directory of the Turf*, Mrs Nagle observed that she 'views with some amusement the fact that the present-day troubles and woes of racing cannot be attributed to women holding licences – as was so widely predicted when they were with-held.'

41. FORGOTTEN WIZARD

It is one of jump racing's strangest and most remarkable success stories, but today few remember the man who could boast of sending out more Grand National-winning runners than Ginger McCain and who modelled his strategy on the training of human athletes, which he had previously done, concentrating on cross country runners.

'He had a genius for developing the qualities of athletes whether human or equine,' said the *History of Steeplechasing* in 1966.

Tom Coulthwaite, a teetotal, non-smoking Lancastrian, was born in 1861 and was himself a talented athlete and rugby player. He began training in Carlisle before moving to Rugeley where he became a popular figure who would hand out meat to local miners and boots to impoverished children as well as routinely paying the fares of everyone travelling on the same bus as him.

In 1907 he came to prominence when he sent-seven-year old Eremon, a horse which hadn't raced until the age of six, out to win the Grand National. The horse was ill-fated, though, running free on the gallops and injuring himself fatally.

Coulthwaite stood as a Conservative candidate for the 1908 Council elections but his political ambitions ended in defeat, so he concentrated on the training.

His Flaxley Green stables revealed his long term ambition as he had a miniature Grand National course built there so that he could familiarise his runners with what they would have to face.

His fame spread and Edward, Prince of Wales, stayed at his stables.

In 1910 Jenkinstown landed a 100/8 victory in the Grand National for him. In 1912 his Balscadden won what was then the richest ever hurdles race in the world, worth £4,000. He would later name his home after the horse.

Not everyone was pleased for Coulthwaite, though. In 1913 he fell foul of the then ruling authority, reported racing historian Grenville Davies in his history of racing in

Nottingham. Non-triers were a big problem at the time, and 'the National Hunt Committee took the decision to crackdown (sic) on this un-wanted practice. Many of the game's top names fell by the way-side. One such notable was Tom Coulthwaite who was warned off for 30 years.'

Tom and jockey Bob Chadwick had been the subjects of an enquiry into the running of two particular runners, Bloodstone and Jacobus. Previously he had been severely cautioned for the 'discrepancy in form' shown by his Great Loss over the course of two races. Tom protested his innocence but lost his licence.

He did not have to serve 30 years, however, and was reinstated after a still hefty seven years, in 1920.

He was intent on training a third National winner and was so convinced that Grakle would be the one that he deferred his retirement until he was 70 when the horse duly won the 1931 National.

Both Grakle and Coulthwaite live on in racing history for their National achievements but also because the horse gave his name to Coulthwaite's invention of a type of crossed noseband to control headstrong horses.

As a postscript to this remarkable man's career – he also kept prize pigeons, grew prize winning roses and became an accomplished dancer after being taught by popular band leader of his day, Victor Sylvester – it should be recorded that he never sat on a horse in his life.

He died on January 13, 1948 and was buried at Brooklands Cemetery in Sale. In 1977 a road was named after him in Rugeley – Coulthwaite Way.

42. 'NO WOMEN OR DRUNKS'

… was the controversial message displayed by Barry Dennis at Royal Ascot one year. He explained why he did not want to conduct business with the fairer sex: 'Once a woman came up and asked for a pound each-way on the 1/ 3 favourite. I just gave her back the two quid and another pound and said "pretend it won, and f**k off"'.

43. HAIR TODAY, GONE TOMORROW

Jockey Pat Valenzuela was suspended in July 2004 after failing fully to comply with the terms of his conditional licensing agreement with the California Horse Racing Board, which required him to provide samples of his hair for drug testing should they so require.

So the stewards were not impressed when he arrived at Hollywood Park unable to supply said samples – because the 41 year old Kentucky Derby-winning rider had shaved his body completely hair-free – his head, chest, armpits and pubic areas, the only areas of his body which could provide a sufficient quantity of hair follicles for testing were devoid of the stuff.

He was stood down from all his mounts immediately, despite complaining that 'I was never advised what length of hair to grow. I didn't do a thing wrong. I got suspended for people assuming that I did something wrong.'

44. APPROPRIATELY ENOUGH

Most racing buffs remember that Foinavon was the shock 100/1 winner of the 1967 Grand National – but few recall that the loose horse who caused the 23rd fence carnage which allowed the outsider to pick his way past fallen and refusing horses, was the entirely appropriately named Popham Down.

45. ONCE IS UNFORTUNATE, BUT TWICE IS CARELESS

Rock Roi finished first in the Ascot Gold Cup in 1971 but was disqualified after testing positive for the painkiller, 'bute'. Back he came for revenge in 1972 and duly finished first again – only to be disqualified again, this time for interference. It was the Peter Walwyn-trained runner's final race.

46. SEE MORE, HEAR LESS

Ian Bryant, breeder of 1999 Cheltenham Gold Cup winner, See More Business, was so superstitious that he would stand behind the grandstand with his fingers in his ears to avoid hearing the racecourse commentary when the horse was running – perhaps he may have bumped into Henrietta Knight at some stage, who would go to great lengths to avoid watching her Gold Cup winner, Best Mate while he was racing. 'Hen' also ensured that her horse would win the 2002 Gold Cup by betting a total of £274 on his opponents – 'if Best Mate did not win, at least there might be some money to come back'.

47. LONG DISTANCE JOCK OFF

Exiled in Russia where he was doing a little training and a little riding, John Sharp(e) (reported spelling varies), was somewhat surprised to receive a telegram from Scottish owner James Merry, inviting him to ride the well fancied Thormanby in the next week's 1860 Derby.

Merry, suspicious that any domestic rider might be bribed to lose, had called up Sharp without even telling his trainer, Mathew Dawson, what he had done.

Flattered by the invitation and hoping to strike it rich and make his name back home, Sharp accepted the booking and set off for Epsom, well aware that he would need to shed some 10lbs en route to make the weight.

He caught a Sunday afternoon train to Berlin, arriving there at 5am next morning having jumped off the train at each stop along the way to exercise a little more of his excess weight off.

He arrived at Ostend shortly before noon on Tuesday, exercised a little more, and caught the cross channel boat to Dover at 6pm.

Sharp – who may or may not have been a relative of mine – reached London at 4am on Wednesday and headed for Epsom, arriving there less than a pound below his allotted weight.

It appears, though, that Merry, who had potential winnings of £85,000 riding on his horse, now had a change of mind – possibly because, as some reports have it, Sharp was inebriated – perhaps having unwisely taken a libation whilst refraining from eating, in order to make the weight. Other reports speak of a heated argument between owner and trainer when the intended change of jockey was imparted.

Sharp was, for whatever reason, unceremoniously jocked off of what was now the very well fancied 4/1 second favourite, being replaced by up and coming 18-year-old Harry Custance.

As a sop to the apparently sozzled sot, Sharp was permitted to partner Merry's no-hope 100/1 outsider and second string, Northern Light.

The race was duly run, with Thormanby always up with the pace before going on to win by one and a half lengths, with Northern Light down amongst the 29 also rans.

Merry won his £85,000; Custance received a 'present' of just £100, and later became the only man to win the Derby and also act as starter for the race, while Sharp's fate and feelings are unrecorded.

48. LIGHTNING STRIKES TWICE AT ROYAL ASCOT

A bookmaker was struck by lightning and killed when a massive storm hit the 1930 Royal Ascot meeting just as The Macnab won the Royal Hunt Cup – causing the rest of the card to be abandoned, for the first time in over 200 years.

'Men went pale. Women gazed on the storm with fascinated horror, deadly white' reported the *Daily Herald*.

Twenty five years later lightning did, indeed, strike twice. And quite shockingly. This time the meeting had been delayed from its usual June dates to July because of a rail strike.

The storm broke over the course on Gold Cup day at 4.10pm, with devastating consequences – killing 29-year-old Mrs Barbara Batt from Reading – who had been expecting a baby. 'A twisted and charred umbrella remained. It is believed to have been carried by the woman who died,' reported the *Daily Herald*.

It was later revealed that 50 people were injured, and another killed. Racing was again suspended – only the second time it had happened.

49. RACECOURSE RICK

Musselburgh racecourse held a minute's silence to commemorate the death of Scottish bookie Ricky Nelson in August 2006 – which came as something of a shock to Ricky Nelson himself who was alive and well and present at the track at the time.

Course officials had got their Rickys in a twist – it was fellow layer Ricky Martin who had sadly passed away.

50. UP FRONT PAMMY CHICKENS OUT OF DERBY

Glamorous Baywatch star Pamela Anderson attended the Kentucky Derby in 2001 and 2003 but announced shortly before the 2006 running of the race that she was boycotting the event – 'Like most people I don't want to support cruelty to animals, whether it's forcing horses to race for our amusement or scalding chickens alive for our plate,' declared the 38-year-old self-styled animal rights activist and member of People for the Ethical Treatment of Animals.

Her opposition to the event may well have been fuelled by the fact that the race had just announced its first sponsorship deal, with the elegantly named Yum Brands, the parent company of fast-food operator, Louisville-based KFC.

Earlier in the year Anderson had requested Kentucky Governor, Ernie Fletcher, to remove the bust of KFC founder Colonel Harland Sanders from the state.

'I'm not shocked that KFC is sponsoring the Derby,' said Ms Anderson. 'It is greedy companies using poor animals all the way around.'

Despite her high profile boycott, the Kentucky Derby did nonetheless manage to go ahead, with Churchill Downs spokesman John Asher magnanimously declaring, 'We would certainly love to welcome her back somewhere down the road.'

The sponsorship deal means that for five years the great race will be known as the Kentucky Derby presented by Yum Brands.

51. RUNNING FOR THEIR LIVES – LITERALLY

One of racing's more shocking episodes took place on a Saturday, in October 1852 at Newmarket, when the eccentric and wealthy owner, the Earl of Glasgow, announced that he intended to run six horses the next day, and that 'the losers should pay the penalty of death'.

This was no idle threat for, as contemporary owner, George Hodgman recorded 'a bad horse in his opinion was only fit to be shot. The Earl of Glasgow knew no such word as "hesitation", his thinning out process by aid of the gun being a common topic of conversation at the period.'

News of the Earl's threat 'spread in wildfire fashion' and crowds flocked to the course with a morbid curiosity to discover the horses' fates.

First of them to race was Senorita, a bay filly, in a half mile match against Lord Clifden's Plunkett. Sent off marginal favourite, Senorita ran for her life and won by one and a half lengths.

Next up was Knight of the Garter, a chestnut colt, taking on Lord Exeter's Ilex over one and three quarter miles. After 'a stern tussle did the Knight earn his continued right to corn' by three quarters of a length.

Double Thong, a bay colt took on Lord Clifden's Feramorz and was spared probable defeat and dispatch when the opponent bolted in the wrong direction at flag fall.

Caracara, a brown colt was 1/3 favourite against Sackbut in the next – and as the pair passed the line at the end of the mile no one knew who had prevailed until the number went up – to relieved cheers from the crowd which toasted 'Caracara's health!'

The first four horses had been partnered by Nat Flatman, and now Tommy Lye partnered Caracara's sister, not even graced with a name of her own by her owner who in the past had called his horses 'He Isn't Worth A Name' and 'Give Him A Name'. She was distinctly unfancied with her opponent, the Duke of Bedford's Hesperus Across The Flat starting at odds-on, but 'the odds were cleverly floored'.

Just one of the threatened six had yet to race – another filly without a name, who was spared when the Duke of Bedford declined to start his Ernestine against her, mercifully, 'preferring to pay forfeit'.

Today one might suspect that the Earl's horses were given a helping hand or that it was all a cynical publicity stunt, but the evidence of the day suggests otherwise.

However, 'the strange part of the business was that neither before nor afterwards did luck flow so steadily Lord Glasgow's way.'

52. VAGUELY INAPPROPRIATE

When plastic surgeon, Dr Robert Alan Franklyn bought Vaguely Noble, who went on to win the 1968 Arc de Triomphe, his wife wanted the horse to race with gold painted hooves. The idea was vetoed by the trainer, Frenchman Etienne Pollet.

53. EQUINE EXTRAS

Hoof Healers – large boots filled with ice to combat injury – were invented in 1990 by David Wells of Ontario. Equinair nasal strips of the type favoured by sportspeople, allegedly to widen the air passages, were worn by point to pointer Interpretation at Ottery St Mary in the late 1990s. Equine nappies, now widely available, offer obvious advantages to lads and lasses charged with the mucking out of stables. Equine night lights are available to cater for horses who fear the dark and equine Copper Bracelets are just the thing to fit around the leg of an arthritic animal.

54. JANET MEAT PORTER

Janet Street Porter was moved on by police for being 'provocative' when she tried to sell cooked horse meat to racegoers at the 2007 Cheltenham Festival" "We're too blinkered to see it as fantastic tasting meat," she said.

55. THE TRAINER WHO NEVER WENT RACING

According to his 1961 *Directory of the Turf* entry, trainer (Leslie) Gerald Cottrell was a paragon of virtue – his entry under the heading 'any other details' declared that he 'never bets, drinks or smokes'.

Another 'never' could have been added to the list by the Devon-based handler who began his career as a permit trainer in 1949, when he was 25, but soon decided that going to the races was not for him.

Then into his 80s, the handler of such good horses as Young Inca and Governor General, who named his home, 'Sprinters', explained to me why he abandoned his trips to the sports: 'When you live in the lovely Devonshire countryside, it is not very tempting to join the long queues on the motorways. In the early days of training I went racing with every runner, but often I would come home to find that there was a problem. When I had a bigger string I decided I was much better employed running the yard rather than spending hours going to and from the racecourses. The horses certainly wouldn't run any faster if I was there.

'My wife Peggy enjoyed racing and was only too happy to take my place and the owners seemed happy with this arrangement. 'I have really enjoyed my training career, there is no better occupation.'

56. AND THE ONE WHO DIDN'T LIKE ANY RACECOURSE

Trainer Captain C T A (Sandy) Carlos Clarke – what a name – was a really colourful character, whose early career was spent as a 'film actor, professional boxer, cowboy – Texas and British Columbia, Commando soldier attached to No 4 Commando World War II. Led the Walcheren Raid, November 1944.'

After the War he became assistant trainer to Fulke Walwyn before striking out on his own in Lambourn from 1949 when he was 34, with horses like No 4 Commando, SS Commando and French Commando – can you see the pattern here?

He was no cowboy trainer, though, winning an Ascot Stakes despite acting as his own Head Lad and declaring when asked his favourite racecourse – 'None. Never stay on one long enough. Only stay for my particular race.'

57. QUEEN ALMOST LOST HER HEAD AT THE RACES

Out for an impromptu early morning gallop on the course at Ascot during the Royal meeting of 1954, the Queen had to take evasive action to avoid possible decapitation via a telephone cable across the track which had sagged dangerously low.

58. OFF HIS TROLLEY

Trainer Sylvester Kirk fractured his arms in 2004 – when he fell off a supermarket trolley in Swindon. As you do.

59. BROLLY GOOD RIDE

Irishman, Lleutenant-Colonel W.L.Newell was at Sandown in April 1930, watching the Royal Artillery Gold Cup, a chase run over 3 miles 125 yards when, with only two to jump, one of the remaining two runners left standing, Porphyrion came down, losing his rider Mr E B Skey in the process.

Newell knew the horse well – he had finished second on him in a Chase at Newbury late the previous year – so, 'I ran from the Tattersall's Ring Stand with Bobby Petre (a Grand National winning rider). The gateman let us out and we caught him before the winning post.

'I had on a good Donegal tweed suit and bowler hat, with umbrella,' Newell later recalled. 'Bobby threw me up and I rode back. Evan Skey was on his feet and running; but Max Tylor on a remounted Philippa was now in sight, so he waved – 'Go in'; I turned at the last fence and a mounted policeman tried to stop me but we eluded him and were over.

'It is a long ride in at Sandown through the crowd. We drew the weight and earned £50 for second place, which was a lot of money when pay was only £18 a month.'

43

60. 'WE ARE NOT AMUSED'

Queen Victoria was far from amused when her son, the Prince of Wales, accepted an invitation in March 1868 to attend the inaugural steeplechase for the Prince of Wales's Plate run at Punchestown.

'I much regret that the occasion chosen should be "Races", as it naturally strengthens the belief, already far too prevalent, that your chief object is amusement; and races have become so bad of late, and the connection with them has ruined so many young men, and broken the hearts thereby of so many fond and kind parents that I am especially anxious you should not sanction or encourage them.' He went, anyway.

61. GOOD MANNERS

It was said – by no less an authority than *The Times Literary Supplement* of January 31, 1924 of Old Etonian and Grenadier Guard, Lord Manners of Foston, that he 'rode in only two races in his life, and won each of them. They were the Grand National of 1882, which he won on Seaman, and the Grand Military Gold Cup of the same year, which he won on Lord Chancellor. Hundreds of men have tried for years to win these races, but have never succeeded.'

62. GRAVE MISTAKE

Australian owner Susan Bell was an eccentric, superstitious figure who was obsessed with the luck-giving properties of rabbits' feet and who once celebrated the victory of her horse Hisign's debut win at Newcastle by throwing a drinks party for 40 of her friends. Before the horse had raced.

Bell, who would always wear green at the track and who married on Friday the 13th in the year 1913, claimed to be guided by a witch from Honolulu. When she had a fancied runner, Enthuse, contesting the 1944 Doncaster Cup, she demanded that co-owner and family friend Captain Walter Bell together with trainer Ted Hush must each take a rabbit's foot with them into her local churchyard and stay there overnight in order to bring good luck.

Somewhat reluctantly, the pair agreed and passed a long, cold night sitting on a headstone, shocking the life out of innocent passers-by.

Enthuse finished second.

63. DUEL PURPOSE STEWARDS

Perhaps it meant something else in those days. Perhaps English gentleman riders were touchy types. But when Capt George 'Jonas' Hunt believed himself to have been insulted after riding a beaten horse called Benjamin at Baden Baden in 1865, the affair went to the stewards – who decided that the only solution was a duel, using pistols,

A Frenchman named Monsieur Thomas had 'shouted out to him in a most offensive way "You have played your game well, Capt Hunt."' The suggestion was that Benjamin had not been 'off'.

This, explained Charles Voight, a chronicler of such exploits, was an 'insult'.

Incensed, Hunt had demanded an explanation and received another insult, whereupon he 'pulled the Frenchman out of his carriage by his nasal organ, which was unusually long' and punched him with his right fist.

The Frenchman demanded satisfaction, preferably via swords. Hunt wanted pistols and referred the decision to the stewards who ruled in his favour.

Discovering that Hunt, a veteran of the Battle of Balaclava, was a crack shot who 'invariably put his chamber-candle out with a Palais Royal pistol', Thomas apparently had second thoughts – when Hunt's seconds went to arrange the details, they were 'at once tendered an apology' and it was explained that Thomas had been under the influence of drink.

The duel was dropped, Hunt returned to the course next day where he rode a winner and was 'cheered for his spirited conduct.'

64. PEN NOT MIGHTIER THAN SWORD, AFTER ALL

Alistair Down, Claude Duval, Peter Thomas, Paul Haigh and other controversial journalists like to sharpen their pens and wield them to great effect against the great and good of the racing world.

The great and good of the racing world quite often feel like wielding something somewhat more dangerous than a pen back in the direction of racing journalists.

Few ever go to the lengths to which French jockey Ludovic, Duke of Gramont-Caderousse did in 1862 when an English racing writer named Dillon, son of an English reverend, wrote critically of his ability in the saddle, in the pages of French newspaper, *Le Sport*.

The Duke demanded satisfaction from the pen-man and the two, together with their seconds, met for a duel with rapiers in the forest of St Germain , near Maisons-Laffitte.

The encounter was brief and bloody. Dillon was run through the body by Caderousse's weapon, and expired on the spot.

As a result, Caderousse had to face a trial, in which he was acquitted but ordered to pay Dillon's mother 3,000 francs, plus a similar annuity.

65. KILLER

He rode nearly 5000 winners – amongst them five Kentucky Derbies – but US jockey Eddie Arcaro was notorious for a 1942 race, the Cowdin Stakes, at Aqueduct, during which he was so outraged at being carved up by rival rider Vince Nodarse that he promptly deliberately and quite openly rode the other man and mount into the rails in full view of spectators and stewards.

Called in to explain his potentially fatal actions, stewards were expecting excuses and justifications for his action when they asked the volatile Arcaro why he had done it, but were told bluntly: 'I was trying to kill the son of a bitch.'

He was suspended for a year and when they both retired, he and Nodarse became golfing partners.

66. WHIPPED INTO SHAPE

Skiving off school to watch Lester Piggott win the 1976 Derby on Empery is a painful memory for trainer Jeremy Noseda, who was found out.

'I was sent to the headmaster and got six ferrulas. This was a Jesuit school and the ferrula was a whalebone covered in leather. You got six of these on the hand, and it made all the blood vessels come to the surface where they had broken. I didn't regret the ferrulas because Lester was my hero.'

67. SEEING RED

Noted for his own colourful sartorial flamboyance, trainer Rod Simpson once trained a horse called Fortune's Guest, who was violently allergic to a certain colour – 'If he saw anything red he'd attack it. Buses, people with red jumpers, he was unbelievable. If he passed a house with a red door he'd go into the garden and kick the door. I had to try and train him around missing the postman every morning.'

68. BRAZIL GOES NUTS AT THE RACES

Former Scotland striker Alan Brazil, now presenter of the talkSPORT Breakfast Show, has never made any secret of his love of racing and penchant for the occasional wager.

He revealed in his 2006 autobiography, *There's An Awful Lot Of Bubbly In Brazil*, that while he was playing for Manchester United he went racing at York with 'a bundle of notes, some £4,000 bulging in my pocket' which he planned to put on his favourite jockey Pat Eddery who was riding a filly called Rye Tops.

But Eddery got stuck in traffic and was unable to take the mount, with Brian Rouse called up to deputise. Brazil decided to stick to his guns – 'when the race got underway I had put every penny on her.'

On the run in, Rye Tops was ahead by a fast diminishing two lengths and scraped home by a head – 'it was one of the most frightening but ultimately euphoric experiences of my life on the racecourse.' The day got better as a trainer tipped him the last winner of the day – 'by the time I left the course I was carrying my money in four Sainsbury's carrier bags. I had a total of nearly £40,000 in cash. At the time I was earning between £200 and £300 per week.'

Now Brazil faced another problem – 'my wife Jill had no idea that I dealt in such large amounts of money when I went to the races'.

How to explain the windfall to her? He went home and 'stuffed the bags full of money into a plastic bin full of leaves' in his garage.

Alan went back to York for the next two days of the meeting and met up with a pal from whom he had intended to buy a Jaguar with his winnings – 'Unfortunately, by that time I had lost all the money I had won over the last forty eight hours.'

69. RACING'S X FACTOR?

There are two very important races in Japan that trainers don't have to bother entering their horses for – because whether they run or not is nothing to do with them.

Instead, the runners are voted for by the racegoing public. The contests are the Takarazuka Kinen run at Hanshin, and the Arima Kinen, run at Nakayama.

The races are extremely important and prestigious – Japanese equine superstar Deep Impact has contested both of them.

Racing Post international racing specialist Paul Haigh explained that 'the fields are chosen by popular ballot. If a horse doesn't get enough votes, he doesn't run, regardless of whether connections want him to.'

Haigh asked, almost rhetorically, 'It works so well it does make you wonder why we couldn't do it here.'

70. AFTER TIMER

It sounds like every gambler's unreachable dream – being able to bet consistently after the race has been run. As far as I am aware there is only one punter to whom such a concession has been made – by the eponymous William Hill to the eccentric owner and mega gambler, Dorothy Paget.

Ms Paget owned the great Golden Miller, five times winner during the 1930s of the Cheltenham Gold Cup and also winner of the Grand National. An enormously wealthy heiress, she was also a very strange lady who liked to turn day into night and vice versa. But she also enjoyed a bet, and when she gambled she did so for big numbers.

She would risk tens of thousands of pounds a time on her 'banco' bets – confident tips from her trainers. Her standing instruction was to bet enough to make her a profit of £20,000 per bet. This caused a sensation once, when she took it into her head to back a horse which went off at 1/8 odds – meaning she had to risk £160,000 to make her twenty grand.

So convinced was William Hill of her honesty – and possibly so keen was he to keep her business – that he allowed her to place bets of up to £20,000 a time on horses – usually her own – which had already run in their races when she rose for the day, late in the evening.

Ms Paget, who died in 1960, backed winners and losers by this method, but her bookmaker's trust was never misplaced and her own integrity never called into question.

71. MORE BANG FOR YOUR BUCKS

Salisbury racecourse in the late 18th century boasted a unique way of informing spectators that a race was off – a musket was fired as they started, and again at the one, two and three mile posts.

72. FIRED UP PREACHER

These days the Cheltenham Festival is one of the most heavily hyped meetings of the year and the course can seem to do no wrong. However, it is worth recalling the days when there was a very strong campaign launched to prevent racing from taking place at all at Cheltenham.

It was led by a man of the cloth, Francis Close who was, in 1827 the just promoted vicar of the Cheltenham parish church of St Mary's, from whose pulpit he whipped up his congregation – 'I verily believe that in the day of judgement, thousands of that vast multitude who have served the world, the flesh and the devil, will trace up all the guilt and misery which has fallen on them either to the racecourse or the theatre,' the reverend declared on Sunday, June 17.

He emphasised his message by posters declaring that 'The Heathen festivals of Venus and the Bacchus are exceeded on a Christian race ground.' He hit out at racecourses as places where 'prostitution, licentiousness forsake the lurking place and stalk abroad in all the impudence of emboldened profligacy', presumably overlooking the fact that such reasons were exactly why many people made a bee-line for the racecourse!

At this time Cheltenham races were run on the Cleeve Hill course and soon meetings there were being disrupted by Close's parishioners who would abuse racegoers and riders and hurl objects at horses and jockeys.

Despite their actions racing was again scheduled for 1830 – so they burned down the stand, resulting in the abandonment of the course and its relocation to nearby Prestbury Park in 1831.

Close pretty much succeeded in having flat racing stopped at Cheltenham, but the jumping fraternity was made of sterner stuff.

73. WILDLY STRANGE

Few Derby winners have enjoyed a ride in a wheelbarrow, pushed by their owner's butler within minutes of being born.

Wild Dayrell came into the world just after midnight, one day in April 1852, the first foaling at Francis Popham's stud, toasted by a bottle of wine, and moved to a warmer box by the prescient, night-capped butler, who declared he would love 'to wheel the winner of the Derby once in my life.'

Named after a disreputable 16th century owner of Littlecote near the Hungerford estate – which he was reputed to haunt – where the colt was foaled, he was sold as a yearling, but bought back as a two-year-old after showing no potential. However, he soon improved and became well fancied for the Derby although bookies fielded against him before the owners were offered £5,000 to scratch him, thus saving them from a hefty payout.

Although his horse-drawn van was sabotaged before he was put in it, Wild Dayrell duly raced, and won the Derby, but so disillusioned was Popham at what had transpired that he declared he would quit racing. Following his Blue Riband triumph the locals wanted to celebrate as was traditional in the Lambourn area, with a resounding peal of the church bells. The Rev Robert Milman, no fan of racing, forbade it.

The bellringers locked themselves into the bell tower and pealed away regardless.

74. BY ROYAL BAAPPOINTMENT

Hurdle racing was born, so it is said, when a bored Prince of Wales, out riding on the South Downs in or around 1810, encouraged his companions to jump some convenient sheep hurdles.

75. THAT'S HANDY

The 1751 edition of *John Pond's Racing Calendar* included the rules for 'A post and handicap match' which require concentration to digest.-

'A Handy-Cap Match is for A, B and C to put an equal sum into a hat, C, which is the handicapper, makes a match for A and B which, when perused by them, they put their hands into their pockets and draw them out closed, then they open them together, and if both have money in their hands the match is confirmed; if neither have money it is no match; in both cases the handicapper draws all the money out of the hat; but if one has money in his hand and the other none, then it is no match; and he that has money in his hand is entitled to the deposit in the hat.'

76. IF YOU WANT TO GET BEAT, GET BOXED – BY 'GREATEST' JOCKEY

John Francome, the former champion jump jockey, outraged many of his colleagues amongst the riding fraternity, purely by admitting that the occasional race may not be run entirely on its merits:

'It happens. It's life. Join the real world,' said Francome on BBC Radio 5 Live's Sportsweek show in July 2006 – and you might have thought he had suggested that all jockeys were paedophiles or beat their wives and girlfriends – and, perhaps, boyfriends, too, such was the sharp intake of breath and exhalation of abuse towards him.

Three jockeys immediately rushed into print with a joint statement – 'As some of the most senior jockeys in the weighing room, we do not recognise the sport that John Francome is describing' in a letter to the *Racing Post* which might as well as have been signed 'Three Blind Mice' rather than 'Kevin Darley, Richard Hills, Michael Hills'. They compounded their, to be kind, naivety, by adding, 'This is no message to give to young jockeys starting out on their careers. It should be made clear to them that there is no fixing of races'.

Even Kieren Fallon weighed in with an opinion in his *Sportsman* column: 'Nobody would suggest that in years gone by, when there were no starting stalls or cameras in front, back, sideways and above, it didn't happen, but it couldn't do today.'

The fact that Francome, dubbed 'Greatest Jockey' by John McCririck, had qualified his Comment that ' I should think it happens about half a dozen times a year – where you watch something and you think 'I cannot believe that the stewards haven't had them in' by adding 'When you think how many races there are, it's actually not a lot.'

Bruce Millington, Sports Betting Editor of the *Racing Post* noted wryly, 'I would have thought the world of racing should be queuing up to thank Francome for having put up such a conservative estimate of the level of crookedness in British racing.'

But almost lost in the controversial furore which followed were Francome's thoughts on how races might be manipulated – 'The simplest way is ground that doesn't suit them, or a distance that's too far.' He elucidated on how a jockey might ensure that his horse did not win a race – 'If you want to get a flat horse beaten you'll be trying to get boxed in and get in all sorts of trouble – there's an art, but I've seen jockeys who can get boxed in in a four horse race.'

77. RAINED IN

Goodwood's Ham Stakes in 1870 was run in an absolute deluge. After the race when the jockeys weighed in, several were found to be overweight.

They claimed that it was due to the rain their colours had soaked up. The stewards debated whether they should void the race before finding, 'on returning to scale three jockeys were found to be overweight, but the stewards declared the race valid as the jockeys weighed out correctly and the difference had been caused by the rain.'

78. STARTER FLAGGING

A June 1871 meeting at Croydon sorely tested and eventually overcame the patience of the official Starter, recorded *The Sportsman* at the time – 'For one race there was a delay at the post of an hour; for another, three quarters of an hour; while for a third, after waiting till nearly 8 o'clock without being able to get the jockeys under control, the Starter threw down his flag and returned to the weighing-enclosure, and the race was declared void.'

79. LE JOCULAR CLUB

If the Jockey Club had a reputation for anything, it was not for the light-hearted, fun-loving nature of its members. Yet, when the French established their own equivalent, the French Jockey Club, or Race Committee of the Societé d'Encouragement in 1833, its leading figure, and President, was an eccentric, wealthy Parisian, Lord Henry Seymour, who was of English descent despite never having set foot in that country.

Born in 1805, Seymour was a rider and owner who imported many top racing men from England into his country.

But, when he died in 1859 no one, other than five members of the French Jockey Club, attended his funeral – possibly because of his love of practical jokes. He would, said French Jockey Club historian Robert Black, 'administer drastic medicines furtively to his dearest friends and derive intense enjoyment from the very unpleasant results.'

And if that wasn't enough to establish just how he became top dog in French racing, well, how about this: 'he delighted in the humane and ingenious pastime of giving away cigars with something explosive inserted in the extremity, and watching the effect when a light was applied by unsuspecting smokers.'

But although Seymour – who would drive around Paris in a coach with four horses, postilions, outriders and bugle horns – left nothing at all to his long-suffering servants when he died, he did leave annuities to five of his favourite racehorses, together with an instruction that they should 'be exempt from saddle work.'

80. WHAT A SICKENER

She was one of the greatest of the early French fillies, but French Derby winner, Gabrielle d'Estrees met one of the most unlikely ends of any racehorse when she died of mal de mer, or sea-sickness.

'Though horses cannot vomit they can suffer terribly from mal de mer,' wrote Robert Black of the mare who was sent to England to visit top stallion Gladiateur in 1867 only to fall sick and die on the return trip.

81. SUICIDAL SORNETTE

It seems unbelievable that a horse could commit suicide. But that is believed to be the way in which top French filly Sornette, described by her trainer and rider M Pratt, as being of 'peculiar temper', met her end.

Having won the Grand Prix de Paris, making all the running in 1870, she was taken out of training in the next year, but when 'she was turned loose in the happy breeding-grounds of Villebon,' recorded 19th century French racing historian, Robert Black, 'she tore like a mad thing, and a blind one to boot, down an alley where was a heap of stakes and, being unable to stop herself – even had she desired to do so – ran herself through the vitals, and died almost immediately; a clear case of suicide committed in a state of temporary insanity.'

82. PLUS ÇA CHANGE – TROP CHER!

The prices paid for yearlings cause sharp intakes of breath today when Godolphin or Coolmore shell out mega-bucks for their colts and fillies.

But not much has changed. In 1876 it was said of English racehorse, Sidonia that 'the ridiculous price of 2,400 guineas was paid as a yearling.'

83. DRAGON FIRED UP

One of the early major turf figures was Tregonwell Frampton, Master of the Horse to Royalty including Georges I and II, William and Anne.

Frampton was 86 when he died in 1727 and the story is told of him that he owned a celebrated colt called Dragon, which he matched against an equally highly thought of mare for a substantial stake.

Dragon duly won, whereupon the owner of the mare issued a challenge against 'any gelding in the world for double the sum'.

Frampton accepted the wager and declared that he would produce a gelding to take on the mare the very next day.

Overnight, he had Dragon gelded, reappearing the next day to again beat the mare.

'It is stated that he (the horse, not Frampton) succumbed soon after the race,' declared the report of the occasion in the Lonsdale Library's 'Flat Racing'.

84. DENNIS' MENACING WILL

Dennis O'Kelly became famous as the owner of the first equine superstar, the unbeaten Eclipse who dominated the turf in the late 1760s and early 1770s. O'Kelly was a huge gambler who was actually outlived by some fifteen months by Eclipse, who died in February 1789.

When O'Kelly died from gout, a symptom of his riotous living style, he left a will whose beneficiaries were his brother Philip and nephew Andrew. In the will he stipulated that should either of the pair 'at any time after my decease lay any bet or wager, or make any match or matches whatsoever for running any race or races upon any course, public or private, they shall forfeit and pay unto my executors and trustees the sum of five hundred pounds of lawful British money to be by them deducted and retained for their own use and benefit out of the property.'

Andrew O'Kelly certainly owned and raced horses after the death of his uncle – whether he managed to avoid paying the price demanded seems not to have been recorded.

85. SHOCKING REMEDY

When the great Ormonde, winner of 16 races, including the 1886 2000 Guineas, Derby and St Leger, showed a tendency to 'roar' during his races, the Principal Veterinary Surgeon to the War Office, Mr George Fleming F.R.C.V.S., suggested to owner Lord Westminster that 'he had the horse treated by electricity in the hope that function would be restored to the muscles which abduct the larynx'.

Reports said that he was 'treated with the electric sponge but although he absorbed enough electricity to illuminate the entire neighbouring town of Newbury, no improvement was achieved, and on foggy mornings it was possible to hear him breathing half a mile away.'

Assessing this somewhat alarming sounding remedy, J.B. Robertson, M.R.C.V.S., confirmed, 'the treatment was unavailing. Ormonde made still more noise when he was put into strong work'. One owner who came up against Ormonde, Captain Machell, complained 'He is not a horse at all, but a damned steam engine.'

However, the great horse made little or no noise when he was the star attraction at a reception held at his owner's Grosvenor House gardens in Park Lane in London to mark Queen Victoria's Jubilee. In the presence of the Prince and Princess of Wales, four kings, two queens and a smattering of foreign royalty, he happily munched on carnations offered by the Queen of the Belgians and geraniums from an Indian prince.

86. BATTLE OF EPSOM

Racing relations between the English and the French were somewhat strained during the 19th century, particularly as there was a certain amount of protectionism going on in France where they forbade foreign runners to contest most of their major prizes.

However, the French would often send raiders over to aim at top English races, albeit the quality of the home contenders was always supposed to be superior.

However, in 1879 a French raiding party came over to compete in the Rosebery Stakes at Epsom.

Leading French owners often enlisted top British talent in their stables, such as trainer Thomas Jennings, originally from Cambridgeshire but who had trained in Italy and France, whose Paul's Cray and Phenix were well fancied for the race, the latter partnered by another Englishman, James Goater. Jennings had prepared the horses at Phantom House in Newmarket.

But the rank and file of British race crowds did not appreciate such 'turncoats'.

Phenix, though, seemed to be the obvious favourite, but his odds drifted from 4/6 to 2/1 and he was beaten by his former hurdle-race countryman, Paul's Cray.

If there was one thing the racegoers hated more than a French winner, it was a French winner beating the French runner they had expected to win.

A contemporary witness takes up the story – 'Two or three thousand ruffians, belonging to what has been called by a describer of the scene "the worst scum of the earth", showed an unmissable intention of tasting blood and of forthwith lynching Mr T Jennings and Mr James Goater.

Howbeit, Mr Jennings – being about 60 years of age – promptly knocked over one or two of his more aggressive enemies and made good his retreat into the paddock, whilst the police took charge of horse and jockey, and so imminent murder was prevented.'

Jennings had experienced similar scenes before – after his Fille de l'Air won the 1864 Oaks she had to be escorted to the winner's enclosure by hired prize fighters.

His 1865 Derby triumph with Gladiateur was hardly popular and also in 1879 Jennings came to blows with top English handler Mathew Dawson when the latter 'intimated that the other was doing his country no service by training for French owners.'

87. JULIE'S SIX OF THE BEST

She was undoubtedly the greatest ever female jockey – but she may also have claims to being racing's greatest fighter!

Julie Krone burst on the US racing scene in the early 1980s and soon proved that she could punch her weight as a jockey against all comers, male or female. Her feisty attitude saw her involved in some high profile punch-ups.

*MIGUEL RUJANO tried to drown Krone in 1986, throwing her into a swimming pool and holding her under after they had clashed at Monmouth Park when, during a race he 'hit me right in the face with his whip'. He split her ear open. After the race she retaliated and threw a punch at him. 'He fell into a cooler, dumping water everywhere.'

After escaping the drowning attempt she threw a poolside chair at her attacker who was subsequently suspended.

*YVES TURCOTTE 'took his whip out and hit my horse across the face with it'. Krone threw her saddle down and launched herself at him when they returned to weigh in. They both got into trouble – 'Yves for hitting a horse, me for hitting a jockey.'

*JAKE NIED was a little known jockey who, after a race 'grabbed me by the shirt and broke the necklace I was wearing'. Krone resisted the temptation to fight back on this occasion – 'it's frightening to have a guy screaming and grabbing you. I just walked away.'

*MARY ANN ALLIGOOD was impeded by Krone's mount during a race. She screamed 'I'm going to get you'. This was one lady Julie did not want to take on, 'She was really mad and I was afraid of her.' So she rushed off and hid in the first aid room. 'I was more afraid of her than of any male jockey.'

*ARMANDO MARQUEZ 'reached over during a race and grabbed my reins, preventing my horse from winning' in 1988 at Garden State Park. 'His actions could have seriously hurt me, my horse, or other riders'.

Again, Julie held herself in check and did not react, but Marquez was disqualified and suspended.

*JOEY BRAVO and Krone 'got into a prolonged scuffle' during a September 1989 race at Meadowlands in which he manoeuvred her and her filly, Mosquera, dangerously close to the rails. Desperate to extricate herself, I reached over and hit him.' He then hit her horse in the face with his whip.

As they passed the post they were pushing each other. At the scales 'he took a swing at me and connected'. She hit back before a trainer intervened and pushed Bravo over. Then Krone pushed him into a metal railing. 'It's impossible to know who knocked his teeth out, the trainer or me,' she said in her autobiography, *Riding For My Life*.

They were both fined and Julie was suspended for 15 days. Eventually, said Krone, 'I learned that no one is ever on the right side in a fight.'

88. WRONG NUMBER

Desperate to discover the fate of his £2 treble, in 1991, Middlesex lorry driver Barry Yates dialled a premium rated telephone service to listen to the commentary of his final selection, which won, landing him a £50 windfall.

He rushed off to celebrate, forgetting to put the phone down. The bill for his 44p a minute call came to £500.

89. THE GREATEST GAMBLE EVER?

It just might have been the biggest gamble ever. At this distance of time it is difficult to judge, but there is no doubt that the cunningly plotted scheme which saw a 200/1 outsider's odds collapse within 24 hours to 5/1 at the 'off' of a pretty big event was a rare animal indeed.

The anonymous author of *The Gambling World*, who styled himself 'Rouge et Noir' was writing in 1898, close enough to the actual events to give his account a ring of truth.

The horse involved was the Irish-bred colt, Winkfield's Pride, a three-year-old allocated a weight of 6st 10lbs for the Cambridgeshire of 1896. He was trained by Classic-winning jockey turned trainer, Foxhill-based W T (but known as Jack or Nat) Robinson and owned by J C Sullivan. The stable was known to enjoy a tilt at the bookies.

The horse did not have a great deal of exposed form, although the word was that he might be useful, so there were many shrewd observers keeping an eye out for any sign of support which might hint at stable confidence.

'But no sign came, and nothing leaked out one way or the other,' wrote Rouge et Noir, 'a master hand at the game was pulling the strings and biding his time'.

That time came with only three days left before the race at a time when 'the 'Special' *Evening Standard* on the Saturday reported Winkfield's Pride 'returned in the betting at Tattersall's at 200/1 offered'.

Offered, but at that point, not taken.

'The race being run on the following Tuesday, all the world and his wife thought that the horse had been badly beaten in his trial, or had broken down, and that these forlorn odds were merely the prelude to his being scratched'.

Now, though, the plotters were ready to pounce – 'Winkfield's Pride, as a matter of fact, was as fit as a fiddle, having done all the stable had asked him so brilliantly that the 200/1 offered was merely a blind, preparatory to a big commission being quietly worked at a given hour on Monday all over the kingdom, at Manchester, Birmingham, Liverpool, Nottingham and all the other provincial betting centres.

'The poor country bookies were "had" to a man, for with the "knocked out" quotation – 200/1 offered – in Saturday's Special staring them full in the face, they looked upon all would-be backers of the horse as "mugs" and on their proffered money as simply 'treasure trove'. So they went on laying the long prices, until every solvent layer's volume was skimmed of its cream, ere they began to tumble to the situation.'

The sting had been perfectly implemented – 'Dire was the consternation and loud the anathemas of the layers who'd been had and great was the rush to "get out" and cover themselves at any price, with this effect that the forlorn 200/1 chance was found landed at 9/1 taken and wanted.'

Winkfield's Pride went off as 5/1 favourite in a large field and 'with lucky little Nat Robinson on his back, jumped off with the lead, made the whole of the running and won in a canter by three lengths – landing a fortune for his backers!'

Rouge et Noir concluded that this was a coup which, "knights of the pencil" will recollect with rueful countenances for many a long day.'

90. RACING WITHOUT JOCKEYS

Greyhounds do it, and those who are critical of the efforts of jockeys might wonder why there are no races for horses unburdened by the efforts of a human being on their back.

I have unearthed one report of such a contest.

Racing writer D W E Brock described the event in 1949 – 'In Italy, the land of heroes, our oldest ally bar one, at least one race is run by horses with no jockeys on their backs, their places being taken by spiked balls dangling at the horse's sides.

'This jockeyless race in Italy is started by the simple process of giving one horse a crack on the behind with a whip; off he goes, and off the others go too. Of course, the faster they go the faster do the nice iron spikes prick them and so ad infinitum. The great point of the Italian race is that the course is absolutely straight, and it is impossible for a horse to deviate.' No, it won't catch on.

91. CHOPPED UP

Surely the only Derby winning jockey to become a karate black belt, Alan Munro, who won the premier classic on Generous in 1991, gave up the sport in 2000 to hone his karate skills in Japan.

Munro, who also studied kung fu in Indonesia, returned to racing in 2005 but was forced to endure time on the sidelines in 2006 after suffering convulsions during a flight in August of that year.

While taking time off for a medical review the 39-year-old, who has also converted to the ancient religion of Taoism, told the media, 'At least I'm back into karate and I'm getting a lot of pleasure from it.'

Perhaps not while he was achieving his black belt, however – 'To get that you have to fight 15 people in a day. I had seven bells kicked out of me. I was throwing up after the fourth fight, but I got through.'

He even contested two international events in Japan and Greece before deciding to move back into racing.

92. ARC AT THIS

As if it wasn't enough to see an army of some 5,000 Japanese racegoers flooding to Paris to launch perhaps the race's biggest ever gamble, which forced their equine hero Deep Impact to start at 1/2 – having touched 1/10 – in the 2006 Arc de Triomphe, when 9/4 was the returned 'industry price' with British bookies, thus pushing winner Rail Link out to 23.6/1 on the PMU when 8/1 was the going rate with the layers, we then had an extraordinary mix-up over the time in which the race was run.

Having been given the official race time as 2m 31.7s racing journalists were soon disputing it. James Willoughby in the *Racing Post* wrote, 'French authorities have made a huge mistake, which they must investigate.'

He had clocked the time some five seconds faster on video re-runs. The difference between the two timings amounted to some 27 lengths, or 80 yards.

Within a day, France Galop officially corrected the time to 2m 26.3s, blaming 'a technical problem.'

93. BUCK'S DUCK UP

Frank Buckle was a conscientious and effective jockey who rode 27 Classic winners in his career which ended shortly before his Feburary 1832 death.

But he had to fast for most of his working life and in 1828 he had to put up 5lb overweight on the fancied Rasselas for the Goodwood Gold Cup after having been unable to resist dining on roast duck the night before – and just being touched off in the race by Miss Craven.

Racing character General Grosvenor was moved to verse to record a message to the horse's owner, Lord Mantcharles:

"Good Heavens!' one cannot help laughing to think

How the weight of a duck made a jockey's scale sink.

How a Gold Cup was lost for so trifling a matter,

I shall faint when next I see a duck on a platter.

Pray take my advice for I wish you good luck – Keep Buckle next time a whole mile from a duck."

Ironically, Buckle, who weighed 3st 13lb when he first rode in 1783, was well known for his habit on the last day of each season of dining heartily on goose to mark the end of his fasting agony.

94. BRA-VO

'I can't think why I was wearing it. I've only got one and it normally only comes out on special occasions, like when I'm trying to persuade an owner of the advantage of having horses with me' – trainer Tor Sturgis was glad she just happened to be wearing her Wonderbra when A P McCoy contacted her in autumn, 2006, to tell her that one of her horses, an un-named three-year-old, had escaped from her Kingston Lisle yard, and was outside his house. Sturgis, who later related the yarn to *Daily Telegraph* racing journalist Marcus Armytage, came to collect it but, without a head collar, and wearing no belt, had to improvise by using her underwear as a lead.

The horse is something of a local celebrity, having already disappeared on another occasion, only to turn up at the nearby Star Inn in Sparsholt.

95. DOUM (EN) ED?

Corroborating details are few and far between, but Britain's favourite French jumps trainer apparently had something of a dramatic introduction to the world, even though he presumably recalls little about it.

However, during a feature in Cheltenham's official guide to the 2005 Festival, writer J A McGrath remarked, that the then 64-year-old trainer was 'born by the side of a road in wartime France.'

96. SIR PETER BEATS THE DEATHLIST

At the start of each year, the website 'deathlist.net' selects 50 celebrities which it believes may expire in the forthcoming 12 months and invites visitors to the site to give their opinions of their choices.

During, and at the end of, each year they discuss how successful or otherwise they have been in tipping winners – ie, deceased celebs.

In the 2005 list, Sir Peter O'Sullevan, better used to appearing in polls of best known/loved racing figures, made a surprise appearance at Number 48 in the deathlist.

Unlike 12 of the others on the list, Sir Peter stayed the course so successfully and in such vigorous health that he was deemed unworthy of inclusion on the 2006 or 2007 list.

He can be comforted to know that he is at time of writing the only racing figure to have featured on the site.

97. KRISTAL CLEAR GAMBLE

Despite laws forbidding gambling and despite the objections of a disapproving rabbi, a 5,000 signature petition against it, and demonstrations by animal-rights activists, Israel's first race meeting was held at the Nir Yaffe stadium in Afula, in the country's Gilboa region on Wednesday, October 11, 2006.

With a collection of tents and a makeshift grandstand, thousands turned out to watch the action – 'People are running here into the stadium, it testifies there's a need and they want to support it' said Danny Atar, head of the Gilboa Regional Council.

Police arrested five demonstrators who got on to the course.

Despite having permitted the contruction of racetracks in 2004 the Israeli parliament did not lift its ban on gambling, despite which Israelis do gamble online, and managed to do so on the race meeting.

Chief Rabbi, Shlomo Amar issued a religious ruling, calling horse racing 'a frivolous activity'.

Israeli businessman Ronen Kristal has invested some $700,000 in the track and believes that to get it up and properly running would create 3,500 jobs.

98. HERE WE GO, WIFEY

The biggest field of the day at Hereford's mid-October 2006 meeting was the 28 who turned out for the annual Wife Carrying Race, run over 80 metres.

First run in 2005, the 2006 event attracted fourteen couples, with Lynden and Jodie Bateman (no, I'm not sure which is the husband and which the wife, either!) sprinting to victory, first time out. They won their combined weight in cider.

99. SURELY SUN MISTAKE

When an old tote building was demolished at Cheltenham several years ago, no one realised the consequences, which became apparent the first time they next raced on a sunny afternoon and the jockeys quickly realised that as they came down the steeplechase course home straight they had to contend with the sun shining straight into their eyes.

Since then the course has struggled to come up with a solution, with some bizarre ideas being put forward.

The most practical solution has become the omission of affected fences with, for example, six being dropped from the 17 jumps of the New Year's Day Unicoin Homes Chase, leaving the run-in longer than that of the Grand National.

Jockeys have blamed the conditions for falls in big races but suggestions that a cloud of steam could be released at the appropriate time to obscure the sun, or that a screen should be suspended between two tethered blimps, were deemed too Heath Robinson for implementation.

The obvious answer is not to run the chases at times likely to encounter this problem, but for television and radio schedule reasons that is a non starter.

The much respected Timeform annual, *Chasers & Hurdlers 2005/6* may only have been partly joking when observing that Cheltenham officials were consulting the Sports Turf Research Institute – 'It is to be hoped that corrective measures will be taken sooner rather than later. Perhaps someone, somewhere, is developing equine sunglasses!'

100. RACING'S BEST BAD TASTE STUNT

It had elements of *The Producers*' about it. The stunt dreamed up by Suffolk Downs racecourse in Boston, USA to bring the race fans flocking to its meeting in June 1970 was almost beyond parody.

Still basking in the success of their re-enactment of the Ben Hur Chariot race, complete with togas and long whips, in which they had staged two five chariot heats (after the 2nd and 4th races) and a five-chariot final after the 8th, featuring four of the actual chariots used in the Hollywood film, *Ben Hur*, bosses at Suffolk Downs decided to go one better – with a re-enactment of Custer's Last Stand.

Top man at the track, Bill Veeck had ignored the fact that the actual anniversary – the 94th – of the massacre was June 26 and went instead for June 6. The re-enactment was to be enhanced by the running of the Custer Memorial Stakes, a $35,000 turf race.

Posters were printed up; 'No kidding? Custer gets another chance? History may repeat itself. Might not, though. Who wins? Well, come on out and find out!'

Veeck had persuaded ' The Improved Order of Redmen of Massachusetts, representing 29 tribes' to re-enact the battle of Little Big Horn – not only would they be playing the Native American roles, they were also supplying Custer's troopers.

The night before the race, explained Veeck, 'they set up their Indian villages around the infield lagoon, complete with teepees and campfires.'

Prior to the chariot race someone had stolen a chariot wheel. Prior to the Custer re-enactment someone stole a teepee.

'As the morning of Little Big Horn Revisited dawned, we were ready,' said Veeck. Thirty five horses were being shipped in. The re-enactment schedule was charted out minute by minute. The 7th race was off at 4.42 and once finished, the action was to take place before the 8th.

The 7th Cavalry troopers circle on the far side of the track, as an Indian brave rushes to alert Sitting Bull to their presence.

The troopers ride down to the Indian settlement, only to be ambushed by the Indians who surround and attack them, chasing survivors up the course.

As the runners for the Custer Memorial Stakes leave the paddock and complete their race a group of Indian braves emerge with prisoners who are tied to stakes in full view of the crowd.

A representative of the Improved Order of Redmen makes the after-race trophy presentation and now, the piece de resistance, described by Veeck – 'that's the signal for Chief Crazy Horse, accompanied by an honor guard of braves, to come charging down the stretch holding a yellow-haired scalp aloft on a long spear. As they gallop past the winner's circle the spear is dipped just enough so that the Sachem (or leader) can grab the scalp and place it on top of the trophy before he hands it over to the owner of the horse that has won the Custer Memorial Stakes.'

Has there ever been anything like it seen before or since on a racecourse?

Well, no – and, fortunately for all concerned, I should think, this never took place, either. Not for want of trying but, as Veeck explains, because 'early on the morning of June

6 it began to rain. It rained and it rained and it rained. And then it poured. An absolute deluge. There was nothing to do but call it off. We were washed out, that's all. Custer should have been so lucky'.

Tastefully classy, eh? The only comparable event in England was the Buffalo Bill Wild West show held at Northampton racecourse in 1903.

101. PHAR OUT SOLUTION

Almost 75 years after the 'crime' was committed, evidence was produced which appeared to corroborate the theory that Australia and New Zealand's greatest equine hero was murdered by arsenic poisoning in order to save illegal US bookies from a huge payout.

The1930 Melbourne Cup winner, the first to go off at odds-on, Phar Lap was shot at before the race although the attackers were never caught. He carried 9-12, 9lbs more than any other four-year-old had ever humped to victory.

So good was Phar Lap that in 1931 the Victoria Racing Club altered the conditions of some races in an effort to 'stop' the horse. Given 10-10 in the 1931 Melbourne Cup, not even the great champion could overcome the weight. He finished 8th.

The plan was now to take Phar Lap abroad to prove his status as a worldwide equine champion and he was sent off to America for the rich Agua Caliente Handicap in New Mexico on March 20, 1932. He cruised home by two lengths, starting 6/5 favourite for the 10f race and collecting over $50,000 prize money.

Phar Lap was taken to California for a rest but on the morning of April 5, 1932, was found to be ill and running a temperature. The horse deteriorated rapidly and died after haemorrhaging blood from his lungs.

At the time the accepted theory for his demise was that he had eaten grass which had been sprayed with weedkiller. But no other horse stabled at the same place was affected.

In October 2006 the *Australian Daily Telegraph* ran an exclusive story claiming that 'scientific tests using breakthrough technology have uncovered evidence the legendary racehorse was poisoned with arsenic' and that 'the startling revelation adds credence to the theory Phar Lap was killed on the orders of US gangsters who feared the champion would inflict big losses on their illegal bookmakers.'

The arsenic theory was backed up by tests on hair from the horse which was on a

2mm sliver of hide cut from his preserved skin, with Australian Synchrotron Research Program scientist Dr Ivan Kempson telling the paper 'You will never get a 100% definite answer, but we can't explain it by any other way than the scenario of poisoning.'

Not everyone agreed – Percy Sykes from an equine centre in Sydney said, 'I would say there was much more chance of him dying of travel sickness or natural causes'.

Others believe that Phar Lap's stable lad Tommy Woodcock gave the horse a widely used tonic containing minute quantities of arsenic which would account for the substance's presence.

One thing is for sure – the horse had great heart – and all 14lbs of it remains on display in the National Museum in Canberra while his hide is at the Melbourne Museum and his skeleton in the Museum of New Zealand.

102. BEAR NECESSITY

The Associated Press, news agency, reported on Tuesday, October 24, 2006, that 'a wild bear attacked three racehorses on a practice run in central Sweden but was forced to retreat into the forest with a broken leg and a bruised ego.' The incident took place near the town of Ransater.

103. TAKE YOUR MEDICINE, TERRY, IT'S GOOD FOR YOU.

Exhausted, in a state of collapse, and suffering from stomach cramps after an heroic ride on Fred Rimell's French Excuse to win the 1970 Welsh Grand National, Terry Biddlecombe staggered into the weighing room looking for medical assistance. The doctor duly obliged, albeit somewhat unconventionally, giving him 'a mixture of Guinness and salt, which was revolting!'

104. HOPELESS HERO WAS NO LOSER

Racing fans have always taken great horses to their hearts – particularly jumpers who stay around the scene for several years. So it is no surprise when an Arkle, Desert Orchid, or Red Rum, captures the public imagination, and causes huge crowds to turn out whenever and wherever they run.

More difficult to explain is the way in which a serial loser called Quixall Crossett became so popular that he had his own fan club, newsletter, film script and website yet ran up a string of 103 career defeats without managing a single victory.

Named after a former Manchester United striker, Albert Quixall, the horse raced for 11 years, never troubling the judge, landing his biggest pay-day when finishing fourth – 57 lengths 4th – to Dublin Flyer in the 1996 Peterborough Chase and winning £1,500. And in May 1998 he had his closest brush with success, finishing 2nd to Toskano at Wetherby.

By 2001 the story of racing's most popular loser had really taken off, with the tabloid press playing it up. On the eve of his 100th outing, astrologer Jayne Headon was brought in to try to conjure up a win – 'Looking at Quixall's chart I can see that at the time of his race his moon forms an angle with Uranus'. The horse duly delivered the expected century of defeats at Southwell on July 22, pulling up.

He raced three more times before being mercifully retired after his assistant trainer, Geoffrey Sanderson, had parted company with Ted Caine who trained Quixall for his daughter Karen Woodhead, when they disagreed over keeping the 16-year-old in training.

Perhaps the greatest achievement of Quixall Crossett's career was the way in which the horse gave three people who had suffered terrible tragedy, the will and wherewithal to carry on. Ted Caine and wife Joy had been driven to despair by the 1994 death of their 26-year-old son, Malcolm, while Sanderson's two-year-old son Adam also died.

Observed writer Jeremy Grayson, who used to contribute to the horse's website, when the grand old horse passed away in his 21st year on October 5, 2006: 'Quixall got all three of his carers back on a more even keel, out to the racecourse and mingling with people again.'

105. TRAGIC PREMONITION

Ayr based trainer John McGuigan was over 80-years-old when penning his book, *A Trainer's Memories* in 1946, in which he told how a jockey who had lived with him and his wife for 13 years met a tragic end – which he seemed to have predicted.

Ernest Wells Williams, known as Mick, had always had a 'dread' of Kelso racecourse, but had been asked to ride there for an owner called Mr Henderson for whom a week earlier he had ridden a winner at Carlisle, so felt obliged to accept the mount, Master William, in the April 19, 1909 chase there.

'When he left Ayr for that fatal meeting at Kelso, my wife bid him "good day and good luck" recalled McGuigan, 'and his parting words to her were "It's not good day – its good-bye." The horse fell, killing himself and his jockey.

106. BARELY PAST THE POST

Gordon Richards, then 40, landed one of his most remarkable victories on April 24, 1945 at Salisbury on the Aga Khan's Leventina in the Barrow Stakes for two year olds.

With two furlongs to go the horse's saddle slipped. 'Richards managed not only to ride the filly bare-backed, but to win the race; he had a great reception when he returned, with all his gear intact,' reported the *Bloodstock Breeders' Review*.

107. TIMELY PROBLEM

Hunstrete romped home in Chepstow's Usk Plate, the 3.05 on June 3, 1962, beating Miss Daynor and Count Down Basie in a four runner race.

However, it transpired that the starter had sent the field off at one minute past the hour as his watch was wrong.

The stewards deliberated and ruled the race void – ordering it to be re-run at 5pm.

Jockey G Lane took Hunstrete back to the post for the re-run, only to discover that his three rivals had all been scratched, leaving him with a walkover to 'win' the race for the second time that afternoon.

108. WEIGHED OUT

Captain Wentworth 'Wenty' Hope-Johnstone was a top gentleman rider of the late 19th century, who twice rode in the Grand National and also twice won five races in one afternoon – at Dunfermline in 1877 and Burgh-by-Sands in 1885.

But Wenty's oddest victory came in a chase at Musselburgh in which he actually passed the post in second place, recalled author Charles Adolph Voight in his book, *Famous Gentleman Riders* – 'he was winning easily when something dashed up, went the wrong side of a post, and was never caught.

'An objection was a matter of course. "You went the wrong side of a post, you know" said the Captain as he was about to get into the scales. "Oh no, I didn't" replied the other. He took his seat in the chair, and – fell forward, dead!'.

109. GRAND GESTURE

THE Duke of Hamilton fully expected his horse Cortolvin to win the 1867 Grand National. The night before the race he popped into Liverpool's Washington Hotel, much frequented by racegoers and bookies, where 'he made a number of people back his horse'.

Whether he had partaken of a glass or two is not recorded, but Welsh trainer and jockey Tom Rees described how the Duke 'went to the bar and said to the lady attendant, "I shall put you on a thousand pounds that my horse wins tomorrow"'

She had no idea who he was, but the horse duly won and the Duke returned to make good his promise – albeit not at his own expense, because 'instead of keeping his word by means of a cheque he went round the room collecting and borrowing money from those present, in bank note and country notes, in all sorts of conditions, dirty, clean, crumpled, pieced together with stamped paper and otherwise.'

He handed over the money to the barmaid who, 'left her situation, married an engineer and went off with him and her £1,000 to America, much to the grief of the hotel proprietor, who said the Duke had been the means of robbing him of the best book-keeping barmaid he ever had.'

The Duke did, however, personally reward Cortolvin's jockey, Page, with a 'present' of £500.

110. RACING'S PRIVATE EYE

Generally credited with being the most scurrilous publication of today, *Private Eye* delights in criticising and sniping at the powerful and wealthy of our society.

Way back at the end of the 18th century such activity was perhaps somewhat more dangerous than it is today. However, one author was moved to write a book taking a close look at the early membership of the fledgling Jockey Club, and speaking out about the morals and activities of those entrusted with the good of racing.

The book, *The Jockey Club, or A Sketch of the Manners of the Age*, pulled few punches and the anonymous author laid about barely disguised targets such as 'Old D__k V-n-n' who just might have been Captain Richard Vernon, winner of the second ever Jockey Club Plate with his Crabb, of whom it was alleged; 'He is notorious for denying bets when the race has been decided against him.'

Earl G——n——r was damned with extremely faint praise – 'His lordship never performed a generous action in his life and but once a just one – and that was when he attempted to hang himself.'

Of the D-e of B——d the book declared: 'Unlike other young men, instead of following the turf as an amusement, he reduced himself to a level with the lowest blackguard, by a scandalous zeal to convert it into profit.'

The Earl of Derby is dismissed as 'our gouty peer'. Sir C B——y (Bunbury, perhaps) is accused of sharp practice when selling horses – 'Lavish in the encomiums on his stud, many a young Nobleman has been the dupe of his eloquence on these occasions, and many are the advantages the worthy Baronet has derived from thence.'

You can see why the book rapidly became a best-seller of its time, and why one of the targets therein, one Charles 'Louse' Piggott (sometimes Pigott) (any relation, one wonders?) responded in print himself in an effort to prove that the anonymous critic of the Jockey Club was an ungrateful debtor who had himself written begging letters to members.

Pig(g)ott, whose racing colours were 'yellow, shot with red' to match, he said, his eyes, reportedly fell into debt himself and died in jail in 1794.

111. RUNNER-UP DISQUALIFIED – PLACED SECOND!

Vacarme went past the post first to win the 1983 Richmond Stakes at Goodwood from Creag-an-Sgor in second, and Godstone in third.

Vacarme, the 1/3 favourite, ridden by Lester Piggott, was disqualified and placed last, having been found guilty of interfering with Godstone. So Creag-an-Sgor moved up to become the winner. Except that stewards ruled the horse had caused accidental interference to 14/1 shot, Godstone, who was therefore moved up ahead of that runner, getting the race thanks to Vacarme being thrown out, with Creag-an-Sgor placed second behind the new winner.

112. LATE HARVEST

When The Harvester won the 1894 Victoria Derby in Australia, he had to survive a stewards inquiry called immediately after the early afternoon race after two of his rivals posted objections. Forty witnesses were called before the placings were confirmed and punters could finally be paid out – at 8pm that night.

113. STUNG INTO ACTION

Polynesian won the second leg of the American Triple Crown, the Preakness Stakes, in 1945, but early in his two-year-old career he had been badly affected by a condition called azoturia, which produces a tenseness of the loin muscles, making urination difficult and leaving the hindquarters virtually paralysed.

Polynesian would have to be literally man-handled and dragged into and out of his stable, standing stock still wherever he ended up.

Although the azoturia had been cured, Polynesian could not be convinced that movement would no longer be painful, and it seemed he would never race again – until one day when a swarm of hornets appeared in the stables and targeted Polynesian. One sting was enough – once he felt that he took off, sprinting away from the buzzing insects. He was cured, and went on to become a champion sprinter, winning 28 of 58 starts.

114. THE FIRST VIRTUAL RACING?

Hong Kong was occupied by the Japanese from the early 1940s, and towards the end of that period, horses for racing were in short supply.

So, inventive officials at Happy Valley decided to supplement their cards by introducing races for wooden horses, made of three-ply, 15.5 inches long and 8.5 inches high. The runners were 'galloped' down a contraption of wires, strung in front of the grandstand.

And they even introduced handicapping – penalising easy winners by removing weights so that they would slide down the wires more slowly.

115. BET YOU CAN'T PRONOUNCE IT

The recent discussions over how the name of top jumper Kauto Star should be pronounced, reflects a debate of many years ago, which ended up as a most unusual wager.

Leading politician Lord Palmerston paid 65gns for a filly, Iliona, who landed a substantial gamble by winning the 1841 Cesarewitch.

The success of the horse sparked a massive public debate on how best to pronounce the name of the horse – with a short, or long O? Most opted for the long version, with Classical scholars favouring the short.

Eventually, with large amounts of money riding on the outcome, the matter was referred to an undisputed expert, the Master of Trinity College, Cambridge – who upset the odds, by ruling in favour of the short O.

Now, how do you think one should properly pronounce the racecourse named Southwell?

116. JEEVES' CUNNING PLAN

Evans the Butler was extremely loyal to his master, 75-year-old Lord Berners. To the extent that he had scraped together £10 from his meagre savings and risked the total amount on His Lordship's 1837 Derby outsider, Phosphorous, at odds of 25/1.

He stood to win a life-changing amount of cash. So one can imagine his feelings when His Lordship called Evans to him several days before the Derby, and handed him a letter to be delivered to the racing authorities, withdrawing Phosphorous from the great race as the horse had recently been found to be lame.

His Lordship himself, famous for his 'Run, I always run' response to enquiries when asked whether one of his horses would be contesting a particular race, was reluctant to withdraw Phosphorous as he had invested somewhat more than his butler, and would have won at least £30,000 had the horse triumphed.

Evans took the letter and withdrew to a local hostelry where he considered his options before deciding that he would take a chance, risking his employment in the process, by not delivering the letter, just in case the horse's injury cleared up.

Lord Berners, famous for always wearing a huge, grubby, white hat and frock coat made of green baize, assuming the letter had been delivered and that the trainer would automatically assume the horse to have been withdrawn, dismissed the entire matter from his mind.

On Derby evening, having been pursuing various business interests during the day, Lord Berners arrived to dine at his London club, to be greeted by an effusive waiter offering congratulations and thanks – 'We all backed it, my Lord, and had a good win'.

'Backed what? Won what?' asked Berners, baffled

Upon being informed that he meant Phosphorous and that the horse had won the Derby at 40/1, Lord Berners was so delighted that he handed over £100 to be divided amongst the club servants, and decided not to mention the matter of the withdrawal letter to Evans, whose own delight and relief can hardly be imagined.

This is the version of the story told by respected racing writer Guy Logan in his 1928 book, *The Classic Races of the Turf*, and whilst others exist, including one told by Lord Berners' nephew and successor to that title that he had visited the lame horse's stables and had him walked around for several hours, during which time he became sound, I prefer to believe that it was Evans wot won it for his Lordship!

Whatever the truth, there is no argument that this was the first Derby started by flag, the last run on Thursday and the only one written about by Disraeli in his novel, *Sybil*. Phosphorous never ran again and Lord Berners was dead within ten months.

117. ROYAL DISCLOSURE

The consequences of the disastrous failure to ensure adequate viewing for all patrons at the refurbished Ascot racecourse when it was reopened for the 2006 Royal meeting, were vividly illustrated in January 2007 when the course announced that for the first time the public would be able to buy tickets for the previously exclusive Royal Enclosure at the meeting.

'One of the greatest breaks with tradition since the ban on divorcees was lifted in 1955,' lamented Andrew Pierce in the *Daily Telegraph*.

But the move had been made inevitable by errors in the design of the new Grandstand, and other viewing areas, and £10 million had to be found to correct them. 'The parapet was so high there were reports that the Queen, at 5ft 4ins, was not tall enough to see over it' reported the *Telegraph*.

'We have gone from the Sport of Kings to the Sport of Chavs,' harrumphed one unidentified Ascot member.

118. STEWARD'S NUMBER'S UP – SORRY, DOWN

Steward Desmond Donegan was passing the numbers board at a 1992 point-to-point meeting at Peper Harow in Surrey when a gust of wind blew the board down, knocking Donegan out cold.

As he was being revived, one passer-by, recognising the victim and perhaps the recipient of the outcome of a disputed stewards' inquiry, was heard to remark, 'It couldn't have happened to a nicer man.'

119. CHARLIE HAS A BALL – OR TWO

Having failed to win a race at the Cheltenham Festival for ten years and seen three of his highly fancied five-strong contingent well beaten on the opening day, trainer Eddie O'Grady knew just what advice to give his jockey, Charlie Swan as he prepared to partner the remaining two runners on day two of the 1994 Festival.

Take A Run was in the 30 runner Coral Cup, and Mucklemeg in the last race, the Bumper.

'I told him in plain English that he was to sit patiently for as long as possible ... I said he was to ride with balls of steel,' remembered O'Grady.

Swan listened, and brought Take A Run through very slowly, only hitting the front after the last, winning at 11/1.

Mucklemeg started favourite and cruised into the lead two out to win by three lengths.

Some weeks later when the excitement had died down, O'Grady presented Swan with a memento of the great day.

It was a small piece of board covered in green baize, embedded in which were two metal balls.

An inscription read: 'Balls of Steel. Time For A Run and Mucklemeg. Cheltenham Festival 1994. Thanks. Edward.'

120. TRAINERS ARE HUMAN(ISH), TOO

Trainers are often perceived as being aloof, obsessive weirdos, but they can be as human as the rest of us – and that is well illustrated by the answers some of them give in the annual *Directory of the Turf* publication when asked to nominate their favourite recreations. The 2006 edition featured French Anglophile handler, François Doumen, answering, 'Finding new ways of never taking a holiday', while Michael Blanshard dug around for the answer, 'Archaeology'. Dai Burchell's choice was, 'Walking around castles', leaving me to wonder whether he ever goes in ... Henry Cecil declared 'Shopping', while G C H Chung's 'Peninsula war' left me baffled ... Simon Earle nominated 'bullfighting' while ladies Lucinda Featherstone and L J Mongan are kindred – and tough – spirits, both selecting 'kick-boxing' ... Mrs 'Mouse' Hamilton-Fairley opted for 'parties', while P J McBride is clearly a chap after my own heart with his choice of 'record collecting – vinyl' ... B A McMahon recreates via something called 'Para-motoring' while Philip Mitchell is happy just 'surviving' and Jamie Poulton rocks out to 'heavy metal and punk music'. However, the majority of them opt for boringly conservative recreations like golf (although Peter Winkworth at least admits to 'playing golf badly in Portugal' leaving me wondering whether he plays it any better anywhere else), polo, skiing, tennis, shooting, fishing and that sort of stuff.

121. PROMISCUOUSLY OWNED?

A winner on 2006 Victoria Derby day at Flemington racecourse, three-year-old filly, Permaiscuous, boasted 45 owners, 44 of them female – from a syndicate called 'Ggees,EveryGirlWantsAPony,PoniesAreAGirlsBestFriend' – along with one 'token' male.

And they all squeezed on to the podium for the after-race presentation after the black, pink ribbon and cap colours had blazed a trail down the 1,600 metre track, partnered by jockey Damien Oliver.

122. ARCH ENEMY

William Archer, elder brother of great flat jockey Fred, was himself no slouch, and made a reputation for himself in the saddle – albeit his strengths were over the jumps.

One day in spring, 1878 he watched a coaching accident take place outside his parents' inn in Cheltenham, the King's Arms, and took it as a warning that he should not ride at the local track on the next day.

His down-to-earth father, William senior, would have nothing to do with such superstitious nonsense and persuaded his son to fulfil his engagement in the hurdles race worth £5 in prize money – which he did, only to be fatally injured in a terrible fall.

123. COOKED UP

When noted turf authority, Sir Theodore Cook started his researches for his book on the first great superstar of the turf, Eclipse, born in 1764, unbeaten in 18 races contested from 1769, and who died in 1789, he made an appeal for information about the whereabouts of the horse's skeleton. He received information about six different skeletons, two horse skins and 19 hooves.

What is now believed to be Eclipse's skeleton has been on display at the National Horse Racing Museum in Newmarket and is owned by the Royal Veterinary College which, in 2005, had to deny stories that an attempt to clone the great horse from DNA would be undertaken.

So far as is known, Sir Theodore, whose book was published in 1907, found no evidence of the whereabouts of Eclipse's bosom buddy, a parrot whose speciality was psalms and popular songs.

124. A RACEY RECIPE

In order to raise money for the Moorcroft Racehorse Welfare Centre, racing figures were approached for their favourite recipes, which were made up into a book, Turf Trough, published in 2006.

One recipe attracted rather more attention than the others, however, given that it did not seem to involve a great deal of food preparation other than the purchase – or perhaps not – of a banana. It was by Irish jockey-turned-trainer Arthur Moore, whose 'mixing instructions' for 'Banana Bread' were as follows: 'Look into laughing eyes. Entwine two loving arms. Spread well shaped legs slowly. Squeeze and massage milk containers very gently until fur lined mixing bowl is well greased. Add banana and gently work in and out until well creamed. Cover with nuts and sigh until well relieved. Bread is done when banana is soft. Be sure to wash the utensils and don't lick the bowl.'

125. GIVE HIM SOME CREDIT

Classic-winning former trainer Peter Walwyn was baffled when his effort to stand a number of racing friends a pre-Christmas lunch were thwarted when his credit card was rejected at Lambourn's Pheasant Inn.

Marcus Armytage, the *Daily Telegraph* racing writer, revealed why – 'in order to get his credit card in his faithful old wallet he had taken the scissors to the oblong piece of plastic and trimmed it up accordingly, snipping off a few edges here and there' – and rendering it absolutely useless for the purpose for which it was intended. Oblong?! Was it an Egg card?

126. OOPS, SHE'S DROPPED IT TOO EARLY

All horses have their birthdays on January 1, so the earlier in the year they are born, the more mature they will be when they come to start their racing career as a two or three year old. And it is absolutely vital that they do not deliver just before the first day of the new year.

Broodmare, Magical Romance, cost her owner Lady Serena Rothschild a world auction record of 4.6 million guineas in late 2006 when in foal with her first offspring.

So, connections were, to say the least, a little miffed when the mare gave birth prematurely on December 21 at Newmarket's Banstead Manor – at least ten days too early and 24 earlier than anticipated.

'What might have been a blaze of publicity for the sport has ended in farce,' wrote Sue Montgomery of *The Independent*, because, 'in 2010 when her body clock says she should be lining up for the 1000 Guineas she will officially be a four year old.'

Montgomery went on to declare that the early birth could be considered 'a matter of huge embarrassment' to an industry attracting serious investors.

'Under the current anachronistic system her value, as a racehorse anyway, is virtually nothing,' explained Ms Montgomery.

It was suggested that the foal could be sent to race in Australia where a thoroughbred's age dates from August 31, with a 31 day leeway permitted.

James Wigan of London Thoroughbred Services, the Rothschild's agent, commented: 'This case has brought only bad publicity, but I hope it will highlight the need for some sort of change.'

127. STEWARDS HAVE WINNERS' WHIP-ROUND

Perth, Australia owner George Towton was so fed up at waiting to receive the £50 winnings his horses had picked up whilst racing at Western Australian track, Wellington, in 1888, that he served a writ on the Turf Club there.

Club Secretary, Mr D A Hay, panicked as the cash-strapped operation could not afford to pay out so, in desperation he had to organise a whip round of £8 from each of six stewards to bail the course out of trouble.

128. FIVE TO TWO CERT

Formby-based trainer Peter Grayson had all five of the declared runners for the 6f Photo Books From Bonusprint.com Nursery at 2.45 at Lingfield on Saturday, December 30, 2006. It was believed to be the first time such a thing had happened on the flat.

Not everyone was happy at the thought of one trainer being responsible for every runner in a race. The trainer himself, for one, 'It's a trainer's nightmare' he said, 'It will be a juggling act to keep the owners happy. The intention is to run all of them.'

Others muttered darkly about the opportunity for skulduggery; some bookies seemed to have reservations – 'We'll certainly be taking care not to miss anything' said Neal Wilkins of VCbet – although the BHB seemed happy – 'It is a race like any other and there should not be any integrity problem. May the best horse win.'

Come the day of the race, though, only two of the five went to post for the race – three of them had mysteriously acquired vet's certificates excusing them from competing. Before the race, Grayson went out on a limb, predicting, 'My horse will win.'

Of the remaining pair, 2/1 favourite Grange Lili, ridden by Robbie Fitzpatrick duly saw off 7/2 shot Foxy Music. Not everyone was happy about the running of the race, with the *Racing Post* commenting 'It looked like a piece of work on the home gallops and as such hardly deserves entry in the form book.'

In August 2004 Jimmy Lambe had saddled both runners in a novice chase at Cartmel.

129. VOODOO THREAT

Disgruntled punters often make their feelings known to beaten jockeys – it comes with the territory. But a more sinister, perhaps unique, threat emerged to female riders in December 2006.

It was revealed that leading jockey Hayley Turner had been sent death threats and hate mail, while female apprentice Frankie Pickard also received disturbing mail – 'It was like a voodoo thing, with all sorts of things on. There are some nutters out there,' said her agent, Richard Hunter.

Turner received drawings of a grave, marked RIP, along with a Tarot card signifying death and a note warning 'I'm going to get you.'

Police were called in to investigate.

130. UNPRECEDENTED IMPACT

We reckon the likes of Red Rum, Desert Orchid, Best Mate and Persian Punch were pretty popular horses, but how many of the population as a whole would have stayed up to the early hours to watch any of these great runners in action?

Well, it is a pretty sure bet that we could not have matched the level of devotion displayed by the Japanese, to their own equine superstar, Deep Impact. When the horse contested the 2006 Arc de Triomphe, not only did thousands of Japanese follow him to Paris, making sure he started favourite in the process, but an estimated, staggering 16.4% of the entire population stayed up or got to watch him finish third in the race.

131. HELLISH CHRISTMAS

Tony McCoy must be a hellishly difficult chap to live with at the best of times as he goes about his single-minded way of proving himself to be the greatest ever jump jockey.

But at the festive season, he is literally 'hell-ish' to live with if his answer to a question asking 'What do you want for Christmas?' in December 2006 is to be believed, as he replied: 'A jar of Hellman's mayonnaise – I have to have it on everything!'

He wasn't the only racing personality to answer the question, posed by the *Racing Post*, with trainer Marcus Tregoning requesting, 'I would like Beyonce in my stocking' while John McCririck asked for 'some money to be able to buy Newcastle United and John Francome fancied 'stilts for when I go racing at Ascot'. C4 presenter Jim McGrath said he 'would like to be Tiger Woods for a day'.

132. JOCKEY WITH A SCREW LOOSE

Most observers of national hunt jockeys are convinced that they must have a screw loose to want to earn a living in such a dangerous, potentially fatal manner.

Jumps rider Wilson Renwick confirmed that suspicion when, towards the end of 2006, he was ruled out of riding – because he had a screw loose.

Renwick's agent, Richard Hall explained: 'When Wilson broke an ankle he had a plate inserted, but unfortunately a screw came loose and started rubbing against his boot when he was riding, causing him a fair bit of irritation.'

133. MOVING STORY

When Malton-trained Cyprian was aimed at the Oaks in 1836 she was walked to Epsom. After the race, connections decided to go for the Northumberland Plate in Newcastle. She also walked there – and won, despite having tramped some 300 miles.

Later that year Elis became 'officially' the first horse transported to the races in a six horse-drawn van, travelling from Goodwood to Doncaster to win the St Leger.

Such an unprecedented sight was this that en route people 'declared that a wild beast of fearful ferocity was locked up inside, others that a terrible criminal was being sent to the assizes for trial.'

134. SNOW EXCUSE FOR BAD BEHAVIOUR

Racegoers were admitted to Gwacheon, Seoul racecourse in South Korea on Sunday, December 17, 2006, where they were expecting to watch the country's biggest race of the season, the Grand Prix.

The weather was wintery, and the Korean Racing Authority suddenly announced at 11.50am, to a stunned crowd of some 12,000, that heavy snow had left the track unsafe and that the 12-race meeting was abandoned.

Racegoers were not best pleased: 800 of them rioted, and burned down ticket booths, smashed glass, assaulted racecourse staff and, perhaps most outrageous of all, 'threw snowballs in a violent manner.'

Eighteen people were arrested and others were barely placated by the offer of free tickets for a future meeting and a voucher for a racing magazine!

135. PLAGUED BY INSECTS

Locust swarms caused the abandonment of race meetings in Narrogin and Mount Barker in Western Australia in December 2006.

136. JAILED SAUNA OR LATER

Racehorse owner Hugh O'Donnell, well known for his string of runners whose names often included the word 'Mental', amongst them Finmental, was jailed in late December 2006 for six months for running a sex for sale sauna.

O'Donnell claimed that the property in Glasow was a centre for autistic children, that lap-dancing poles were for the assistance of disabled visitors and flashing disco lights were aids for the children while chains, shackles and mirrored ceilings were purely for decoration.

137. BATTEN DOWN THE PUNTERS

In 1997, visitors who flocked to the Epsom Downs on Derby day were attracted by the odds being offered by racecourse bookie John Batten.

Helped out by an assistant, Al, the generous layer was offering top price about the favourite Entrepreneur and good odds for other runners including the eventual winner, Benny The Dip.

After the race, won by the 11/1 shot a crowd of some 80 punters formed, waiting to collect their winnings. But Batten and his mate had fled the scene, leaving the winning punters an estimated collective £40,000 out of pocket.

Despite a photograph being widely shown by the media no trace was ever found of 'Batten'.

138. LEAPING INTO THE FRAME

Malton trainer William Garforth made an early impression in his career with Euryalus, a chestnut horse he sent out to win decent races at York, Wakefield and Northallerton in 1774.

The colt also won twice in 1775 but was eventually sold to stand at Beverley for a Mr Thompson who recorded a remarkable incident involving Euryalus who 'in the year 1789 made an extraordinary leap through an open window in his stable into the yard, at the Rose and Crown Inn, to a mare which was standing there at the time. The window was only 2ft 9ins high, one foot eight inches broad, and about four feet and a half from the ground; and, what is most singular, he did not receive the slightest injury, or in the least damage the window.'

139. STRANGE HORSE DEATHS

In 1828 it was reported that 'Marla, by North Star, dam by Gohanna, entered for the Gold Cup at Liverpool, was burnt to death at Newcastle on the evening of April 11, owing to a spark from a candle having ignited her litter. The poor animal was literally roasted alive' ...

1927 Melbourne Cup winner Trivalve died from a snake bite ... 1967 Champion Hurdler Saucy Kit died in 1980 whilst covering a grey mare ... in 1990, American chaser Uptown Swell was drowned when stung by a bee whilst swimming ... a year later jockey Willie Hernandez was thrown by his mount at Calder in Florida. The horse bolted straight into the infield lake and drowned. The horse was called Lucky Ben ... although Fetchinni collapsed and died whilst in the stalls awaiting the start of the Micklegate Selling Stakes at York in October 1992 the horse had come under orders, thus was officially declared to have been a runner ... We're In The Money, and English River, both listed as 'dead' in the form book both raced at Ascot and Nottingham respectively on November 18, 1988.

140. EARLY EQUINE FENG-SHUI?

The art of feng-shui has become fashionable in recent years, but there is some suggestion that at least one observer of the racing scene was in sympathy with the ideals of the Oriental system.

In May 1828, Mr R Darvill of the 7th Hussars, published the first volume of his *Treatise on the Care, Treatment and Training of the English Racehorse*, in which he suggested that all stables should be placed with their fronts to a southern aspect – 'from observations which I have made in attending sick horses, I am of the opinion that horses, when consistently standing in stables in which the doors and windows are placed so as to front the South are not so liable to constitutional diseases – the distemper, for instance – as those which stand in stables, the front of which may have a North-eastern aspect.'

141. MELBOURNE CUPSET

After helping make racing history when his horse Delta Blues became the first Japanese raider to win the Melbourne Cup, the horse's owner, Katsumi Yoshida, whose runner headed a one-two in the race for the land of the rising sun, decided to take the trophy back to his hotel on the local train, despite his inability to speak English – or even Australian!

He sat amongst impressed racegoers from the 106,000+ crowd, of whom I had been fortunate to be a member.

The 2006 Melbourne Cup, for which there is a parade of bands, previous winners, and current trainers – amongst them, Luca Cumani – through the streets of Melbourne, boasted a number of strange features – for example, Delta Blues' jockey Yasunari Iwata had never left Japan before. He prepared for the event by watching a DVD of the previous year's event.

Not everyone was impressed by the Japanese 1-2: 'The crowd found it difficult to relate to the Japanese, they could have come from Mars for all they care,' said leading Aussie owner, Paul Makin.

Aidan O'Brien's well fancied raider Yeats, partnered by Kieren Fallon, was blessed by a Catholic priest prior to the race, run in slightly unseasonal, chilly conditions, which resulted in six racegoers being treated for mild hypothermia by the St John first aiders – 'Some were just inappropriately dressed for the weather.'

In the crowd was singer Diana Ross, whose bodyguard (!) caused much ridicule to his charge when he blocked a racegoer emerging from a toilet, telling him 'Diana Ross is about to walk this way and no one is allowed to look at her'. 'Oh purr-lease!' scoffed top Aussie paper *The Age's* diary column.

Singer Chris Isaak who was spotted deep in conversation with Shane Warne, serenaded the crowd with a song prior to the race getting underway.

Nelson Mandela was invited to the Cup by the owners of New Zealand-trained and owned Mandela. The great man was otherwise engaged.

Most innovative touch of the day? Perhaps the introduction of plastic champagne bottles to get round the no-glass rules in the grandstand. I can confirm that there was no obvious adverse effect on the contents.

142. NOT SO FAST, COBBER

Reclusive trainer Jack Denham, whose relationship with the media over the years had been frosty to say the least, thawed out rapidly, after watching his Natski just pip the massive, 18 hands mare, Empire Rose, on the line in the 1988 Melbourne Cup.

A beaming Denham, renowned for his serious bearing, spoke happily to the gobsmacked journos, whom he had previously disdained, until the point that the official result was announced – 'Empire Rose first...'

Nine years later, jockey Greg Hall – favourite quote 'everything's ticketty-boo' – stood up in his irons and roared with excitement as his Doriemus went past the line, locked in combat with Might and Power, ridden by Jim Cassidy. Hall, a previous winner on Subzero in 1992, was convinced – as was most of the crowd – that he had prevailed. He celebrated as the owners hugged in the grandstand – until Might and Power's number went up as the winner.

Might and Power's trainer? Reclusive trainer Jack Denham.

By the way, Doriemus' sire was a horse called Norman Pentaquad which never raced because he was born with a deformity – a large, protruding bone on his leg which made him look as though he had five feet – hence his name, from 'penta', Greek for five; and quad, Latin for four.

143. MANFRED MANIAC

When he was good, he was very good. But when Manfred was bad, he was dreadful.

The Aussie runner peaked in winning the 1925 Victoria Derby by 12 lengths. But he refused to race on six of the 28 occasions he went to post – although he won half of those he condescended to take part in.

But his most extraordinary display came in the AJC Derby, for which he started 2/5 favourite, before refusing to start until a reported seven seconds after the rest of the field had gone – leaving him a furlong in arrears.

The combined efforts of jockey Billy Duncan, plus the clerk of the course, finally 'persuaded' Manfred to start and by halfway he had caught the tail-ender. By the home turn he had reached the leaders and he then stormed to victory. His reported time of 2.28.5, allowing for his seven second delay, was two seconds inside the then record.

In 1926 the Western Australian St Leger was won by Jolly Odd, ridden by W Sibbritt – despite the fact that his mount had actually turned the wrong way at the barrier start and set off in the opposite direction before the jockey could persuade him to race the right way – whereupon he stormed through the field to win by just over a length.

Manfred next refused to start in Melbourne's Caulfield Guineas but was still made 7/4 favourite for the 1925 Melbourne Cup in which he was beaten by a mere half a length.

He had a lay off before running 3rd and then refusing to start in consecutive races.

After running up a string of four straight wins he disgraced himself once too often by refusing to race on consecutive Saturdays in February 1927 and was retired to stud where he sired Melbourne Cup winner The Trump.

144. DRIVEN TO DISTRACTION

Racing was banned at all UK tracks other than Newmarket after May 31, 1918, during the First World War.

That racing had been taking place at various venues up until that point had been a contentious issue, and when the 'War' Grand National had been run at Gatwick, *The Times* got very shirty when it ran a story suggesting that 'motor cars in plenty' had driven racegoers to the course, in direct contravention of the fuel rationing prohibiting such pleasure jaunts at the time.

This provoked a stern rebuttal from no less a figure than the Chief Economy Officer of the Petroleum Executive, who fired off a missive to the Editor of *The Times*, putting him straight – 'On the completion of necessary inquiries it has been ascertained that there were not more than 15 motor cars on or near the racecourse during the races. The drivers of the cars on the course were examined by the Police as they left, and all but one were found to be officers on short leave or invalided members of His Majesty's Forces holding special permits under Paragraph 6 of the Motor Spirit and Gas Restriction Order, 1918.'

So, stick that in your paper and print it! Ah, but what about that 'all but one' ?

'The driver of the remaining car was summoned to appear at Reigate Petty Sessions on a charge of using motor spirit for driving a motor car from a race Meeting.'

145. YOU'RE TOO GOOD – CLEAR OFF!

When English jump jockey Thomas Pickernell – who would ride in 17, and win three Grand Nationals – went to live in Australia in 1855, shortly after his 20th birthday he decided to do a little stewarding, and then to take a few rides while he was there.

Soon he was booting home the winners and, in the process, putting the noses of a number of Tasmania's top jockeys out of joint.

In particular the former cock o'the walk there, David Richardson, became so frustrated at being beaten by the 'Pom' in-comer that he started an anti-Pickernell petition, then dashed off a letter to the local paper, demanding Pickernell's disappearance:

'Though willing to allow Pickernell's qualities as a jockey to be of the first order, I am bound to suggest that, were Mr Pickernell's coolness, skill and judgment displayed in discovering that by offering his services gratuitously to the proprietors of racehorses he is depriving poor men – and some of them with large families – of their usual and legitimate and only means of subsistence, it would be more creditable to that gentleman than taking the opposite course and would entitle him to and ensure him the award, not only of every praise and the respect of every well-wisher of the Turf, but that of the community generally, particularly those who are depending on horse-racing for support.'

Not only is this a contender for the 'longest sentence ever' award, it is also perhaps the first example of the Whingeing Poms being beaten at their own game!

146. EMUS BANNED

'Racecourse Emus (people systematically picking up betting tickets) will not be tolerated on the Australian Jockey Club's Racecourses. Anybody found so operating will be deemed to be an undesirable and will be banned from the Racecourse and dealt with according to law.' I was a little surprised to see this announcement – endorsed by 'A A King, Chief Executive' in the race programme for the Royal Randwick, Sydney, Australia, meeting of Saturday, November 25, 2006, which I was fortunate enough to attend. The same rule had also been highlighted in the cards for Flemington in Melbourne, where I had also watched the Victoria Derby and Melbourne Cup meetings. Odd sort of rule, though. Presumably, if I am stupid enough to lose my winning ticket then no one else can collect it, so the winnings will go begging and will stay in the bookies' satchels or the Aussie tote's (TAB) capacious pockets. I'd rather someone picked up the ticket and made use of the money, really.

147. NOT SUCH A HAPPY BIRTHDAY

It might have made for a happy birthday for owner/rider Nolan Byrne when he partnered his chaser Winsley in an Amateur Riders' event at Cheltenham on October 25, 2006. But jockey Byrne celebrated both his debut ride, and his 21st by putting up nearly as many pounds overweight on his mount. Punters and racegoers were not best pleased as the partnership went off at 33/1 and unseated at the 7th.

Those who had backed the horse in the morning without knowing how much overweight would be carried – 20lbs – complained on the Betfair Forum.

But Byrne, who rode at 10lb above his stated normal riding weight of 11st – dismissed them – 'I put up the overweight because he is my own horse and I wanted to ride him.'

Paul Struthers, of the Horseracing Regulatory Authority, commented: 'There is no rule that dictates how much overweight someone can carry.'

Perhaps, thought many, there should be. Not, though former BBC commentator Julian Wilson who, declaring 'is no one allowed any fun nowadays'? lambasted the 'losers and low-lifes who, for the main, contribute to the betting exchange chatrooms,' for vilifying Byrne.

148. HOW HARRY NETTED QUEST

After hurdler Desert Quest had won to put himself into the Champion Hurdle picture in late 2006, pro gambler Harry Findlay, who bought the horse to run in his mother's name, revealed how he had financed the purchase of the horse via a hefty bet on a tennis match: 'I laid out £400,000 to win about £300,000. When Andre Agassi went a break up in the third set I had another lump on Roger. If he'd lost, I wouldn't have been in the comfort zone to buy a horse.'

Findlay also revealed that it had not been easy to establish himself as a successful high-rolling gambler: 'In trying to get by on gambling without a job I was almost considered a rogue. I was potless a million times and homeless, too, after my Mum threw me out. I've lost everything including my freedom, my self-respect and that of my friends and family. I've frightened myself badly.'

149. TIED DOWN

Prue Hayes, long suffering wife of top Aussie trainer David Hayes, revealed how her husband deals with 'a bad day at the track' shortly before the 2006 Melbourne Cup. Revealed Prue in *The Age* newspaper, 'Not only does he come home grumpy but he invariably takes off his tie, cuts it into small pieces and goes straight to bed – even if its only 7pm.'

Mind you, it is a wonder they ever got wed, as on the first date, Hayes, a former crack athlete, showed off to his new girlfriend by taking her to the local athletics field where he 'showed her his triple jump run up.'

150. NO LAUGHING MATTER

When Australian comedian Tony Rickards, who appears on stage under the name Con Marasco with an act which features plenty of topical racing-related comedy, visited the stables of top Aussie breeder Neville Duncan, at Oakland Park Stud near Busselton, he was bitten on the backside by a then un-named yearling.

Rickards was impressed with the aggressive youngster and tried unsuccessfully to raise the cash to buy him. But when Duncan got round to naming the colt, he remembered the biting incident, and called him Marasco – 'so that every time the horse went past the post he could feel awfully sick about it'.

And he was, as the horse hit the headlines as a four-year-old in 2006, clocking up wins in top races and pushing his value up towards the stratosphere.

151. DEAD HEATED MOMENTS

Jockey Bobby Don experienced the unique feat of being involved in three dead heats on one card when his Satansnameisrufus, Early Christmas and Bicker's Boy had to share the honours with, respectively, Ramsey's Straw, Cletos Easy and London Town at Santa Fe track, The Downs on June 18, 1983.

The first quadruple dead-heat on record was at Hove in 1851 in a chase, when Defaulter, Reindeer, The Squire and Pulcherrima were ruled to have crossed the line inseparably together.

The first such outcome in a flat race was at Newmarket in 1855 on October 22 when Overreach, The Unexpected, Gamester and Lady Go Lightly went past together.

Prince Ming and All India dead-heated in Morphetville, S Africa's Baker Hcp, on May 13, 1964 – then did so again in the Birthday Cup at Victoria Park on April 10, 1965.

At Rockhampton in Queensland, Australia on September 9, 1922, Bay Hart and Sir Ross dead-heated three times in the Second Division Hcp – after which stakes were divided.

On January 29, 1994 father, Rodney Durden, and son, Craig Durden, dead-heated on 66/1 shot St Adam and 9/2 favourite, Sazerac, in a hurdles race at Bendigo, Australia.

152. FOR FLOCK'S SAKE

After five jockeys were dislodged from their mounts when a flock of seagulls – the birds, not the rock band – flew into the runners as they entered the home straight for the Goldenway Handicap at Sandown, Australia, on March 30, 2005, the event was declared a no-race. In August 2007, two Canada geese were killed when a gaggle of the birds landed on the track as the runners at Wolverhampton sped towards the home turn.

153. ANYTHING YOU CAN DO

After Brisbane jockey Colin O'Neill won on Summer Park at Rockhampton on October 1, 1973, his wife Pam went out and won the next race on Rocky Way, completing a unique double for a married couple.

154. PAYNEFUL

Eight members of the Payne family were active jockeys in the 1990s in Australia, with four of them – Therese, 24; Maree, 22; Bernadette, 20 and Patrick, 19; all contesting one race for the first time at Warrnambool on July 8, 1994.

Siblings, older sister Brigid, younger brother Andrew and younger sisters Cathy and Michelle all rode and won races with Patrick on Besta Besta, beating Therese on Initial Red into second and Maree on Locharn into third at Bendigo on December 28, 1993.

The three did exactly the same again on November 17, 1994 at Ballarat with Andrew and Bernadette also having mounts in the race as a record five of them competed in the same contest.

155. SLEEPING ON THE JOB

Trainer Nigel Twiston-Davies is apparently a martyr to sleepwalking, an unwanted affliction which has in the past reportedly resulted in him waking up naked in hotel corridors and which in October 2006 left him needing stitches in his head and painkillers for rib and back injuries, after he tumbled on to a brick wall after opening a bedroom door and falling several feet.

Hearing the news, rival handler Philip Hobbs was somewhat less than sympathetic – 'I suggest he wears a parachute in bed in future'.

156. TRUTH IS SOMETIMES FICTION

Everyone knows that the first Melbourne Cup winner, Archer, was walked over 500 miles by his lad, David Power, to contest the first running of the race in 1861. They even made a film about it in 1985, Archer's Adventure. However, shipping records show that the horse travelled from Sydney to Melbourne on the ship, The City of Sydney ... everyone knows the first Derby was run at Epsom in 1780 – ah, so what about the Derby Plate run at the Isle of Man from 1621? ... everyone knows Richard Dunwoody, one of the greatest jump jockeys of all time could never have won the Derby. Except that he partnered Misaaff to win the Jersey Derby in 1990 ... everyone knows the first British evening race meeting took place at Hamilton Park on July 18, 1947 – er, unless you count the one they ran at York in 1784 – 'the fifth race was run in the dark', or the one at Baltinglass, Ireland in December 1791 'when lights were erected at each corner of the course to direct the runners' reported the *Irish Racing Calendar* ... everyone knows American jockey Tod Sloan introduced the 'monkey on a stick' style of riding to England when he arrived in 1897 – until they learn that black, Kentucky Derby-winning jockey William Simms was here a couple of years earlier and was the first to demonstrate the technique ... everyone knows racing has always been the Sport of Kings – yes, but only since 1918, discovered Reader in English at Oxford University, Gerald Hammond, explaining that the phrase first referred to War; then Hunting ... everyone knows Bruce Hobbs became the youngest ever Grand National-winning jockey when partnering Battleship to victory in the race in 1938 – everyone, that is, except for Irish jockey Reggie Walker who was on runner-up Royal Danieli. Despite the verdict going to Battleship after lengthy deliberation by the judge, Walker went to his grave in 1951 convinced that he had been deprived of at least a dead heat.

157. GAMBLER

A chemist called Gamble created a sensation in Melbourne in 1879 when he advertised for 'subscribers' to buy shares worth £1 each in selected horse races.

Each subscriber could select his own horse, and the first prize pay out would be one half of the total amount subscribed, to be divided amongst those selecting the winner. Second prize would total three tenths of the prize money, and third one tenth, leaving one tenth as profit for Mr Gamble.

Punters – and the media of the day – loved the new-fangled idea. The authorities were not so enthusiastic, and police searched his chemist's shop and arrested Mr Gamble.

The authorities wanted to take Mr Gamble's system under their control and run it at racecourses.

But every time he was released, Mr Gamble promptly organised another subscription race, until, eventually, the might of the law stepped in to put a stop to his enterprise.

158. AS TOUGH AS IT GETS

The conditions for the 1828 Rathcroghan Steeplechase, run over five miles at the course in Roscommon in Ireland, suggested there were few tougher events ever contested.

The race was a sweepstakes of £10 each, with 30 sovereigns added. 'During the run six stone walls, five feet high and 18 inches broad at top are to be leaped, independent of other obstacles – 4yos to carry 10st 10lb; five 11st 8lb; six and aged 12st'.

Thirteen went to post for the race, run on March 18 and witnessed and recorded for posterity in *The Sportsman* magazine by 'One of the Boys of the Redmond's.'

The race was ultimately won by Charles French's Tiger, carrying 12st, described as 'a flea-bitten grey of great power and equal to carry 14st with hounds.'

The racegoer described the crucial stage, in which 'the race lay between Tiger, Barony Boy and Highflyer, who was leading until they came to the last wall but one, which Highflyer and Tiger took in fine style, but Barony Boy struck it with his knees and gave himself and rider the most frightful fall I ever witnessed. The horse charged at it gallantly, and from the force with which he struck it, he performed a complete somerset in the air, landing on the top of his head, and then rolling over his rider, who I am happy to say, was not much hurt, though at the moment I thought both horse and man were really kilt. I believe this was the only fall which took place in the race. After the fall poor Barony Boy was no more seen.'

As Tiger and Highflyer fought out the finish, the former got home by a head ' a thing only rarely witnessed at the finale of a steeple chase; and some good judges say that Highflyer would have won had he not been jostled by a horseman just after he leaped the last wall.'

Some things haven't changed in almost 200 years in Irish racing, though, as the correspondent noted, 'The race was scarcely over, ere it began to rain in torrents – I fully looked forward to a mighty "wet night" – and "faith!", I was not disappointed, for here hospitality holds sway!.'

159. TOMMY LYES IN WAIT

There are few reports of the riding tactics employed by jockeys in the earlier days of racing, but an eyewitness account of the Ascot Gold Cup victory of the Tommy Lye-ridden 8/1 chance, Bobadilla in 1828 reveals that at least one rider was using his wits to conjure up victory.

Reported the *Sporting Magazine* of the June 4 race, 'So near a dead heat was it between the two (Bobadilla and Souvenir, partnered by A Pavis) that Tommy Lye, brought expressly from the North to ride on this occasion, had recourse to a little stratagem that I never before saw practised, and which, I have no doubt, gave him the race.

'He was on the farther side from the (Judge's) chair; but at the instant before coming to the winning post, he suddenly threw himself forward in order to attract the eye of the Judge. It had the desired effect and Bobadilla was declared winner, by a head only.

'Lye's riding in this race, and the little Yorkshire finish which he gave Arthur (Pavis) at the end, has put him up as a jockey many points in the estimation of our South Country judges of riding.'

160. SHOERLY HEEL POLISH THINGS OFF

Santa Anita racetrack in the US ran the Eddie Logan Stakes on December 30, 2006 – possibly the first race sponsored in honour of a racecourse shoe-shine attendant.

Eddie Logan has worked at the track since 1934, and course president Ron Charles paid tribute to him: 'He's still brightening the life of everyone who passes by his shoe stand.' 96-year-old Eddie was delighted, 'I am just so honoured – now, if I can just pick the winner.'

161. VIEWING PROBLEMS

Ascot was forced to spend millions of pounds in an effort to improve viewing from certain areas of the course after being inundated with complaints following the reopening of the course in 2006 after the building of a new grandstand.

But complaints about viewing facilities at major courses are far from a modern phenomenon. In 1868, the *Broadway* magazine criticised Epsom – 'There was a day, certainly, when this Grand Stand was first opened, that everybody had something like equal main and chance. If he came early he got a good place, but by this time every good place is bespoken, for the whole front of the building is occupied by private boxes.

Anybody, unless he happens to be "somebody", has, therefore, the Hobson's choice of a bird's eye view on the leads (sic) above, where he gathers a very imperfect notion of the race, or the crush of the lawn below, where, by adopting the tactics of a Perfect Cure, and continually jumping up into the air, he may, peradventure, recognize the colour of a jacket, and delude himself into the idea that he has seen the Derby run for.'

*In the same year, the Derby was almost postponed for a number of years after a dispute arose when a Mr Studd purchased 'some property, including a certain portion of the Derby course' and refused the Epsom authorities offer of remuneration for permission to use that part of the track. Eventually a late compromise was arrived at.

162. LIFE'S A BECHER

Becher's Brook, the Grand National obstacle, is named after Captain (Martin) Becher, who fell into the water there in 1839 whilst riding Conrad. Few know that he remounted, only to fall at the second brook, and fewer still know much more about this man, son of a Norfolk farmer, and who received his courtesy title from the Duke of Buckingham.

He was a decent rider over jumps and hurdles and in 1829 rode 700 miles in a fortnight to get to the meetings where he had rides. He was also the life and soul of parties, showing off his party-piece of running round a room without touching the floor – even kicking the ceiling – whilst imitating the sounds of animals. In 1832, he was arrested on suspicion of being a body-snatcher because of the coffin-shaped driving box on his buggy.

In October 1835 he won twice on the same horse, Vivian, at Aintree's first ever all-hurdles race meeting. In 1836 he won the St Albans Steeplechase, a big race of the day, on one of his favourite horses, Grimaldi – only for the animal to drop dead shortly after passing the post. Becher kept a souvenir of the day which he would proudly show off to friends – one of Grimaldi's forelegs.

Becher retired in 1847 after a fall at Doncaster, in which he broke his thigh in two places. He then became Inspector of Sacks to the Great Northern Railway. He died in 1864 and was buried in Willesden Cemetery, aged 67.

163. THE SECOND RACING SUFFRAGETTE PROTEST

Most people in racing are aware of the controversial death of suffragette's rights campaigner, Emily Davison, during the 1913 Derby in which she brought down King George V's colt, Anmer, sustaining fatal injuries in the process.

But few are aware of a similar incident which took place at the Royal Ascot meeting later that same year, during the Ascot Gold Cup.

As the runners turned for home, 1912 St Leger winner, Tracery, was going well, four or five lengths clear when, as an eyewitness account records, 'emulating the example set by the militant suffragette whose rash interference with the runners in the Derby had thrown the field into confusion and led to her own death, some demented fanatic rushed out from the trees brandishing a revolver in one hand and a flag in the other.

'Whalley, the rider of Tracery, tried to avoid the lunatic, but failing to do so, he and Tracery were brought down.'

The previous year's winner, Prince Palatine, had to jump over Tracery, after which he swerved across the course, stood stock still, then started again – and won the race in the record time of 4mins 21 and three fifths of a second.

The 'lunatic', a man called Hewitt whose revolver was loaded and whose flag was that of the suffragette movement, was severely injured.

164. DOGGED EFFORT

Each-way backers of Lord Astor's Swift And Sure had every reason to be barking mad after the horse finished fourth, one and a half lengths behind third placed 2/1 favourite, Colorado, in the 1926 Derby, won easily by 11/2 shot, Coronach.

For 9/2 second favourite, Swift And Sure, ridden by R A 'Bobby' Jones, was badly interfered with when a dog ran loose on to the track, as they entered the straight, costing the horse at least the distance by which he failed to make the frame.

165. MONTICELLO MIRACLE

BLINDED in his right eye during a U boat attack in 1942 when he was in the US Navy, Don Karkos overcame his disability to work with horses and in racing.

In December 2006, aged 81, he was celebrating 16 years at Monticello Raceway where he was working as a paddock security guard, checking in horses and helping out in the barns.

As he helped prepare a horse called My Buddy Chimo for an early morning workout the colt lowered his head before raising it suddenly and butting Don, just above his blind right eye.

Don was thrown back against a wall and stunned by the incident.'Being kicked is part of the job, but I've never been hit that hard.' He went home to recover – where he suddenly became aware that sight had returned to his eye.

'I love that horse. Hey, right now, I'm loving it all,' Don told reporters.

166. NO CORN-Y RACING JOKE

Cornish comedian Jethro became the unexpected owner of the only living full sister to triple Gold Cup winning jumper, Best Mate.

Looking for 'something they couldn't get their hands on' to provide him with a pension, he was watching TV racing from Cheltenham when he 'realised someone must be producing these winners.'

This encouraged him to get involved in assembling a stable of jumps broodmares, near Okehampton, where his pride and joy is Flying Iris, bought in Ireland – 'Where can you buy a full sister to Best Mate?' he asks rhetorically. 'You can't, Flying Iris is the only one. I bought her at three and put her in foal straight away.' She's like the Mona Lisa, the only one in the world.'

Yet the 'world's funniest Cornishman' as he describes himself, who has already sold a yearling filly for 180,000 euros, finds racing no laughing matter – in fact he has never been to the races in his life – 'those huge crowds would put me off. I'd much prefer to sit beside my fire at home and watch them winning on TV' he revealed in December 2006.

167. COMMENTATOR'S NIGHTMARE

The 1883 Paris Grand Steeplechase was won by Too Good, partnered by aristocratic Hungarian jockey, Georg Maria Gobert Graf Erdody von Monyorokerek und Monoszto – who also fortunately, answered to 'Count George'.

168. FOR ROWING, READ RACING

Once upon a time the Oxford and Cambridge Varsity Boat Race had a serious rival – the Oxford and Cambridge Varsity Horse Race.

Few are aware of it today, but back in the 1860s the two great universities took each other on on the racecourse.

'In days gone by Oxford undergraduates had a race at Moreton-in-the-Marsh Steeplechases to themselves,' wrote racing writer Charles Adolph Voight in 1925, 'It was called the Trial Stakes and had its origin in being a sort of test race to see which of three horses should represent Oxford against Cambridge when there was an Inter-University Steeplechase. These began about 1861.'

Records of these contests are few and far between, but it is recorded that in 1865 Oxford won, courtesy of Mr Leathes' Marchioness who got the better of Mr Wentworth's Proposition, representing Cambridge.

169. BLAZING SADDLES

At a jumps meeting staged at Kilkenny in Ireland in 1896 the four runners and riders in the main chase of the day, being run over three miles, had a shock as they approached the open ditch fence on the far side of the course – for it was blazing merrily away, having been torched by local 'scoundrels'. Undaunted, three of the four jumped it and, unperturbed, carried on round and did so again on the next circuit, by which time it was merely smouldering.

170. EARL-Y WARNING

When the Earl of Chesterfield breathed his last in 1773, his 79th year, the reading of his will was eagerly awaited.

In the will was a generous bequest to his godson, albeit with strings attached: 'In case my godson Philip Stanhope shall at any time keep or be concerned in keeping any racehorse or pack of hounds, or reside one night at Newmarket, that infamous seminary of iniquity and ill manners, during the course of the races there, or shall resort to the said races, or shall lose in one day at any game or bet whatsoever the sum of £500 then in any of the cases aforesaid, it is my express will that he, my said godson, shall forfeit and pay out of my estate the sum of £50,000 to and for the use of the Dean and Chapter of Westminster.'

Not all of the 'Chesterfields' were anti-racing and the succeeding Lord C George, the 6th Earl, owned the 1838 St Leger winner Don John and the 1838 and 1849 Oaks heroines, Industry and Lady Evelyn. He reportedly spent the latter stages of his life – he died in 1866 – when he had disposed of much of his huge inherited fortune, gazing into space through a telescope manoeuvred for him by a butler.

171. STRANGE EARLY HISTORY OF IRISH NATIONAL

A 'five bob' horse won the second ever Irish Grand National, run in 1871 over three miles. Owner Thomas Yaden Loyd Kirkwood of Carrick-on-Shannon rescued filly Mabel Grey from the knacker's yard for that amount, renamed her The Doe, under which name she romped home at 10/1 – then produced 1881 English Grand National winner, Woodbrook ... in 1873 Scots Grey was neck and neck with The Torrent as they raced to the finishing post. But Scots Grey's saddle slipped and the horse bolted into the course betting ring, scattering the bookies before rider Garry Moore got the horse back on course to finish second. He was third next year, but won in 1875 – although the official verdict that he had beaten Mickey Free on the line came too late for the young clerk from Dublin who had backed him big-time with money which wasn't strictly speaking, his to bet with. Convinced the horse –

and his bet – had lost, he fled the course and committed suicide ... 1876's Irish Grand National was won by, er, Grand National ... the 1885 winner, Billet Doux, was only an average winner, but owner, Polish-American, Count Eliott Zborowski, went on to suffer one of the great bizarre deaths. He was killed in a freak motoring accident in Nice in 1903 when one of his cufflinks became entangled in the drive-chain of his motor vehicle.

172. FAMILY FAILURE

Trainer Frank Dichlera from Mullimbimby in Australia had great hopes of his filly Ruby Queen when he sent her our for her first racecourse experience on October 29, 1988. Alas, the inexperienced runner trailed in last of 12.

Frank's optimism was far from dented and he sent Ruby Queen back into the fray – again and again. And again. And again. Fifty nine times she raced. Fifty nine times she was unplaced. She won a total of zero prize money and was beaten on average just over 13½ lengths every time.

Frank reluctantly retired the horse, but soon had the career of her daughter, Midnight Ruby, to look forward to. It was a shorter career than Mum's. Only three races, but Midnight Ruby kept up the family reputation. Unplaced each time, no prize money won, beaten on average just over 30 lengths per race.

Undeterred, Frank introduced Ruby Queen's son, King Ruby, to the track. He was a real chip off the old block. Forty five races. Never placed. No prize money. Beaten just over 19 lengths on average.

Frank gave up on the family – and possibly went off for a ruby.

173. LOCO PUNTER WENT OFF THE RAILS

Keen punter Brian Bonnay was given a hot tip for the 2.50 at Lingfield, but realised he would struggle to get to the bookies in time to place his bet.

So the 32-year-old Darlington man, a keen amateur athlete, decided that the only way to get to his local betting shop in Northallerton would be to run along the local high speed railway line. Even though the shop was 14 miles down the track, Brian set off alongside the line. As he jogged along, startled train drivers reported a 'madman' on the line, and high-speed trains were forced to slow down to 20mph to avoid hitting him. Brian stopped en route to ask astonished track workers whether he was on the right lines.

Eventually, Transport Police were sent after him in a diesel, and managed to collar him nine miles into the trip.

Brian was most annoyed that he was unable to get his £50 bet on the tip, which was called, appropriately enough, Express Service – until he found out later that the Bill O'Gorman-trained four year old had been beaten.

Brian was duly hauled up in front of the local beak in January 1993, where he was fined £40 with £100 costs for trespassing on the railway.

174. DARK OUTCOME

Top stayer, Dark Secret came into the stretch at Belmont Park, USA, with the 1934 Jockey Club Gold Cup, run over two miles, at his mercy.

As he stretched towards the line there was a sudden hitch in his stride and rival Faireno closed to within a head as the pair flashed across the line.

Dark Secret immediately pulled up in obvious distress; his right foreleg had been broken, yet he had run on to the finish in what came to be hailed as perhaps the bravest ever equine performance on a racetrack. He was immediately put down.

175. LOWE POINT

'Gallant Man, in hand, and saving ground to the last three eighths mile, moved up determinedly in the early stretch, reached the lead between calls and was going stoutly when his rider misjudged the finish'.

That is the dispassionate description of what happened when jockey Bill Shoemaker came to win the 1957 Kentucky Derby only to stand up in his irons before the post and end up beaten a nose by Iron Liege.

You'd have expected Gallant Man's owner Ralph Lowe to be incandescent with rage. But he knew it was going to happen.

He had told people before the race that he had dreamed his colt lost the race because the jockey stood up in the stirrups prematurely. He readily forgave Shoemaker but might not have been so understanding, one suspects, had he not been a Texas oil millionaire.

It was all the stranger considering that Shoemaker had won the race as recently as 1955 on Swaps and went on to do so three times more on Tomy Lee in 1959, Lucky Debonair in 1965 and Spend a Buck in 1985.

176. LESTER CASHES IN

Lester Piggott made a big impression when he visited the Doomben racecourse in Brisbane, Australia, winning a top race there.

So much so that the Brisbane Turf Club's official history, published in 1989, made a point of recording that, having won the race and been presented with a trophy, Lester 'indicated he would have preferred money'.

Turf Club chief, Sir Clive Uhr, a man once imprisoned by the Japanese, was heard to remark to a fellow official, 'Tell that bloke, if he's so unhappy about the trophy we'll buy it back from him.' And they did. For 100 Aussie dollars.

The history does not record whether Lester received the trophy after winning the 1969 International Stakes for which he had been booked to ride Alby Pratt-trained Prunda, only to request a switch to the trainer's other runner, Panvale after that horse made Lester's look very slow indeed in a public gallop.

Piggott changed his mind and stayed where he was when Pratt whispered to him that Panvale had been fitted with ultra light, wafer-thin horseshoes for the gallop, in order to encourage better odds for Prunda – who stormed home like the good thing he was.

177. DOWN THE DRAIN

Having hosted only three meetings after its gala opening on May 20, 1933, the brand new Doomben racecourse in Brisbane, Australia, was forced to close down.

Someone had forgotten to fit vital drains. Fences had to be pulled down and stretches of turf ripped up before the track could re-open several months later.

Another Aussie racecourse found its inaugural meeting called off, when the first scheduled race meeting at Roeburne in the north west of Western Australia, due to be run in mid 1867 had to be postponed until August of that year – due to a local food shortage.

178. SWORDID INCIDENT

Ralph Topping, now a director at bookies William Hill, visited a Glasgow branch where he worked some 30 years ago and was surprised to be greeted by one of his old customers.

Surprised, because Ralph had been working as relief manager in the shop the last time he had seen the man – with whom there had been a disagreement over a disputed bet.

Recalled Ralph, 'He was the brother of a Glasgow gangster. He disappeared – then came back looking for me, clasping a samurai sword.'

Having survived the incident, Ralph mused, philosophically, 'Thirty years on the guy is still a regular. Just shows how loyal customers can be.'

179. BROLLY GOOD? NOT REALLY

Five thousand spectators had flocked to see South Australian course Thebarton's Grand Annual Steeplechase on September 19, 1854 and were in good heart as the well fancied Duke of Wellington forged to the front.

But hopes of a payout for those who had backed the animal were dashed in bizarre fashion as a woman in the crowd rushed on to the track and thrust a parasol at horse and rider – causing the Duke to jump sideways and come down on top of its unfortunate rider.

180. JUST LIKE AINTREE, THEN

'Young virgins, according to custom, appeared in a state of nudity; many of them had wild flowers stuck behind their ears, and strings of beads round their loins; but want of clothing did not seem to damp their pleasure in the entertainment'.

This description of part of the crowd at a race meeting – which also included 'a few naked boys, on ponies without saddles who rode over the course, after which the second and last heat commenced' – at Kiama in West Africa, was contained in an 1832 book, *Discovery of the Termination of the Niger*, by an author named Landers who wrote, 'The racecourse was bounded on the north by low granite hills; on the south by a forest and on the east and west by tall shady trees' – almost an African Goodwood by the sound of things – and the jockeys wore 'trousers of every colour, red leather boots and white and blue turbans. The horses were caparisoned with bells, tassels and charms'.

It all sounds quite familiar. Oh, except that, 'the jockeys carried spears, which they brandished madly.'

181. CARRY ON RACING

1000 guineas day on May 8, 1945, coincided with V E (Victory in Europe) Day as the Second World War came to an end – but no one at Newmarket was prepared to allow a show of emotion to get the better of them. Stiff upper lips were the order of the day, reported the Bloodstock Breeders' Review of the year, looking back on the occasion – 'The exterior circumstance of the greatest victory in history was not allowed to interfere with the conduct or decorum of the Meeting. The Stewards did not exchange hats, nor did the bookmakers pay out any bonuses. Even the white and red flag, flying above the winning post, was not replaced by a Union Jack. The crowd left in an orderly manner after the conclusion of the last race and proceeded on its homeward way. All the lights were up again after five and a half years.'

182. BURN OUT

Eddie 'The Fireman' Birchley, who had indeed been in that profession, set out to douse Australian bookmakers in the late 60s and early 1970s via the oft-tried but seldom successful tactic of placing vast sums on so-called, odds-on good things.

Birchley quit the Brisbane Fire Department and initially was very successful at Queensland tracks where the TAB system guaranteed a minimum 10% profit on all winning bets, meaning that the shortest price a horse could pay out at was effectively 1/10.

By hammering away at the 'certainties', 'I soon knocked that off – the Queensland government had to change the law,' boasted Birchley.

By now he was betting up to $100,000 a time – 'I'll always be happy to lay 1/3 or 1/4 as long as I think the correct price is 1/100.'

He won $77,000 on Elle at Moonee Valley in December 1973 and in November 1974 plunged $208,000 on Caboul at Flemington, forcing the price down from 2/7 to 1/6. He laid $50,000 to win half that on Debbie-Jo at Rosehill, and $60,000 to pick up $15,000 on St Louis Blue at Warwick Farm.

Birchley burned the bookies for $200,000 in a three day conflagration at Flemington in early 1975, backing a horse called Lord Dudley so heavily that the mechanism on the bookies' boards couldn't show the price the horse had shrunk to.

Having laid out $1m to win $200,000 the scheme inevitably began to go wrong as he dropped stakes of $105,000; $75,000 and $60,000, leading him to believe that the horses he was backing were being deliberately stopped or got at and threatening to produce sensational evidence to support his claims to the Australian Jockey Club – but nothing materialised.

Making another bid for glory in 1975 he blew over $70,000 on beaten Cap d'Antibes in the AJC Oaks at Randwick and $60,000 on Juanita Gay in Melbourne.

It was the beginning of the end and Birchley's blazing betting career was damped down until in 1980, aged 49, he poignantly fell foul of the law over a trivial case of stealing goods worth less than ten dollars.

183. EAT YOUR HEART OUT, ROD

Trainer Rod Simpson is well known for his flamboyant fashion sense – but even he might have had to give best to a handler from the mid 1920s, R 'Moppy' Gordon, who was a frequent visitor to Chepstow where he would 'grace the paddock swards' by 'wearing yellow suits, red socks, yellow shoes, multi-coloured bow ties and to complete the picture usually turned up in a yellow Rolls Royce,' according to course historian, Pat Lucas.

184. REARLY UNLUCKY

Renowned stud groom, Harry Sharpe told a story of one of the least likely equine fatalities which could be imagined.

Writing in the 1945 *Bloodstock Breeders Review*, the author of *The Practical Stud Groom*, recalled an American stallion, Hand Grenade, foaled in 1915, who 'had an accomplishment (?) which, I learned years later, led to his death.

'When brought out from his stable for inspection, he would rear straight up on his hind legs and click his forefeet together like castanets. 'Showing off once too often he overbalanced, fell backwards, broke a hind leg and had to be destroyed.'

185. JOHNNY'S WINNING GAMBLE

He may have been one of the most appropriately named of jockeys, but Johnny Gamble nearly found himself in big trouble for living up to his name.

The jump jockey was at Newbury between rides, wearing a dark suit and trilby hat one day when he decided to ignore the rule which prevents jockeys from having a bet and went into the ring to have a flutter. Whilst there he spotted out of the corner of his eye a steward looking towards him.

Worried that he may have been rumbled he made himself scarce, only to hear over the public address system an announcement calling for 'the jockey Johnny Gamble to report to the stewards' room after the second race.'

Thinking quickly Gamble, who lived nearby ran to the exit and hailed a cab to take him home, where he quickly changed into slacks, a sports jacket and flat cap before dashing back to the course.

Once there, recalled his riding pal, the Grand National-winning jockey John Buckingham whose finest moment was on board the 100/1 shock outsider Foinavon and who retired in 1971, Gamble 'reported to the stewards' room as instructed, and the man who had spotted him in the ring looked at him with some surprise, muttered 'Sorry, there's been a mistake' and let him go.'

186. WINNER CARRIED TWO JOCKEYS OVER THE LINE – TOGETHER

Leading Australian jockey Ted Bartle rode in many top races in that country during the 1930s and 40s, retiring in 1947. On March 22, 1930 he rode six winners at Moorefield. But in later years he recalled his part in an almost certainly unique incident which took place at Bathurst racecourse. Bartle was riding the heavy odds-on favourite in a maiden when fellow jockey Barney Porter was deemed surplus to requirements by his inexperienced mount who promptly deposited the rider across the neck of Bartle's runner.

'I carted him past the post, then got him back on his mount before we returned to the Judge,' remembered Bartle, but 'He called it a dead-heat – I reckon I won with 16 stone.'

187. NEW YORK TRAINER TRIVIA

• **Knockout** New York trainer Peter Vestal tried his hand at boxing prior to racing – fighting as a middleweight he had 38 bouts, winning 23, 15 by knockout.

• **On The Right Road** New York trainer Howard Tesher was a little surprised to learn in 1993 that one of his horses, Cox's Sword, was not at the Belmont Park track where he was supposed to be – but that he had somehow managed to find himself, riderless, running down the Hempstead Turnpike during the morning rush hour. The horse then 'merged onto the cloverleaf heading to the Cross Island Parkway.'

'Luckily,' said a relieved Tesher later, 'he was smart enough and well trained enough to run with the traffic instead of against it.'

Cox's Sword was apprehended on the return leg of his journey and brought back safe and sound.

• **Bleached** In a bizarre incident in 1991, trainer David Whiteley's Slew's Ghost had bleach thrown in his face by a security guard. He recovered, though, and won his next outing at Saratoga.

188. VOW OF SILENCE.

Top French trainer Andre Fabre has refused to speak to the French media – other than when he wins the Arc de Triomphe, which he has done several times – since winning the championship there 19 years ago.

As Colin Mackenzie of the *Daily Mail* says, Fabre 'regards the *Paris Turf* newspaper with as much respect as his dog Basil reserves for the Chantilly trees.'

189. GREAT TURF FRAUD

A wealthy French widow called Madame de Goncourt, living outside Paris in 1876, was targeted by two English con men who convinced her that they could supply her with racing certainties – for a certain consideration, of course.

Harry Benson and William Kurr eventually extracted some £30,000 from their target.

As French racing historian Robert Black commented in 1886, 'This shows how deeply the sport of horse racing – especially as a medium of investment – had impressed the French mind by this time and how widely spread among all circles of French society was the fancy for the Turf as a pecuniary speculation.'

Eventually, Madame de Goncourt realised what was happening and 'had recourse to the law'. Scotland Yard was called in, and identified Benson, who had been detained in Amsterdam. Superintendent Adolphus Williamson sent up and coming Chief Inspector Nathaniel Druscovich to bring him back, which he seemed to find an unaccountably difficult task. Meanwhile, Sgt John Littlechild caught up with Kurr in Edinburgh.

The pair were eventually tried for what had become known as the Great Turf Fraud. Benson, described as an 'accomplished swindler, of good birth and education who was much esteemed in the Isle of Wight' was sentenced to 15 years penal service, Kurr to ten years; three other defendants were also convicted.

Now, though, Benson began to 'sing' in the hope of receiving a reduced sentence, and his sensational claims revealed that top cop, Inspector John Meiklejohn had been accepting 'bungs' from Kurr to keep him one jump ahead of the law, and that the policeman had encouraged Druscovich to accept money from Kurr to repay debts, while another leading detective, Chief Inspector Palmer was also dragged into corruption claims.

Eventually all three policemen – Meiklejohn, Druscovich and Palmer – were sentenced to two years jail, and the scandal almost wrecked Williamson's career. As a result of a fraudulent tipping scam the whole of the Detective Branch of Scotland Yard was reorganised.

190. WINNING ON TWO LEGS

Diamond Jubilee, winner of the triple crown of 1900, and owned by the then Prince of Wales, was a temperamental type. He was ridden as a three year old by his former stable lad Herbert Jones, the only person who seemed to be able to calm him down.

In his first race as a two year old he kicked a racegoer and tried to savage his jockey, Watts who, in his next outing, he threw before bolting.

Having won the 2000 Guineas and Derby it was hoped that he was a reformed character, but prior to the Leger he took 20 minutes to saddle and then insisted on walking on his hind legs almost constantly whilst waiting for the start – trainer Richard Marsh's 1925 memoirs, *A Trainer To Two Kings,* features a remarkable photograph of the horse looking like a circus performer.

He won the Leger at 2/7 but never won again.

191. SUITS YOU

Former champion jockey Michael 'Muis' Roberts came to Britain from his native South Africa, where he became a popular figure.

Catherine Jenkinson, who looked after him and other apprentices when the 1954-born Cape Town man was starting out at the Jockeys' Academy gave an insight into his character in her 1994 autobiography; 'Once he won a race for an owner who was a wholesaler in menswear and part of the present for winning was any suit Michael cared to choose. The black grooms adored Michael because he was so decent to them, unlike most. One of the grooms was to be married, so Michael took him and had the prize of the suit made for the groom instead of himself; and then he bought the shirt, tie and shoes for him. This groom had never owned a pair of trousers in his life. Michael swore him to silence.'

When Roberts came to England and won the championship he landed a £10,000 windfall for his agent Graham Rock who had rung up a bookie at the start of the season and asked what price was on offer for Roberts. He was told 100/1 and asked if he could have £100.

He could – and did. I should know – I took the bet.

192. WINNIE'S ROYAL WINNER

Racing fan and owner, Winston Churchill vetoed his officials' plan to stage the Queen's Coronation in 1953 on Derby Day due, officially, to the Princess Elizabeth's love of the sport – (but almost certainly as much because of his own!) it was reported in documents finally revealed in 2007.

193. YOU BET THE ENGLISH ARE COMING

Firmly committed to state-run betting visa the Pari Mutuel, the French did permit bookmakers to operate there at one time.

A former stud groom, an Englishman called Palmer, opened 'Palmer's New Betting Rooms' in Paris upon the inception in 1833 of the French Jockey Club.

Twenty years later there was a veritable invasion by British bookmakers. Historian of French racing, Robert Black, explained in 1886: 'England contributed to the formation of a permanent betting ring in France. England turned France into a sort of Botany Bay for bookmakers and list holders. The Betting Act of 1853 for the suppression of betting houses (in England) led in the first instance to the emigration of parasites of the Ring to Paris, with betting agencies all over the Rue de Choiseuil.

England transferred some of the 'nuisances' just as she had transmitted many among the advantages of the Turf. The more disreputable emigrants' example was followed by their more reputable brethren who liked the climate, or the language, or the society, or the cookery of France.'

Among the first of the English bookmakers to thrive across the channel was one Mr J B Morris, owner of 1854 St Leger winner Knight of St George, who 'won quite a reputation by eating – not four and twenty blackbirds baked in a pie, but four and twenty ortolans at a sitting.' Ortolans are sparrow-like songbirds apparently eaten bones and all.

Black was not the greatest fan of bookmakers or 'this gigantic betting business, this unproductive industry, the alchemical institution for the extraction of money without value received.'

194. OVER IN A FLASH

Top French owner, the Duke de Castries lost six of his potentially talented racehorses in an extraordinary fashion at his Saint-Georges stable in 1883.

A storm broke out. 'The stud-groom had been serving out the oats to the youngsters (yearlings), standing by twos in each box, an iron-lined manger running from end to end of the whole building and supplying all the boxes,' explained writer Robert Black.

'When he reached the last box, having served out the oats, he was all of a sudden thrown down underneath a colt which fell – struck with lightning – atop of him, and which he discovered to be stone-dead, whilst his stable-companion was safe and sound. And, strange to say, it was so in every compartment; one – the one with its muzzle in the manger – had been struck dead by lightning, the other had escaped. If both had been able to feed at the same time, the whole 12 – instead of six – would assuredly have been killed.

The names of five of the killed are given – Czarda, by Salvator and Czarina; Gargantua, by Stracchino and The Garry; Mic-Mac by Gilbert and Merry May; Tape a l'Oeil by Salvator or Saladin and a dam not mentioned, and Vis-à-vis by Uhlan and Vignone.'

195. CAN'T SEE THE POINT MYSELF

Hong Kong racing authorities were baffled after discovering a device buried on the track at the Happy Valley racecourse in March, 2007.

The remote-controlled apparatus, which included twelve metal tubes, each a foot long and containing a dart, was designed to fire the chemical-filled arrows at horses as they emerged from the starting stalls for the three scheduled 6 furlong sprints.
It was deliberately hidden under the grass close to where the stalls were to be positioned

for the forthcoming Wednesday night meeting. The tubes were wired together and linked to a remote receiver and were discovered when a course official checked out the track before racing.

A police source commented: 'the device was almost certainly related to betting and could be linked to organised crime syndicates or triads.'

It seems likely that the plan was to shoot tranquillisers into the bodies of horses the gang did not want to perform at full capacity.

196. FRENCH BRED

Gladiateur was the French hero of 1865 after he came across the Channel to win the 2000 Guineas and the Derby before landing the great French test, the Grand Prix de Paris. He then returned to England, winning at Goodwood before landing the St Leger.

But this first genuine Gallic great might never have existed but for some cunning work at stud when it was first decided to mate his sire, Monarque with Miss Gladiator, because the male had taken a great aversion to his intended female partner and refused to have anything to do with her.

Yet he was smitten by another mare, Liouba, so, said a contemporary report of the coupling, 'to bring Monarque to consent to the union from which Gladiateur was to spring, he had to be left to feast his eyes – in an ecstasy – for a while upon his favourite; he was then blindfolded and Miss Gladiator was substituted for the Liouba of his choice.'

197. LADIES ONLY

Saratoga racecourse claimed in 1894 to have 'the only race-track betting ring in America for women.'

Author Edward Hotaling described the area: 'Trimmed in natural woods and opening into 'retiring rooms' for its customers, the women's ring had a counter behind a wire screen at one end, where three bookmakers operated, with their ticket sellers, cashiers, and a blackboard giving entries and odds. This operation was connected to the main ring by telephone, a man down there monitoring the boards and flashing the odds back upstairs.'

But this concession to the ladies was not quite as philanthropic and thoughtful as it might have seemed. As investigative journalist of the day, Nellie Bly, revealed when she paid a visit: 'The other day, when a horse won with odds something like 200/1, I have forgotten the exact figures, there had been two bets sold in the women's room, and the odds were only 40/1.'

Hotaling confirmed this scandal – 'the women got worse odds' – giving another example of a horse 400/1 in the ring paying only 40/1 to a female punter.

198. LADY WEIGHTER

The arrival on the scene for the first time in living memory of a female Clerk of the Scales sent the 1831 *Sporting Magazine* into something of a tis-was when she was spotted at Blandford Races:

'I could not help thinking it rather outré to see a fair lady weighing the jockeys,' blushed their scribe, 'and when they came to change their jacket or put on a flannel sweater or two to make them preponderate in the scale, to see them standing as cool as cucumbers before the fair damsel, or, at least, full in her view, with doeskins all unbuttoned' – ooh, matron! – 'I deemed it a pretty particular considerable tarnation queer sight.'

199. HILLS TOPS

Thursday, September 14, 2006 was something of a red letter day for the Hills family, as trainer Barry sent out a winner at Pontefract ridden by his grandson Patrick – whose father Richard also enjoyed riding a winner on the same card. While over at Yarmouth, Richard's brother Michael was booting home a double at Yarmouth – both of which were also trained by Barry, who is evidently still hankering to land the bet he struck back in 1988 at odds of 1000/1 to a £35 stake that he and/or his family will go through the card at a British race meeting.

200. BLINDING RESULT

Active during the mid 18th century, jockey John Metcalf from Knaresborough was quoted at 20/1 when he took on a fellow Yorkshire sportsman over a 3m flat course for 100 guineas a side.

The course was a circular one, which spectators reckoned would not suit Metcalf's riding style – after all, he was completely blind.

Nonetheless there were posts at intervals around the course and Metcalf took the precaution of standing a man by each one who rang a bell as Metcalf and his mount passed by, thus guiding him on his way – to a shock victory.

201. THE CRUELLEST CUT

Foaled in 1846 and a useful racecourse performer, Vatican contested both the Derby and St Leger, finishing unplaced and third respectively. Despite continuing to race at a high level until he was six he was a temperamental character and when he went to stud at Hambleton near Thirsk for Mr William Stebbing, he became almost uncontrollable, revealing a savage streak, reducing Stebbing almost to despair – 'I cannot cure him, do what I can.'

The horse had to be restrained – one witness reported that he was 'roped and chained from every side, and he screamed, roared and kicked.'

By 1858 Stebbing had employed a lad, Albert Barker, who struck up a relationship with Vatican and calmed him down. However, Barker left to go abroad and Vatican reverted to type, breaking one man's arm and breaking ribs of another.

'It was then that Stebbing conceived the diabolical idea, to have Vatican blinded,' reported racing writer John Fairfax Blakeborough, going on to record the almost unbelievable cruelty which resulted.

'Holmes, the Thirsk vet was sent for. The whole of Stebbing's staff was requisitioned, Vatican's legs were drawn from under him, and as soon as he fell on the straw in his box, two men sat on his head and wads of chloroform-soaked cottonwool were pressed over his nostrils till for once the savage was tamed for the nonce.

'With heated irons, Holmes then performed one of the cruellest operations to which a racehorse was ever subjected. He burned out both Vatican's eyes, so that when the poor brute regained consciousness, he was not only stone blind but in terrible agony and a ghastly spectacle to look upon.'

Worse was to come, though, as owners refused to send their mares to the horse with the awful reputation, and in 1859 he was put down – being subjected to further indignity when he was shot by one Jim Humphrey of Kilburn 'who affected the dress of a highwayman and was invariably followed by a number of black retriever dogs.' Vatican's body was borne away to be fed to Humphrey's pack, dragged away on a flat cart.

202. PHEW! ADIEU TO YOU, TOO, MY LORD

In his 1778 memoirs, *Adieu To The Turf*, Willoughby Bertie, the 4th Earl of Abingdon, a keen gentleman rider, described his method of managing weight loss, which consisted of sweating off his excess poundage by donning seven waistcoats and burying himself in a dunghill.

203. A COLOURFUL DICK

One of the top 'gentleman riders' of the day, Richard Ten Broeck, turned up at Warwick on Friday, November 23, 1866, to take on Mr Reginald Herbert in a two mile match.

Ten Broeck on three-year-old Douro was 5/6 favourite to beat Herbert's older Garus, conceding a stone.

It was Ten Broeck's appearance which qualifies this race for inclusion in these pages. He rode out on to the course 'garbed in a pair of yellow breeches, Duke of Wellington boots with enormous Mexican spurs, a flaming set of brand new orange colours, black belt, and a post-boy's cap several sizes too big for him, armed with a tremendous whip, and smoking a huge black cigar.'

It is not recorded whether he was smoking the cigar all the way round, but he was beaten by two lengths.

204. BETTING ON TECK

What was at the time the largest bet ever struck on an Irish racecourse almost caused a Royal scandal.

The brother in law of the future King George V, the philandering gambler, Prince Francis of Teck, had managed to lose £1,000 to bookmaker John James when, in June 1895, stationed in Dublin with his regiment, he went racing at The Curragh, determined to wipe out his debts at one fell swoop.

He decided that the four runner Stewards Plate for two year olds in which Bellevin was hugely superior to his three rivals was ideal for the purpose, and instructed James that he would have £10,000 on the favourite at odds of 1/10. Bellevin was beaten by Winkfields Pride – who went on to win the Cambridgeshire while Bellevin never won again.

The Prince was now eleven thousand pounds in debt. Ruin, scandal and disgrace lay in wait – forcing the future King – at the time Duke of York, to intervene and pay off his ne'er do well in-laws debts.

205. LESTER'S MEDICAL MUDDLE

Returning to home shores to race at Doncaster in September 1981, Lester Piggott, who had been racing in America, Germany and France in recent days, realised he had forgotten to bring with him his medical record book.

In an effort to avoid detection, he told the first weighing room official who asked for it that he had already shown it to a second. And when the second requested sight of it he told him he had previously produced it for the first.

All went well, until the two conferred and discovered that neither had seen the book.

The normal fine for not producing the log was £7 but because of his attempt to hoodwink the officials they topped his punishment up to £100.

206. BUCK OFF

Former England skipper and then current Manchester City manager, Stuart Pearce repaid Lambourn trainer Carl Llewellyn, who was training three horses for him, by attending his September 2006 open day – and being thrown from the back of Weathercock House Stables' bucking-bull machine on several occasions.

207. CLARION CALL

Bookies were at a loss to understand the sudden plunge on the previous year's 9th placed Melbourne Cup runner, Clarion, to win the 1898 race. His realistic odds of 20/1 were shortened consistently as the cash kept on coming.

By the time word reached the layers that the money was inspired by the recent publication in an Aussie paper of a dream reportedly had by a woman that Clarion won the Melbourne Cup but that she herself died before the race, Clarion was priced in single figures.

Then the un-named woman was reported to have died, as predicted as this early 'Friend of a friend' story did the rounds.

Clarion went off as 5/1 favourite – and finished 10th.

208. SELIM MILES BETTER?

The first winner of the Irish Derby, Selim, in 1866, was perhaps the most short-term prolific Classic winner ever – the horse had won a Royal Plate at The Curragh, the day before making history, and English owner James Cockin raced him victoriously in royal plates at the course on the next two days.

There had been an earlier attempt to inaugurate a race of this type and stature, run from 1817 – 1824 and which was called, I kid you not, the O'Darby Stakes.

209. KILLED BY HIS OWN HORSE

Captain William George Middleton, one of the most popular sporting personalities of his day and an outstanding gentleman rider, was killed during a race – by his own horse, while still on its back.

Middleton – known as Bay – won 29 races on his own chestnut gelding Lord of the Harem, including 17 consecutive wins between November 1882 and April 1884.

On Saturday, April 9, 1892 Middleton partnered his own gelding, Night Line, in the Midland Sportsmen's Cup at Kineton Valley.

There were five runners and, when close home, Night Line pecked on landing over a fence. Explains writer Charles Adolph Voight in his *Famous Gentleman Riders*, Middleton 'was brought forward, and the horse, throwing his head back, caught Middleton on the chin with such force as to break his neck. 'Bay' must have been dead before he reached the ground.'

210. BOG STANDARD CRISIS

The Irish Turf Club members were over the moon when they discovered that King George IV had agreed to attend the special Royal Meeting they had organised to take place at the Curragh in his honour on Saturday, September 1, 1821 as part of his state visit.

Preparations were put in hand and all was deemed to be perfectly organised – the Royal Stand was in place, the Banqueting Room set up, course officials were fitted out in Royal livery, all at a cost of some £3,000.

Until, as word came through to the organisers that His Majesty had been suffering severely from an upset stomach, as an eyewitness to the occasion described, 'one of the Stewards stood forth with great solemnity in the assembly of managers and said, "Gentlemen, I fear one thing has been omitted, which it appears may be an essential necessary. I mean a water closet."

Panic. Until the Duke of Leinster volunteered to ride the 23 miles to Dublin to collect and bring back a Mr Simmons who was known to be the top – bottom, perhaps?   man in this field.

However, he would need to know the dimensions of the Royal posterior in order to ensure that he came up with an acceptable and efficient piece of work. Step forward Mr Massey Dawson, the MP for Clonmel and the largest such representative, whose dimensions were thought to approximate those of the King.

The emergency operation was duly set in motion and the equipment installed to everyone's satisfaction and relief.

Until – 'when the pump was tried, a trifling oversight was discovered – no water was forthcoming, but only that which poured from the heavens.'

No matter, what could be done had been done.

The King arrived, the first race started 'but before they could arrive at the winning post, his Majesty was obliged to bolt.' All, as one might say, must have 'panned out' satisfactorily for His Majesty appeared content at the arrangements as he presented a Gold Whip to the Duke of Leinster at the end of the day's entertainment, which he said should in future be run for each year.

The organisers of the day's racing were flushed with success.

211. JOCKEY CLUB TOOK NO PRISONERS

Nineteen former prisoners of war jointly bought a horse called Twenty Players which was trained for them by Marcus Marsh in 1946. When the syndicate turned up for a race at Folkestone and requested a course pass each, the Jockey Club decided to introduce a rule limiting the partners in any one horse to four.

212. END OF THE LEVIATHAN

William 'The Leviathan' Davies was the biggest, most fearless bookmaker of the mid 19th century. He changed his career from carpenter to bookie after working at the Newmarket Subscription Rooms and making a note of all the wagers that the members there talked of placing.

He soon realised that most of them were losers and decided that there was a healthy profit to be had.

He quickly acquired his complimentary 'Leviathan' nickname in honour of the huge wagers he laid. His worst ever day was an £80,000 loss when 25/1 shot Daniel O'Rourke won the Derby in 1852 – yet he paid everyone immediately 'with as little concern as he paid his laundry bill'.

But his exit from the sport of kings was strange indeed, as fellow bookie George Hodgman later recorded in his memoirs: 'I dated the beginning of his physical collapse from the day he fell through the dilapidated Grand Stand to the weighing room below at the Rochester and Chatham Meeting.

It was an extraordinary spectacle – that of Davies dangling, hung up by his arms and struggling in vain to touch the ground. He was promptly extricated, but the shock was severer than the bruises. With an idea of shaking off the effects of the accident he ran the circuit of the course twice.'

Matters took a turn for the worse when 'shortly afterwards he was struck on the head with a heavy blunt instrument by some scoundrel intent on robbery.'

That was it. Davies retired with a farewell dinner at Brighton in 1857 after which he became a recluse until his death in October 1879.

213. DERBY DAVE?

Conservative leader David Cameron's father Ian owned a promising two year-old with a Derby entry, Mountain Pride, trained by John Dunlop and there was speculation that he could be less than happy with his racing connection 'because it might make voters regard the old Etonian as a toff,' wrote *Racing Post* 'Anorak' columnist John Randall.

His father's Emerging Market was the 33/1 winner of the Wokingham at Royal Ascot in 1996 – when his Hello won Italy's Gran Criterium. David Cameron himself is reportedly descended from the illegitimate daughter of King William IV, who owned the first three in the 1830 Goodwood Cup.

Father, Ian also co-owned a horse with David's wife Samantha in the 1980s.

214. QUAKING IN HIS BOOTH

Commentating at Hollywood Park in June 2005, racecourse caller Vic 'Goof on the Roof' Strauffer suddenly realised that an earthquake had just begun. He kept his nerve and told listeners: 'We are in the middle of an earthquake here in Southern California – Lady Lucayan tries to slow it down. She leads by two and a half lengths. By the way folks, I'd like you to know I love you all and that horse racing was my first love.'

215. HEAVING BOWL

'One of the six bathroom stalls at Churchill Downs contains not a standard toilet but a wide, rectangular 'heaving bowl' designed to aid in routine regurgitation,': racing journalist Pat Forde on the jockey facilities at the home of the Kentucky Derby in a May 2006 article for allhorseracing.com.

216. BEATEN INTO A ...

'There was a good deal of amusement caused' at the St Leger meeting of 1820 reported Leger historian, J S Fletcher, 'by the appearance of the jockeys in the Cocked Hat Stakes of 25gns each, in which the riders appeared in headgear answering that description, though for what reason no historian is good enough to say.'

The race was won by T Shepherd on Sir W Maxwell's chestnut colt, Monreith.

217. JERRY GOOD TACTICS

Owner Mr R. Gascoigne and trainer Croft were convinced that their horse Jerry had a favourite's chance in the 1824 St Leger, having already won the York version of the contest.

Jerry was being closely watched over in his stable day and night 'and so great were the precautions taken, that it seemed impossible that he could be nobbled by anybody,' noted racing writer, W A C Blew. Yet 'still the bookmakers kept laying against him'

Croft visited the betting room at Doncaster, where he 'was astonished to find the hostility which prevailed against his horse.'

Croft went for a walk to clear his head and was passed by a post-chaise in which he saw Jerry's jockey, Edwards and also one Bob Ridsdale, 'a not too honourable character'.

Now the penny dropped for Croft and Gascoigne – it was the rider rather than the horse who was being got at. So the pair hatched a cunning plan, but waited and kept quiet, taking no action at all.

On the day of the race, Croft, Gascoigne and Jerry were all in place as along came Edwards, ready, in his colours and about to mount the horse, when Croft stepped forward, tapped him on the shoulder and told him: 'Not today, Mr Edwards, thank you; we shall not require your services.'

And immediately, Croft brought forward Ben Smith, their substitute jockey, an ultra reliable and honest jockey who had once won a race in 1786 at York despite having had his leg broken by a kick at the start. Smith rode Jerry capably and effectively, bringing the black colt through late on to victory against 22 rivals at rewarding odds of 9/1.

218. NOT SUCH A SUCKER

The story is told of American George Smith who, in the early 1900s, made his living from selling candy on a stick.

One day he went to the races and backed a runner to win him a substantial sum. When the horse won he decided to commemorate the victory by naming his candy after the winner – whose name was Lolly Pop.

The rest is history.

219. LOGGING IN

When racing began at Hokitika's course on the west coast of New Zealand in 1866, local police chief, Inspector Broham anticipated a certain amount of rowdiness amongst the clientele, which numbered between three and four thousand who were being catered for by 10 publicans' booths dispensing hard liquor.

Many of those attending were miners and Broham had prepared an area under the grandstand where he could detain transgressors. To secure such folk a large log was sunk in the ground and a staple driven in, to which was secured a bullock chain – to which prisoners were handcuffed until they could be dealt with.

220. HEROIC BILL

The late trainer Bill Marshall, a successful handler in Britain and then in Barbados, was a fighter pilot during the War, winning the DFC and in September 2006 he was honoured by a plaque, unveiled by his widow Pamela, at The Royal Mail pub in Lydd to commemorate his heroic feat in saving the town from a flying bomb in 1944.

Marshall was patrolling the Kent skies in his Spitfire when he spotted one of the deadly 'doodlebugs' which wreaked such havoc throughout the land. Noticing that the bomb was about to fall on the town below, he blasted it from short range, risking fatal danger and damage to himself in the process. His action destroyed the V1 bomb, but the blast blew a great hole in his plane's radiator. Marshall somehow managed to fly the plane back to base.

**Derby winning trainer Marcus Marsh served in the RAF as a rear gunner in bomber command and was shot down over Holland in 1941, later taking part in the famous 'Wooden horse' escape.

**Jockey Dick Black and trainer John de Moraville found themselves together in a P-O-W camp in Germany during the War – when they were released they formed a racing partnership, combining for their first winner, King Penguin, at Ludlow in October 1946.

**Four Grand National winning jockeys died in service during the Second World War: Frank Furlong (Reynoldstown, 1935) of Fleet Air Arm ; Bobby Everett (Gregalach, 1929) of the Navy; Mervyn Jones (Bogskar, 1940) of the RAF; and Tommy Cullinan (Shaun Goilin, 1930), serving with an anti-aircraft unit.

221. MAJOR PROBLEM

When Conservative Prime Minister, John Major celebrated his 50th birthday he was showered with presents – amongst them a former racehorse turned stallion – from, naturally, the President of Turkmenistan, Saparmurat Niyazov.

How they gift-wrapped the horse, called Maskat, has never been fully explained, but Mr Major certainly had a problem trying to work out what to do with it!

It stayed in its Turkmen stable for many months until protocol demanded that it be brought to England where it was offered to – but turned down by for being 'too frisky' – the Life Guards. It was eventually quietly moved off to a stud farm in Wales.

222. GOMEZ JUMPS TO IT

Frankie Dettori's now legendary flying dismount upon winning another big race is often said to have been 'borrowed' from US jockey, Angel Cordero, but another rider has better claims to be the originator of the flamboyant – if slightly risky – gesture.

Cuban-born rider Avelino Gomez, six times top jockey in Canada in the 1960s and 1970s is hailed on the Canadian Horse Racing Hall of Fame website as 'the man who patented the victorious high leap from the saddle in the winner's circle'.

His greatest triumph came in extraordinary circumstances, when, having been subjected to threats on his life if he partnered Victoria Park in Canada's big race, the Queen's Plate at Woodbine in 1970, he not only rode, but won, and turned as he approached the post to pointedly stick out his tongue at those who had threatened him.

223. GREAT BOOKIE ROBBERY

Australia's equivalent of the Great Train Robbery was the Great Bookie Robbery, which caused as much of a sensation when it took place in Melbourne in 1976.

Ten prominent bookies had gathered in the settling room at the city's Victoria Club after a successful three day's racing over Easter, waiting for a security firm to deliver them monies held for them at the races.

As the security men arrived at lunchtime, so did six men, some sporting machine guns. Overpowering the guards and the bookies they made off with an estimated 1.4m Aussie dollars.

It was the biggest robbery ever staged in the country, was never solved and eventually became the subject of a TV mini series.

224. ROLE OF THE DUYS

After a hard fought race at Suffolk Downs in the States in June 1993, jockeys Carl Gambardella , 53, and female counterpart Dodie Duys came to blows. They were separated and told to go and cool off – Duys did so in the shower, only for Gambardella to sneak into the ladies changing room to resume hostilities. Both were subsequently suspended for 15 days – well, at least it had been a clean contest.

225. RACING ANTICS

When stewards at Calcutta's racetrack needed to refer back to the details of a decision they had made, following an appeal against it in 1888, they discovered that all the records had been eaten by white ants.

226. THAT'S JUST NOT BUNNY

Rabbits chewed through a vital cable at the rear of the giant TV screen in front of the grandstand at Royal Ascot in 1995 – thus leaving racegoers with a blank screen for the first race.

227. PHOTO FINISHED

Excited owner Leonard Seale watched his horse, Super Sally, flash past the post at Lingfield, in a three way photo finish for the December 1991 European Gold Patrons Handicap.

Waiting for the outcome of the photo, Seale collapsed and died of a heart attack – before the announcement that 11/4 shot Super Sally had prevailed.

228. PRINCE'S HEARTY END

Eighty-year-old Prince Batthyany, the naturalised, Hungarian-born owner of Galliard, well fancied contender for the 1883 2000 Guineas got so excited that on his way up the short flight of stairs to the Jockey Club luncheon room prior to – some accounts say during – the race, he keeled over and died of a heart attack. His horse won.

229. JOCKEY WINS – HORSE SECOND

Riding 11/4 shot Amantiss at Devon in August 1986 jockey Anthony Charlton finished first – but Amantiss finished second.

As the pair approached the post, Charlton somehow tumbled out of the saddle and crossed the line a split second ahead of his horse.

The race was awarded to the second finisher – Slip Up.

*There was a very similar incident at Exeter on October 31, 2006 – Halloween night – when jockey Richard Johnson was urging on Phillip Hobbs-trained Out The Black to the line, still in with a winning chance when, literally a few yards from the line the eight year old 'did a Devon Loch' and just collapsed on his stomach, depositing Johnson on the ground inches from the winning post.

230. BRINGING HOME THE BACON

Rag Time Belle's win at Redcar in April 1992 really brought home the bacon for connections – pig breeder owner Roger Hughes, pig-keeping trainer Malcolm Eckley and bacon farmer breeder Victor Wadge.

231. FOXY LADY AND OTHER UNEXPECTED ANIMATED OBSTACLES

When Julie Krone came to challenge on 30/1 shot Quilma at Gulfstream Park in January 1991 she suddenly realised she had slightly more to do than expected – as she had to jump a fox sunning himself on the back straight. Julie and Quilma still managed to take second place ... two furlongs into the 1991 St Leger the field had to take rapid evasive action to avoid 35 year old Alan Davis and an-eight-year old boy, who were sitting happily on the course ... the 1988 Ulster Derby at Down Royal was delayed while a flock of sheep was cleared off the track ... Capt Frank Taylor was so grateful when a large dog got onto the course at Doncaster during the valuable Scarbrough Stakes, hampering hot favourite Queen of Trumps and allowing Taylor's Ainderby to nip through to victory, that he found the dog's owner, bought the mutt and gave him a life of luxury ... A bullock on the course proved a problem before the 2.15 at Beverley in May, 1989 ... and during the same year jockey Brian Peck suffered a broken arm when his mount at Florence, Kentucky, collided with a deer ... Racing at Nairobi was held up in 1993 until a troop of baboons could be persuaded to move on, while at Adelaide back in 1928 a group of snakes spooked runners going down to the start and had to be dealt with.

232 THE STEWARDS INQUIRY HELD BEFORE THE RACE

Rumours swept the racing world prior to the running of the 1831 St Leger that plotting was afoot amongst certain dubious characters with a view to ensuring the certain well fancied runners in the race would not be permitted to run on their merits.

The suggestion was that certain parties intended to start horses for the sole purpose of interfering with leading contenders.

Becoming aware of these rumours and acting with enviable alacrity, rather than permitting skulduggery to happen and then try to deal with its consequences, the stewards met together to decide what action to take, and duly issued the following, unprecedented statement, dated 'Doncaster, 19th September, 1831' and signed 'By order of the Stewards, J.Lockwood, Jun. Clerk of the Course':

'At a meeting this afternoon of the gentlemen connected with the turf, it being stated that strong and apparently well-grounded suspicions are entertained that a determination has been entered into by certain individuals to interfere with the fair start and just decision of the race for the St Leger, it has been resolved, that in the event of any nefarious act of the kind being attempted, it be strongly recommended to all future stewards, not only to prevent every jockey who has been proved either to have created false starts, or otherwise to have behaved unfairly, during the race, from ever again riding at Doncaster; but that the master of these jockeys, if afterwards proved to have been implicated in such transactions, be prevented ever again starting a horse at these Meetings'.

In the event, the race produced as controversial a result as ever recorded in the oldest Classic, with Lockwood, the Clerk of the Course and Judge calling 3/1 favourite The Saddler as the winner in a very tight finish with 20/1 shot Chorister, only to be over-ruled by his son, who persuaded him to opt for the latter as winner.

Many influential racing folk of the day were never convinced that The Saddler had been beaten.

Not only that, but the Judge placed only two of the 24 runners, while the second best backed horse, Marcus, 7/2, finished last but one with well known jockey Sam Chifney insisting that his mount had been poisoned.

233. NOTE-ABLE CELEBRATION

High rolling Aussie punter, Perce Galea celebrated the victory of his black two year old, Eskimo Prince in the valuable 1964 Golden Slipper Stakes by throwing handfuls of Aussie tenners to the crowd.

Galea was a notorious Sydney-based gambler who suffered a string of heart attacks, after the first of which, in 1963, he was warned by his doctors that the stress of his high stake bets could bring on another. 'I couldn't go to the races and not have a bet. That would be the same as going to church and not praying,' he said 18 months before being hit by the one which finished him off in 1977.

234. STRICTLY FOR THE BIRDS

Aussie horse, Drongo, foaled in 1920, was named after an obscure species of bird. But after a high profile career during which he too often flattered to deceive – he ran in two Melbourne Cups and raced 37 times without ever getting his head in front – his name was hijacked into common parlance where it became synonomous with something useless and slow.

American horse, Gussie Mae, would have qualified for the description 'Drongo' in June 1995 when she had clocked up 85 successive defeats and was set to claim a new US record of 86, eclipsing previous record holder Really A Tenor. Gussie Mae, owned by Kanface Affa, went for glory in a 7f race at Atlantic City – and won.

235. PHEW, RACING'S OFF

Saratoga racecourse announced that its nine race card on August 2, 2006, was off 'because of high heat and humidity' It was the first time in at least 50 years that such a thing had happened, but with the temperature hitting 110F the decision was approved by trainers, jockeys and officials – and copied by Delaware Park, Monmouth Park and Suffolk Downs. In the past there has been a huge variety of reasons for cancelling or abandoning race meetings … because: there are rhinos on the track (Racecourse Road, Kenya, 1903); the

Army wants the course for manoeuvres (Wormwood Scrubs, 1817) ... the King (racing fan, Edward VII) has pegged it – all fixtures cancelled for a fortnight in May 1910; the bookies are all on strike because Winston Churchill wants to introduce a betting tax (Windsor, 1920s) ... there's an industrial crisis (April-June 1921); it's the General Strike of May, 1926 ... there's a rail strike (Royal Ascot 1955) ... the Turf Club wouldn't allow the jockeys to sacrifice a cow to safeguard the course from accidents (Accra, Ghana, 1966) ... tote staff were on strike (Punchestown, 1989); political riots had broken out (Bombay, 1993) ... racegoers are sitting in the middle of the course because the Pari Mutuel staff are striking (Chantilly, 1993) ... 'because of a spillage of aviation fuel on the course' at Newbury in October 1992 when a light aircraft crashed on the flat course just before the 7th race; because there is a bomb on the course – 1997 Grand National ... because it is Princess Di's/Queen Mum's funeral – September 1997/April 2002 ... because torrential rain has washed away the track surface – Southwell, July 2007 ... because the Pope's addressing 400,000 pilgrims on the track – at Randwick, Sydney, in July 2008.

236. DERBY DEATHS

Most people are aware that suffragette Emily Davison brought down the King's horse Anmer when she ran on to the Epsom track during the 1913 Derby and later died although the row over whether she targeted that particular runner still rages to this day. But the Blue Riband event has also suffered the shadow of death on a number of other occasions such as jockey Frank Collinson who rode Pan to victory in 1808 but, en route to Epsom slept in a damp bed and later died of the chill he caught there; bookie Brograve was wiped out when Smolensko won in 1813, so killed himself; and in 1836, the 6th Lord Craven's younger son, Augustus Berkeley Craven, born in 1777, was so distraught after losing £8,000 by betting against winner Bay Middleton, that he shot himself the morning after the race; Humorist won in 1921 but died two weeks later, suffering from a tubercular lung condition.

237. LIFE'S A BEACH (2)

In August 1751 Captain Jennison Shafto rode Cat Cobourne's black gelding to beat Capt Vernon's self-ridden bay gelding for a 100gn purse on the sands at Scarborough where they continued to race for over a century ... they also race or have raced on the beach at Redcar and South Shields in England, and still do at Laytown in Ireland, while Spain's Sanlucar de Barameda is another beach course ... Aberdeen staged racing in 1661 when contemporary reports noted: 'The sea shore is plaine and sandie. At low water there is bounds for hors raices no less than two myls of length.' ... perhaps the earliest record of such sport dates from 1504 when documents speak of 'hors rynning' on the sands at Leith, attended by James IV ... prior to the first regularly constituted races at Liverpool, in July 1827, they had raced annually on the sands, or north shore, of the River Mersey.

238. WHO KNEW?

That ... Peter Scudamore was once an estate agent...David Elsworth worked as a night watchman ... Gee Armytage declined an offer from *Mayfair* magazine to become a nude model ... Charlie Brooks' fledgling football career was shattered when former England boss Graham Taylor rejected him at a trial ... former royal jockey Bill Smith used to work for Moss Bros ... Charles Cyzer combined training with manufacturing Christmas crackers ... trainer John Ffitch Heyes was a former rock promoter who booked Jimi Hendrix for £25 ... Simon Dow was the UK's top rated junior 800 metre runner before becoming a trainer ... rock star racing fan, Pink Floyd's Roger Waters, paid 490,000gns for Northern Hal ... Portsmouth builder Bill Davies has installed stained glass windows in his house depicting Lester Piggott's greatest winners – his garage wall features a mural of the maestro and in his lounge are two three foot high statues of him ... the last moustachioed jockey to win the Grand National was Mr Campbell on The Soarer in 1896 ... King Edward VII introduced the now traditional Panama Hat to Goodwood in 1906 ... Sir Michael Stoute likes to whistle 'My Way' or 'Some Enchanted Evening' on the gallops ... dual Champion Hurdler Monksfield was an inveterate snorer ... that the first Sunday race meeting in the UK took place at Les Landes racecourse in Jersey on August 5, 1984 ... that Michael Matz, trainer of 2006 Kentucky Derby winner Barbaro, carried the US flag at the closing ceremony of the 1996

Olympics having been part of the silver medal winning show-jumping team ... not only that, he once survived a plane crash in which 100 died and was reunited with three people he helped rescue, prior to that Derby victory ... actors Peter O'Toole and Albert Finney are both sons of bookmakers ... film star Judy Garland once had a racing stable named, yes, Over The Rainbow ... Ole Blue Eyes, Frank Sinatra, owned a 1960s winner of the Santa Anita Handicap, Mr Right ... Bing Crosby serenaded racegoers at the Curragh after his Meadow Court won the 1965 Irish Derby with 'Irish Eyes Are Smiling' ... the crooner was also founder-president of Del Mar racetrack ... Lester Piggott once guested on a 1951 radio programme, Calling All Forces, along with Petula Clark and Shirley Bassey ... he was also featured at Madame Iussaud's from 1962-2002 ... that after each running of the Preakness Stakes at Pimlico a painter climbs a ladder to the top of the Old Clubhouse where he paints the weather vane in the winning colours of the owner ... that when Julian Wilson was appointed BBC TV racing correspondent, he beat a certain Michael Stoute for the position ... that happily married couple, top trainer Henrietta Knight, and former top jockey Terry Biddlecombe first met when she was interviewed by him on the Central TV racing feature, 'Terry's Tips' ... that 1867 Grand National winning jockey George Ede – who rode as Mr Edwards – was co-founder of Hampshire Cricket Club for whom in 1863 he scored 1,200 runs ... that jockey Eddie Harty, who won the 1969 Grand National on Highland Wedding spent two years working as a cowboy in America ... that when 100/1 no-hoper Foinavon won the 1967 Grand National his trainer, John Kempton, convinced the horse had no chance, was at Worcester where he had just sent out the winner of a novice hurdle ... triple Grand National winning jockey turned trainer Arthur Nightingall's ashes were scattered over the Derby course at Epsom when he died in 1944 ... 2006 Royal Ascot Aussie raider, Takeover Target, winner of the King's Stand, is regularly fed 'a couple of glasses of beer' as part of his training regime ... that jump jockey turned trainer Scobie Coogan, also owner, breeder and saddler, is an internationally renowned Koi Carp judge ... that the first four home in the historic Newmarket Town Plate, run for some 340 years, receive 8lbs of Powter's sausages ... when Tracy Piggott, Lester's daughter, rode her first winner on August 28, 1988 she wore the boots Tommy Stack had on when he won the National on Red Rum..that when Tracy's dad launched his unexpected 1989 comeback to the saddle he did so in Lima, Peru ... that Sir Michael Stoute received his 1998 knighthood, not for his racing achievements, but for services to tourism in his native Barbados ... that the late trainer David 'The Duke' Nicholson's trademark red socks became a permanent fixture after he wore them for his 1963 Triumph Hurdle victory ... that the original horse names in the board game, Totopoly, were those of the Lincoln winners from 1926 to 1937... that Sheikh Mohammed's great but ill-fated Dubai Millenium was originally named Yaazir ... that Sir Alex Ferguson's first racehorse – and first winner – was named Queensland Star in tribute to a ship built by the yard where his Dad worked ... that when Devon Loch collapsed on the Grand National run-in in 1956, jockey Dick Francis's wife, watching from the stands, did likewise – in a dead faint ... that Sandown Park racecourse was constructed on the site of a priory built by Henry II, all of whose occupants perished during the plague of 1349 That trainer Robert Alner is a keen Status Quo fan – and supports West Bromwich Albion ... Christophe Soumillon, French champion jockey is married to a former Miss France – and owns 20 dogs ... top US trainer D Wayne Lukas started out as a basketball coach ... while Yorkshire trainer Neville Bycroft, 73 in 2006, signed professional forms for York rugby league club in the early 1950s ...the first horse race Sheikh Mohammed ever watched was at Newmarket on May 5, 1967 when he saw Royal Palace win the 2000 Guineas ... that west of Wales trainer Peter Bowen, 48, has not only never flown, he has never taken a holiday

239. FOOD FOR THOUGHT

Trainer Sir Mark Prescott refuses to allow any hot food other than toast or boiled eggs to be consumed at his Heath House yard ... Gay Kelleway once listed her favourite food as 'chocolate body sauce' ... Willie Carson always wanted to become a chef...jump jockey Ron Hyett opened an edible snail farm ... in 1990, US jockey P J Lydon finished third in a race in Manhattan – in which runners had to consume as many ribs as possible within three minutes. He knocked back 25 ... trainer Neville Crump's wife Sylvia's grandfather Alfred Bird invented Bird's custard powder ... renowned chef, Mrs Beeton once lived in the original Epsom Grandstand..jockey John 'Kipper' Lynch's dad was a fishmonger..Edinburgh bookie Victor Gold allowed hard up butcher Iain Hunter to stake steaks on his tips in 1996 ... Olivier Peslier adopted a diet which banned him from eating beef, oranges, grapefruit, broccoli and tuna fish ... owner Duc de Joyeuse prepared his horse for a 1651 match race in France worth 1,000 crowns to the winner on bread made with aniseed and beans, and 200 fresh eggs on the two days prior to the contest which, despite, or because of, his diet, he won ... late 19th century champion amateur rider, George Baird would breakfast on 'weak tea and cod liver oil' ... jockey Willie McFarland opened a pizza parlour in Wantage..trainer Martin Pipe loves bananas – but only straight ones

240. DARN IT! THOMMO NEEDLED?

Somehow managing to step on a darning needle, which passed straight through his foot, racing commentator and workaholic Derek Thompson was not about to let such a pin-prick prevent him from driving to Sedgefield where, in March 2007, he was on commentary duties.

Thommo drove all the way there with the needle still embedded, he told TalkSPORT radio listeners, only consenting to seek medical attention on arrival. He had to be stood down from the commentary box to spend the night in hospital with what his wife Julie called "the male version of pain."

241. LILY NOT IN THE PINK

Lily Langtry, famed actress, beauty and lover of the Prince of Wales, and a native of the Channel Islands, was a keen racegoer in the days when it was not done for ladies to be owners. So, her horses would race under the pseudonymic ownership of Mr Jersey – as whom she won Royal Ascot's Coventry Stakes with Milford in 1892.

She also twice won the Cesarewitch, with Merman in 1897 and Yentoi in 1908.

Whilst in Sydney in the late 19th century she had purchased an Aussie-bred racehorse called Chesney which she arranged to have shipped to England, along with another horse called Kiora.

En route, the steamer in which the horses were travelling, was shipwrecked off Mouille Point, off South Africa's Cape. The two horses managed to swim ashore where they were rescued.

Chesney was acquired by owner Abe Bailey, in whose ownership he won the 1901 Metropolitan Merchants' Handicap at the South African Turf Club meeting held on December 26, 1901. Later becoming unsound he was sent on to England ending up in the Robinson stable at Foxhill.

Chesney's companion, Kiora, was sent on to England after the shipwreck and actually ran in the 1906 Grand National, only to fall at Becher's Brook.

Interestingly, one of the hottest early fancies for this race was Moifaa, who had won the National in 1904 and subsequently been bought by King Edward VII – Lily Langtry's former paramour. Moifaa was said to have been shipwrecked off the coast of Ireland whilst en route to England via his native New Zealand.

However, when Brough Scott recently researched this incident with a view to writing it up in a book, he was unable to authenticate the story.

242. UNGENTLEMANLY CONDUCT

When prominent racing man Christopher 'Kitty' Rowntree won a Cup race at Stokesley in Cleveland in 1791 he little expected that his efforts to receive the trophy would end up at York Assizes after he and the owner of his mount Centaur, Mr Thomas Burdon, were refused the Cup and £123 prize money by the stewards on the grounds that Rowntree 'was not eligible as a gentleman rider.'

Rowntree lived at Middleton-on-Leven, where he kept a pack of hounds, kept horses and enjoyed racing, cockfighting and the society of all manner of sporting men.

Not good enough, old boy, claimed Mr Sergeant Cockle, the counsel for Stokesley stewards, declaring that Rowntree was ineligible as a gentleman rider on the grounds that 'he was blind in one eye, wore leather breeches as his everyday dress and that each market day at Stokesley he dined with the farmers at an inn which charged just one shilling or eighteen pence.'

Mr Sergeant Law, on behalf of Rowntree declared 'A gentleman remains such wherever he dines. Those wishing to withhold the title should have proved not where he dined and what he paid, but that he dined and left without paying. They should have proved not that he went about in leather breeches, but without any breeches on – that would truly have stamped him as no gentleman.'

Rowntree won the case.

243. EARLIEST EXCUSES?

Some inventive and memorable excuses have been used by racing folk, but one of the earliest and most convincing was uttered way back in 1822 by top rider of the day, Sir Tatton Sykes, who had been expected to win on Mr Booth's runner at Northallerton, Joker. Sykes delivered his challenge and pulled his mount up, only to look up and see the remainder of the field setting off on the final circuit, without him.

Unperturbed, the recently wed Sykes, whose bride had been watching on from the stand, informed the somewhat disgruntled owner, 'I am very sorry, sir, but you must blame Lady Sykes, not me, for the mistake; I was thinking more of her than my work'.

Ten years earlier, though, in September 1812 at Tramore in Ireland a Mr Scully objected to a result on the grounds that the jockey riding Young Waxy had struck Mr Scully's horse, Slug during the race.

Young Waxy's rider was ready with his excuse, however – 'the reason for striking Slug was in consequence of Slug having bit his leg, and the blow was given to extricate his leg out of Slug's mouth.'

The stewards accepted the excuse and allowed Young Waxy to keep the race.

244. BOOZE SORRY NOW

Racing and alcohol have been uneasy partners for many a long year. In July 2006, editor of racing magazine, *Pacemaker*, Darryl Sheerer, railed, 'What can ruin the raceday experience is the fear of a day being spoiled by drunken behaviour'. He referred to 'an ugly, drunken brawl' at the Guineas Meeting at Newmarket, and noted 'the Royal Meeting at Ascot was not immune from this kind of behaviour either.'

The record of a meeting organised by one Henry Witham at Pearson Moor in Durham early in the 19th century reveals that such behaviour is far from a new phenomenon.

Racegoer John Nixon recalled 'the meeting was more than usually rowdy. Beer 'ad libitum' had been provided and the liquor was on the racecourse in casks.' Bad move – 'the weavers and other thirsty individuals could not be restrained from making an attack on the beer. The heads of the barrels were knocked in and the rougher element, not having vessels out of which to drink, used their clogs for this purpose'

Nixon concluded, ruefully, 'There was no further race meeting.'

What Darryl Sheerer would have made of Aussie jockey Gary Murphy's reaction after riding Mercator to win 1991's Ballarat Cup in Melbourne, I can't imagine. The ecstatic Murphy announced that he would buy the entire crowd a beer.

There were 13,000 racegoers present and chaos ensued! It is not clear whether he had meant a beer each, or one between them!

245. JUST POPPING OUT, DEAR

There has been much discussion about whether jockeys should be limited to riding at one meeting per day in order to cut down on lengthy travelling times which could subject them and other road users to potential danger.

Sir Tatton Sykes was a top jockey of his day – the early 19th century – but the leading amateur had no compunction about doing what it took to make the ride on a fancied mount.

Records turf historian, The Druid, 'Twice Sir Tatton Sykes rode from Sledmere to Aberdeen, with his racing jacket under his waistcoat and a clean shirt and razor in his pocket, for the sake of a mount on the Marquis of Huntly's Kutusoff and Sir David Moncrieffe's Harlequin, when the Welter Stakes was the greatest race in Scotland; and without stopping to dine, went back to sleep at Brechin that night and reached Doncaster after a six days' ride, just in time to see Blacklock beat for the 1817 St Leger.

'Kutusoff, whom he thought to be decidedly the best he was ever on, did not win that bout, but the victory in the white and black cap of Sir David in '22 squared up his Scottish luck. The 360 miles were done, principally in the forenoon, on a little blood mare, and with the exception of a little stiffness, she seemed none the worse.'

**In 1764, jockey Joe Rose rode at three different meetings – Manchester, Richmond in Yorkshire and Lincoln, on consecutive days, commuting on his own horse, carrying his own racing saddle.

246. MARTINIUS PIPIUS VERSUS PAULUS NICHOLLUS?

We reckon that horse racing dates back some four hundred years or so – but perhaps it is rather earlier than we have believed.

For, the discovery of an inscription from 1376 – that's BC – suggests that the sport has been going on at least since then – when even Peter O'Sullevan would have been just a lad.

It transpires that the chief riding master of the Indo-Aryan state of Mitanni (are you with me, still?) in Mesopotamia was a great authority on training racehorses, and the inscription reveals that the animals were first given a special reducing diet, accompanied by baths and gallops to induce sweating, while 'periodical purges of salt-water and malt-water' were also part of the treatment.

Trotting and short gallops over two or three furlongs were also part of their regular training, which would last for some six months – the duration of the season, one presumes.

The professor from the University of Prague, one M Hronzy, who translated the inscription, declared that 'in view of the methodical nature of the system described, there could be no doubt that it had been evolved as the result of long experience, and might have originated as early as 3,000BC.'

247. SINK OR SWIM

Flamboyant Aussie gambler Perce Galea was one of that country's leading plungers but in 1961 his hefty punt on a horse running in Sydney had come unstuck and he found himself owing leading bookie TB 'Sharkey' Dwyer £1700.

Galea arranged to meet Dwyer at the Clovelly Surf Club to settle up. When he arrived the bookie was swimming – but he suddenly got into difficulties.

Galea raced towards the sea, but fell and banged his face heavily. Nonetheless he dived in, made it to the struggling Dwyer who was on the point of drowning, and dragged him to the beach where they both collapsed, exhausted.

As they recovered, Dwyer, who owed his life to Galea, told the punter – 'If you had kept me in that water for another minute I'd have wiped what you owed me'. He got up, walked to his car, calling over his shoulder; 'See you at tomorrow's settling, Perce.'

248. FAGGED OUT

The Cheroot Stakes, run at Calcutta's racecourse in 1832, boasted a unique set of qualification rules but still attracted 17 runners, despite the fact that race conditions specified that each rider must 'start with a lighted cheroot in his mouth, keep same alight during the race, and bring it alight to the weighing place, or be considered distanced (disqualified)'. Only one rider fell foul of the rules during the mile long race.

249. HEY MAN, CHILL OUT

Trainer Reg Akehurst was convinced there was a sinister and unusual reason for the disappointing performance of his big hope, Loh, in the 1976 2000 Guineas – he reckoned the horse had been doped with marijuana.

250. TAKING THE PISS

Major Leon, a top sprinter, was drug tested after winning a 1969 race in Victoria, Australia. There was consternation when it emerged that the sample, apparently taken from the horse, was 'of human origin'.Connections were fined for 'improper practices'.

251. CASUALTY OF WAR

German Derby winner Alchimist should have enjoyed a leisurely retirement at stud. Instead the horse met a bizarre end when, at the end of World War II, in 1945, the grooms looking after him at Gradiz, the National Stud, where the highly valued stallion was standing, fled in the face of the advancing Russian army.

The almost starving troops could not believe their luck when they arrived and saw what to them was meat on the hoof,

Alchimist was killed and consumed – whether in a rare or well done condition does not seem to have been recorded for posterity – thus bringing to an end that particular bloodline.

252. KEEPING MUM

A unique formbook entry appeared in Weatherby's *Chase Weekly* for a jumps race run at East Devon's point-to point-fixture on March 4, 2006, when Ted One was partnered by Caroline Farrant – 'rider constantly harassed by mother ('do stop keeping on, Mum'); taken down early.' Ted One and Ms Farrant did not perform with distinction and the pair were tailed off last by some 42 lengths – earning the admonition, 'given dreadful ride and should have been censured'. So, perhaps, as they tend to do, Mum knew what she was on about.

253. WAKING THE DEAD

Ireland's *Daily Chronicle* reported on March 17, 1926 that an Irish racehorse had been celebrated at a bizarre wake.

Cannon Ball was the doyen of the local pony racing scene, having sired many of the best ponies in the land and had an unbeaten record of his own at country race meetings.

'He died on Monday in his 38th year. As soon as his death was announced large numbers of people visited the owner, Mr H O'Toole of Leam, Connemara, who was as much affected as if he had lost a near relative. Neighbours had the body taken into the kitchen, where it was laid out on an improvised bier. A half-barrel of porter stood in the corner of the room, and the pony was 'waked' as if it had been a human being.

Soon after midnight the body was placed on a large stable door, which had been taken off its hinges, and was carried by ten stalwart peasants to a grave lined with hay on the owner's farm. There, at the dead of night, the burial took place, and a local bard read the following verse:

'Sleep, brave old pony, thy race is run,
No more with earthly kin you'll mingle;
Dream of racecourse tracks you've won,
Of noble steeds and epic deeds,
And bookies left without a jingle'.

254. PLUS CA CHANGE

As arguments rage about whether there is more, or less, fixed racing taking place than there has ever been, it is cautionary to refer to a report of a 1785 race meeting at Alnwick in Northumberland where the clerk of the course Nicholas Brown's own race record declares, 'A contrived race betwixt the parties, and the prize (£50) should not have been given' ... some seven years earlier at Boroughbridge in the north of England's October 1778 meeting, the top five year old mare Miss Nightingale was expected to win the £50 main contest, but was found dead just before the race. Skulduggery being suspected, she was opened up, 'and in her stomach was found about 2lbs of duck-shot, made up with putty into balls' recorded a contemporary account. One Wm Turner was committed to York Assizes on suspicion, but was acquitted 'for want of evidence' ... even earlier than this, in September 1722 'some malicious persons got into the stable where Mr Pratt's chestnut colt Tosspot (!) stood, and gave him a dose of physic the night before he was to run' at Scarborough.

255. GOING ICEY

Six runners lined up for a race on Tuesday, January 15, 1740, to be run in three heats, each of two miles, taking place near Barnard Castle, County Durham – 'on the frozen River Tees'. In 1607 and 1608 there was 'a great frost' as a result of which horse racing was staged on the frozen River Ouse in York, run from 'the Tower at Marygate end, through the great arch of Ouse Bridge, to the Crane at Skeldergate Postern'.

256. OH, WHAT A GAS, LET'S HAVE A WHIP ROUND

There is no report of the actual racing which took place at Lambton Park in Durham's 1826 meeting, but *The Sporting Magazine's* description of the activity at the track is entertaining, telling of 'a great diversity of amusement ... in addition to racing, the horsewhipping of one groom, and the cutting down of another who had hanged himself, but not effectually, to avoid the anger of his master – both grooms having been detected in malpractices. But the most entertaining occurrence was the extinguishing of the gaslights whilst the gay party were engaged in the mazes of a dance. The joke was not relished by the Head of the Castle who offered a reward of £1,000 for the discovery of the offender.'

257. BEATEN IN A WALK-OVER!

It sounds impossible, but, inevitably, it has happened – horses beaten in a walk-over. And even two horses walking over in the same race. The latter phenomenon occurred at Northallerton racecourse in 1778 when only two of the six declared runners for a four mile event, a sweepstake of 20gns each, turned up. Orpheus and Icelander were there, but connections of Orpheus queried 'the legality of Icelander's nomination'. Eventually, 'both walked over, the owners of each claiming the stakes'.

To return to the seemingly unfeasible defeat in a walk-over, it happened in 1990 at Tweseldon point-to-point when Terry Smith was due to partner Rossa Prince, the only runner in one of the races – only to lose out when the horse bolted and could not be recaptured.

In 1994, Ciaran O'Neill emulated that achievement when he did actually walk over with mount Mister Chippendale at Blankney point-to-point – but was disqualified for failing to weigh in.

And in 1964 Trelawney was the only horse declared for the Queen Alexandra Stakes at Royal Ascot. The entire day's racing was rained off. It was re-scheduled for the Saturday and rained off again.

258. MYT BE A RECORD

Edinburgh owner Mr C Kidd sent his Myton Lad to contest the Hunt Cup at Shilbottle's six race card in Northumberland in 1884. He started as favourite to beat his three rivals but could only finish second to well handicapped Ned, a 300 guinea purchase earlier in his career and half brother to top horse of the era, Isonomy.

However, in the next race the two rivals took on each other again, with Ned given a 14lb penalty, enabling Myton Lad to gain revenge.

Not content with this success, Mr Kidd decided to start Myton Lad for the Hurdle race which was next up – the horse was not impressed with the plan and promptly refused at the first – although his jockey did make him eventually complete the course.

As the runners gathered for the next contest, the Licensed Victuallers' Plate, the crowd was nonplussed to see Myton Lad lining up for the fourth time that afternoon – only to raise the roof – had there been one, that is – as the heroic horse won 'rather cleverly'.

However, connections of another runner objected 'on the ground that they had not gone the proper course.'

The stewards deliberated and decided the race must be re-run.

Coming under orders for probably a record fifth time at one meeting, Myton Lad went out and did it all again, this time getting both verdict and spoils.

However, even this marathon performance by Myton Lad may have been outdone.

An 1863 tome, *Horse Racing* by an unknown author, describes 'a very severe race run over the Doncaster course, September 28, 1797. The race was for £100, in two mile heats, for which seven horses started. The first heat was strongly contested between Stamford, Cardinal and Pepper Pot; the second was a dead heat between Warter and Pepper Pot, Stamford being third; the third heat was won by Pepper Pot; the fourth by Warter; and, astonishing to relate, the fifth was a dead heat again between Warter and Pepper Pot! These two horses started again, for the sixth time or heat, when Warter was the victor. Such an evenly balanced and exciting struggle must have been well worth witnessing; and undoubtedly the animals must have possessed great stamina and gameness.'

259. CENSOR HUMOUR

Owners have tried all sorts of subterfuge in order to slip dodgy names past the powers that be, and most of their efforts have become well known once exposed. However, whether some of the names which seem to have been accepted down the years would have any chance of acceptance today is a moot point.

In 1840, Tadcaster races played host to dual winner Prickbelt, which may just have had an entirely innocent meaning as, no doubt did Sir H T Vane's Little Fanny, an 1809 runner at Northallerton. You have to like the naming of Bedlamite, out of Maniac, half brother to Lunatic, by Prime Minister, which shows that politicians of 1822, when these horses were active, suffered much the same sort of reputations as they do today!

My favourite named horse is a mid 19th century runner called Sweetest When She's Naked, who was on the circuit around the same time as Pudenda.

Perhaps the word had an alternative meaning in 1930 when the Yorkshire Cup was won by The Bastard. The horse eventually ended up in Australia for stud duties, but his name was too 'in your face' for the delicate Aussies, and he was re-christened 'The Buzzard'. Mind you, I suppose many might be unenthusiastic at purchasing 'the son of a Bastard'.

Muff Diver was a 1978 winner in Belgium, around about the same time that Shy Talk was active for several seasons.

In the 1980s a horse called Willy Wank won 18 times, once holding off the challenge of Scorched Panties.

The Julie Cecil-trained Mary Hinge delighted fans of spoonerisms by chalking up five wins during 1993 and 1994. Obviously inspired by that name, Joe Blob and Cunning Stunts were soon to be noted. In 1994 three year old Weigh Anchor gave fast-talking commentators some problems.

New Zealand racehorse Tulsy Tsan was banned from racing in 1998 when the authorities read her name backwards.

Top US owner Mike Pegram, whose best horse in recent years has been Captain Steve, was also the proud owner of the salacious Isitingood, and the innocuous looking Dixie Norma's – innocuous, that is, until pronounced aloud with a prefix such as, for example – Mike Pegram's. Try it.

Jockey Club officials prevented a Richard Hannon late 1990s two year old from running as The Gobbler, so it became Golden Ace. In 2003 the Jockey Club were not happy with a French raider which came over to race here. Trainer Elie Lellouche had been unable to get the name he wanted, Gros Nichons, past the French authorities, so translated that to English and went for Big Tits, which was duly approved.

In July 2005, Owen Byrne of the Jockey Club revealed some of the names which had been rejected as being unsuitable. Chocolate Starfish fell victim to the red pen as it apparently refers to the anus; Jack Meehoff should be obvious to most men and women of the world, while Sofa King Fast was speedily rejected; Wear The Fox Hat was an inventive effort – and eventually called Nameless – while Mrs Merkin – a merkin being a pubic wig – just might have got through had it been mistaken for Mrs Merton, but Far Kinnell didn't get very far through the process at all.

In May 2006, a horse trained by Vince Smith with one undescended testicle won a juvenile maiden race – his name is Juan Bol.

In 2007 a syndicate called the Landing Strip Partnership, gave Weatherbys a few hairy moments, naming a two-year-old Bollywood Style. Innocent enough, but I am indebted to *The Observer* newspaper for explaining that it means 'to have the pubic area shaved and covered with Henna tattoo.' They also own Bush Breakfast. Their colours are white with a black stripe.

And in July of the same year, *Racing Post* reader Jonny Allison commented on some runners he had noticed; "May I suggest a nursery restricted to three entrants – New Balls Please, Cute Ass and Little Knickers. Maybe the owners of Panty Raid could sponsor?' Not all censorship is applied to names with saucy or risqué meanings, and it is impossible to believe that the name of the good Fred Rimell-trained chaser of the mid-1940s, Coloured School Boy, would be permitted now.

260. WEIGHTY MATTERS

The runners lined up for the one mile race at York in 1788 in which Mr Maynard's bay mare was the outsider of two against the 1/2 favourite, Mr Baker's gray horse. Neither horse had a weight advantage – both were set to carry 30 stone!

Victory in the 100 guinea contest went to the second favourite.

In 1867 one-handed Mr Robert Calder partnered his own Lyra in a £200 match over

1m at Wark in Northumberland, against Mr Chirnside's Hurcules. Both carried 20 stone and Mr Calder won, well, handily.

Promoting a new video in the 1990s, hefty comedian Bernard Manning, weighing 18 stone, donned racing silks and rode – or, sat on – a horse called Wolfie.

**Jockey, J Kitchener, who rode the winner of the 1844 Chester Cup, weighed in at 46lbs. His mount, Red Deer, the first three year old winner of the contest, stormed in by some 50 lengths at 7/2, landing a £100,000 coup for owner the Duke of Richmond, carrying just 4 stone. It took Kitchener an additional half a circuit of the course to pull the horse up.

261. WHAT A COINCIDENCE

Perhaps the first coincidence winner in racing history emerged at the 1881 Easter Monday fixture at Birmingham's Four Oaks Park, at which the Lady Wood Two Year Old Plate was won by Lady Wood ... One of the all-time greats of American racing, Man O'War suffered the only defeat of his career in August 1919 – beaten by a horse called Upset ... There never was a more appropriate coincidence bet than on November 14, 1973 when Captain Mark Phillips wed Princess Anne and that afternoon's Royal Wedding Chase was won by Royal Mark ...The 'Thatcher Stakes' run at Lingfield in January 1996 was won by Carrolls Marc. Lady Thatcher's children's names are Carol and Mark ... in July 1989, Chester's Wonderfuel Gas Handicap was won by Burnt Fingers ... on the very day Mr Frisk won the 1990 Grand National, a horse called Mr Frisky won in the US, equalling that country's record of 16 consecutive victories ... after a Spitfire fly-past to commemorate the Battle of Britain at Kempton in September 1990, the Spitfire Handicap was won by 11/2 flier, Blue Aeroplane ... Market Rasen staged the Town Council Novice Chase, won by Corrupt Committee, ridden by A Tory in September 1992 ... Lingfield's Albert Handicap in January 1993 was won by Albert ... the 750 smoking enthusiasts who attended a specially arranged race meeting at Meadowlands Racetrack hosted by *Cigar Aficianado* magazine in the 1990s were delighted when the final race was won by Light It Up ... the horse which reared up and badly gashed Lester Piggott's left eye, putting him in hospital, whilst cantering to the start in Hong Kong in February 1993 was called – Beat Them Up ... five days before the 1992 General Election, the Grand National was won by 14/1 shot Party Politics, while just two days before voting began Political Issue was a 9/4 winner at Kelso ... in July 2006 at a York meeting, Wyatt Earp won the 2.45 race at 13/8, then in the 5pm, the 12/1 winner was Josie Marcus – the name of Western legend Earp's last wife ... Southwell winner in mid- August 2006, Cream Cracker was indeed ridden by Jacob – Daryl of that ilk ... when Tony McCoy made a comeback from an eight week wrist injury at Hereford on September 28, 2006 his first mount, and first winner, was Absolutelythebest.

262. WINE NOT?

Mr T Walker and Captain A Hay decided in 1773 to race from London to York – the former partnering his hackney gelding, the latter hiring Capt Mulcaster to ride aboard his road mare. The stake money at stake is not recorded, but they set off from Portland Street and after 40 hours and 35 minutes in the saddle, Capt Mulcaster arrived at Ouse Bridge in York.

Of his rival there was no sign because, as *Sporting Magazine* later reported, 'Mr Walker's horse tired within six miles of Tadcaster, and died the next day.'

The good Captain's mount thrived on her racing diet, having 'drank 12 bottles of wine during her journey, and was so well on the following Thursday as to take her exercise on Knavesmire.'

263. CHOCKEY

Top Melbourne jockey Harold Badger shocked his weight conscious colleagues in 1939 when he signed a commercial deal to advertise Energy chocolate.

264. ED-LINE MAKER

Ed Cavalho, 10lb claiming apprentice, managed to win a race at the 42nd time of asking when partnering Majestic Moran to victory at Tampa Bay Downs in January 1993 – at the ripe old age of 43.

265. ONE THING OR ANOTHER

Several horses – Glenside, who won the 1911 Grand National, for example – have won races despite having only one eye ... Masked Ball won races despite – as his name hinted – having only one testicle ... Prime Mover won at Southwell in 1993 despite having only one hip ... 19th century jockey Harry Edwards, a somewhat untrustworthy character who would, wrote racing historian 'Thormanby' 'rather make a pony 'on the cross' than get a hundred on the square', was also distinguished by having only the one eye ... in February 1927 jockey George Duller rode Royal Falcon to victory, with one foot clad in a slipper as it had yet to recover from a recent injury ... leading jockey at early Saratoga meetings in the early 1860s was a black rider with one eye, known only as Sewell.

266. SEATS OF POWER

With an estimated sale value of £1,000, five green leather armchairs which had housed the posteriors of the Queen, Prince Philip and other Royals during racing at Newbury, came up for auction in February 1990 – fetching £10,900 from an anonymous bidder.

267. NOT HIS DAY, REALLY

Riding in Macau in March 1992, Tony Ives was weighing in after partnering Mountview to victory when he caught his foot on the bottom of the scales and tripped, hitting a table and knocking himself unconscious. When he came round he declared himself fit to ride Good Luck Swoopy in the next. The horse played up in the stalls, trapping Ives' leg, injuring it so badly that he had to give up his rides for the rest of the day.

268. BEASTLY NAME FOR BEAUTY?

A former finalist in the Miss Great Britain beauty contest was not amused when she discovered that a businessman against whom she had recently won a discrimination claim, had apparently named a racehorse after her.

Emma Nicholson, from Stanley, County Durham, who was sacked after she became pregnant, was very unhappy to hear in April 2006, that her former boss Nigel Gravett, had named his two year old filly, being trained by Peter Easterby, 'Emma Told Lies'. The 25-year-old said, possibly quite perceptively and accurately: 'He's having a dig at me. They may see this as a joke, but to me it's further evidence of the way I was treated.'

Mr Gravett commented, possibly somewhat less accurately: 'As far as I am aware, there is no law about what you can or cannot call a racehorse.'

269. GOLDEN OLDIES

Charlie Whittingham, oldest trainer to win the Kentucky Derby at age 76, applied for training credentials in New York and, despite being bald, listed his hair colour as brown, because 'that's the way I remember it' ... still going strong aged 90 Carl Hanford, trainer of five time US horse of the year, Kelso, commented 'a good horse is dangerous in anybody's hands' in August 2006 as he was inducted into the Racing Hall of Fame ... 92-year-old Mrs Frances Genter became the oldest winning owner of the race when her Unbridled won the 1990 Kentucky Derby. Trainer Carl Nafzger gave the unsighted veteran an impromptu commentary, ending – 'He won it, Mrs Genter! He won it! You've won the Kentucky Derby. I love you, Mrs Genter.' ... Fred Hooper was 95 when his Roman Envoy won the 1992 Kelso Handicap at Belmont Park ... Keep Talking, hero of the 1992 National Hunt Chase was 97-year-old Jim Joel's 12th Cheltenham Festival winner and his last before dying shortly after ... punter Albert Fuller celebrated his 100th birthday on February 29, 1984 – wouldn't that make him really only 25? – by visiting his local William Hill shop in Mottingham, Kent where he backed John Francome, who rode his 1,000th winner over the sticks, Observe at Worcester ... 105-year-old Rosie Hamburger was appointed the *New York Post* racing tipster in the spring of 1996, having started betting 'sometime before World War One'. She died later that year, but her final selection was a winner.

270. THE LONGEST SPRINT EVER?

Swaying Tree, the mount of Eddie Hide, set off in Ripon's Yorkshire Handicap on August 4, 1980 at 4.30 – and finished as the winner of the race, over an hour later, with Jimmy Bleasdale on board.

The 14 runner race had got underway, apparently, as per normal, but after one furlong of the scheduled six, a red flag was waved and six horses and jockeys pulled themselves up. Eight, though, ran on, with Wynbury passing the post in front.

At 4.35 came the announcement that the race was void.

At 4.48 it was announced that there had been a false start.

At 5.04 it was announced that the race would be re-run at 5.30.

At this point nine of the original 14 runners were withdrawn

Wynbury was amongst the five who did line up again but this time Swaying Tree, one of the six who had stopped in the initial running and whose jockey Eddie Hide had since managed to get himself kicked by another horse so having to be replaced by Jimmy Bleasdale, romped home in first place.

271. ASHEN FACED

When popular Aussie jockey Noel Barker died in 1992, following a fall at Randwick in Sydney, his widow Kelly said that she wished to scatter his ashes at Sha Tin racecourse in Hong Kong where he had been champion jockey.

The Royal Hong Kong Jockey refused to permit such a thing, claiming, 'the local feelings on such matters are very strong.'

272. INJURED – BY THE AMBULANCE

A spectator was hospitalised at a Brighton meeting in October 1995 when the course ambulance failed to negotiate a bend and ploughed into the middle-aged racegoer who was later released after precautionary checks.

273. UNDER ORDERS, OFF, HOLD ON, I'M COMING

Towards the end of the 19th century, Clerk of the Course at Birmingham's Four Oaks Park racecourse, John Sheldon, was a very conscientious chap – who would often have to act as Starter – and also as Judge.

Many a time Sheldon would get the runners under way and then jump into his horse and cart and charge off to the Judge's box to declare the result.

Presumably knackered by his work-load, Sheldon resigned in 1886.

274. BODY SNATCHERS

Four men were spotted making off with the body of a dead horse, tragically killed during a race at Birmingham's first – and only – Saturday fixture in May 1908.

The body was traced to a local slaughterhouse where it had been purchased for 5/- (25p). The *Birmingham Gazette* later reported that the gang involved had been 'brought to justice'.

275. LET'S KEEP THE RIFF-RAFF OUT OF RACING

Having taken a close look at the condition of the racing world, the Earl of Derby was so disturbed at what he saw in 1857, that he put pen to paper to appeal to the Jockey Club to do something about it:

'It has become a subject of general observation and regret that the number of men of station and fortune who support the Turf is gradually diminishing, and that an increasing proportion of horses in training is in the hands of persons in an inferior position, who keep them not for the purpose of sport, but as mere instruments of gambling.

'I venture to think that it is your duty as Stewards of the Jockey Club, to exercise a wholesome influence upon the character and respectability of the Turf.

'You cannot debar any man, whatever his position in society, from keeping racehorses; nor do I recommend a vexatious and inquisitorial scrutiny into the character and conduct of those who do so; but when among their number are found those against whom flagrant cases of disgraceful fraud and dishonesty have been legally established, it appears to me clearly within your province to stamp them with your reprobation, and to exclude them from association, on an equal footing, with the more honourable supporters of the Turf.'

The Earl backed up his words by demanding that the Club warn off a particular owner, one Mr Adkins from who 'a sum of above 6,000 pounds has been recovered on the avowed ground that it had been won by cheating with loaded dice'.

It was unanimously agreed at the AGM of the Jockey Club that this resolution should be adopted.

Then, 150 years later in 2007, Goodwood supremo, the Earl of March courted controversy when he told Richard Kay of the *Daily Mail*, 'We have far too many chavs, I'm afraid I would like to see ladies in nice traditional English summer frocks, with linen suits and Panama hats for the gentlemen!'

276. ASPELL ON THE SIDELINES

Perhaps the only jockey who could boast an official fan club – they sponsored a race in his honour at Fontwell – Leighton Aspell stunned them when he quit suddenly, aged 31, in July 2007, after finishing unplaced in a Stratford chase, confessing 'Deep down, I've not been happy.'

277. BRAWL ASCOT

More drunk punters arrested than England World Cup fans' was the unexpected front page banner headline of *The Sun* on June 23, 2006, contrasting behaviour at Royal Ascot, where, it was said, 25 racegoers had been arrested in three days, and at the World Cup in Germany, where, claimed the paper, England fans 'have been hailed the best in the world' for their peaceful conduct with only 13 arrested in three days.

Regardless of the accuracy and selective nature of the figures involved, the story must have made uneasy reading for racing officials with the paper reporting that 'shocked onlookers told how plastered racegoers punched, kicked and even headbutted each other.'

278. WHIFF OF CONFUSION

Punters trying to get paid out on the winner of the 1867 Melbourne Cup, Tim Whiffler, were turned away by bookmakers who told them, 'Sorry, you were on the other Tim Whiffler!'

Fights broke out as confusion raged, for there were two Tim Whifflers running in the race. One of them had won – the one who had become known as 'Sydney' Tim, who went off as 5/2 favourite, because he had arrived from that city to contest the race, and had landed a comfortable victory, beating the local horse, Tim Whiffler – known as 'Melbourne' Tim and a 50/1 outsider – into fifth place.

But, inevitably, many of the unscrupulous element amongst the big crowd for Australia's major race, were prepared to swear that they had been on 'Sydney' even though their betting ticket indicated 'Melbourne'.

Eventually, the situation seemed to be sorted out, but with these two high profile horses being joined on the circuit by a decent horse called Tim Whiffler, performing on the Perth tracks, and 'Sydney' Tim producing a son called, er, Tim Whiffler, which won the Great Northern Derby in New Zealand no one was quite able to tell their Tims from their Whifflers for some while.

Particularly when owner Mr J Moffat announced in 1871 that he had imported from England a horse called, well, Tim Whiffler, who sired 1876 Melbourne Cup winner Briseis.

279. NO APOLOGY AS KING DETHRONED BY ARCHBISHOP OF CANTERBURY

At the age of 81, having never been to a race meeting or placed a bet, and suffering ill health, the Reverend John King was hounded out of office because of the amazing success of a racehorse he owned.

Having become the Vicar of Ashby-de-la-Launde in Lincolnshire in 1822, the Rev King inherited his late father's stud, with strict instructions not to sell or dispose of it.

Rev King discreetly operated under the name of a friend and a nom de course of Mr Launde, but when his filly, Apology, won the 1874 1000 Guineas, Oaks and St Leger, it was the talk of the racing world.

Word reached the Bishop of Lincoln – probably via his Chancellor, the ambitious and zealous Canon Edward Benson, who would eventually become Archbishop of Canterbury. The Bishop was persuaded that he should not be best pleased that one of his underlings should be associated with the immoral world of racing. He wrote a stiff letter to the Reverend, copying in the *Guardian* newspaper.

Facing such public criticism the ailing Rev King had no alternative but to resign his post – and he died shortly after, early in 1875 – with another of his stable representatives, the appropriately named Holy Friar, favourite for the Derby.

The Rev King may well have observed with interest from his Heavenly abode in 1905, the Grand National being won by Kirkland, bred in county Limerick by the Reverend Clifford.

280. WELL, I'LL BE DOGGONE

Dogging is the sexual activity which got former Premiership footballer Stan Collymore into the papers some while back. Those of a sheltered disposition should move on to another story now, but the more adventurous may be intrigued to hear that a number of racecourses are now playing host to doggers – not at the same time as racing is going on, mind you. That might frighten the horses.

As I understand the matter, dogging seems to involve some people doing, other people being done to, and spectators observing.

Whatever, the *Observer*'s racing columnist, 'Tattenham Corner' is so well up on these things that he recently cited 'a website that specialises on the subject' when informing us that Doncaster, although closed for redevelopment at the time, 'is one hotbed of sexual activity'.

He went so far as to tell us where to locate said activity – 'Just after the Grandstand is a road called "the Straight Mile". Dogging is to be had all along the grass and in the wood at the end of the road'.

Transvestites are the dogging attraction 'in parkland next to Windsor' and the other course getting in on the act is Nottingham where it apparently goes on or, perhaps, comes off, 'after hours in the car park'.

Cheltenham and Pontefract are other tracks believed to be targeted by aficionados of such activity.

281. LOST SLEEP

A race was delayed by 26 minutes at Saratoga in the States in July 1991 – because runner Lost Link was on the track in front of the starting gate – fast asleep. The horse had been tranquillised by the track vet after panicking before the race and becoming dangerous. The three-year-old eventually came to, and was withdrawn, allowing the race to go ahead.

282. YOU'RE MY LAST, MY FIRST, MY ... EVERYTHING?

Thirteen went to post for the 3m Rathnure Handicap at Wexford in Ireland in March 1988.

Leader, Lady Daffydown, went the wrong side of a marker, dragging several of the others the same way.

The jockey, Pat O'Donnell on Derry Gowan, went back to take the right course but the loss of ground left him finishing last of the ten to complete the course.

The stewards looked into the race, watching a poor quality video of the action – and disqualifed the first nine to finish – placing Derry Gowan first.

That was not the end of the controversy, though, and when another video came to light, it showed that another runner, Mullakhea, who had finished 6th, had also clearly taken the correct course. The horse's connections appealed to the Irish National Hunt Committee which met several days later and handed the race to Mullakhea, leaving Derry Gowan, who had already finished first and last, now in the runners-up position.

283. STARTER UNDER ORDERS

After a controversy over the result of a selling race at the Curragh in April 1812 which was not finally settled until an entire year later when it was decided that the result should be altered because one of those involved had taken the wrong course, the stewards, the Marquis of Sligo and Bowes Daly ruled that 'there was most reprehensible inattention on the part of the Starter and as a mark of our disapprobation of his conduct we hereby direct that half a year's salary shall be withheld from him.' It seemed a little superfluous that they added that he should exercise 'more caution in future.'

284. CUTTING COMMENTS

Trainer John Scott sent out an incredible 41 Classic winners during his career between 1827 and 1863. A sophisticated man, he enjoyed nothing more than entertaining visitors to stories of his racing days, whilst feeding them a fine meal. He would make a great show of carving a joint of beef with a unique knife, whose handle was made from the shank bone of Rowton – who in 1829 had become his third St Leger winner.

285. CAUSING A FLAP

Carrier pigeons were utilised by news agencies to spread the result of a horse race for the first time in 1825 when word of Memnon's St Leger victory literally flew from Doncaster to London.

286. PIPE DOWN

Trainer Martin Pipe sponsored the 'Am I That Difficult? Handicap Hurdle' at Taunton in January 1997. Of course a man who would only eat straight bananas could never be described as difficult, surely? A man who played his horses Radio 1 all day, who used to 'borrow' samples of other trainers' feeds to check them out and who said of his riding career of one winner. 'My saving grace as a jockey was bravery bordering on stupidity.'

287. BREAST MATE?

Bra firm Triumph International recently ran a competition amongst workers to find a name for their newly acquired racehorse. Won By A Nipple made the short-list but was just touched off by Bosom Pal.

288. STONE COLD CERT

When Irish steeplechasing was in its infancy it appears that spectators came up with a way of ensuring that their fancy was a stone cold cert, according to the report of a race over open fields at Limerick, in February 1833, contested against local riders by Englishman George Smith.

Forewarned that racegoers who had bet against him would not be above hurling stones at him during the race to slow his progress, Smith came up with a cunning plan to counteract this possibility.

The Sportsman magazine highlighted the danger – 'a man has to run the gauntlet at the risk of martyrdom – to put himself in the way of becoming a second St Stephen or, in plain language, being stoned to death.'

Aware of this threat, Smith set off on his mount, Fidler, wearing his jockey kit and colours, but once underway stopped to don an overcoat and hat before spurring his horse into a clear lead. As he approached the fences guarded by the stone carrying spectators Smith shouted at them to move clear as the favourite, who was winning, was just approaching.

Assuming Smith to be an interested party out following the course of the race they did just that, permitting Smith to avoid personal damage and to win the race.

289. FOOD FOR THOUGHT

Brisbane jockey Stathi Katsidis was suspended for three months and fined $A5,000 (£2,000) in late 2006 after describing Chief Steward Reid Sanders as 'a grub.'

290. COLLARED

When jump jockey Jimmy Brogan came down on the flat whilst riding 7/2 favourite Prince Blackthorn in the 1944 Irish Grand National, he broke his collarbone – for the fourteenth time.

291. VIRTUALLY UNBELIEVABLE

Players contesting the virtual racing management game, getminted.com, were selling their non-existent 'horses' for up to four figure sums during 2006, with one named SilverBullet Jonz, 'trained' by Jonz79, sold to fellow 'trainer' Andy Hargie in October, for a staggering and very real £2,500.

292. WARNING

When its not your day, its not your day. Reeling from England's fifth day, 2nd Ashes Test collapse from 69-1 to 129 all out, in December 2006, skipper Andrew Flintoff could have done without the horse he co-owned, and named after him, Flintoff, running and being beaten that afternoon back in England, while on a day that spinner Shane Warne had caused havoc amongst the England batsmen, Warne's Way was a 9/2 winner on the same card.

293. GOLDEN GLORY

Neville Sellwood, who rode Delta to win the 1951 Melbourne Cup, was rewarded by owner, Sir Adolph Basser, with a gold Rolls Royce.

294. GET THE PICTURE

Martin Molony was the Tony McCoy of his day – single-minded in his quest for winners. The Irish rider criss-crossed the channel, chalking up winners prolifically – in 1950 he notched up 116, one off the all time record in Ireland, whilst also finishing runner up to his own brother Tim in Britain. So, when a win was there, he went for it.

As Martin galvanised Dominick's Bar, an 8/1 shot, for a late run to the line in the 1950 Irish Grand National he could see only one obstacle in their way as he battled to catch leader Stormhead on the run-in. That obstacle came in the shape of a newsreel cameraman who had strayed to close too the action.

'His stupid fault' reasoned Molony, who galloped relentlessly on, bowling the cameraman over as he got up to win by two lengths.

295. VICTORIA'S SMASHING TIME

Queen Victoria, at the time a Princess, was introduced to racing by her uncle, King William IV, who took her to Ascot and even introduced her to betting – she won a chestnut mare called Taglioni from him in a wager.

On June 15, 1854 Victoria, by now Queen, was at Royal Ascot where, reported The Times, during the New Stakes, 'just as the horses reached the Royal Stand, Her Majesty in her eagerness to see the race, not perceiving that the window where she had been standing, had been put down, leant forward rather hastily to look out, and broke a pane of glass with which she came into contact.'

However, after Prince Albert died in 1861 Victoria never again went racing.

296. STRAIGHT UP, SHE'S A WINNER

Cousin of Lester Piggott, brother of top jockey Bill Rickaby, Fred Rickaby became a leading trainer in South Africa, and in 1950 had planned a betting coup on his horse, Lady Valerie 'We thought that if we put up the stable apprentice the punters would imagine the filly was not fancied. William was a nice kid, not overburdened with intelligence, but had good hands and horses seemed to run for him'

The chosen race was a poor quality six furlong handicap. 'I planned the commission myself. Three 'mugs' were supplied with ready money and I organised some out-of-town bets at starting price. It worked like a charm and the filly started at 20/1.'

William wasn't told what was afoot until he was in the parade ring, when he was advised, 'Your only danger is that you might swerve and cause interference. Jump out of the gate and keep straight, that is all you have to do. I don't mind how far you win.'

Rickaby watched as Lady Valerie was slow away but moved into a good position with only four runners ahead of her.

'William was unconcernedly sitting still behind them. With a furlong to go he must have been fifteen lengths behind the leaders. He then shot past the horses he was waiting behind and with Lady Valerie making up ground as if she had just jumped in, got up to finish third, beaten a length and a neck.'

Rickaby was apoplectic. 'For fear of exploding with rage, I avoided William until we got home.'

Once back at the stables he demanded an explanation. 'Well, sir' said William , 'I was not quite so well away as about four horses around me and they were close together in front of me. I daren't pull round them, because you said I must keep straight. You know, Mr Rick, I'd have won easily if you hadn't told me I must keep straight.'

This incident hastened Rickaby's eventual decision to give up gambling.

297. PUFFED OUT

In 1922, the Newmarket stewards held an enquiry into the smoking habits of jockeys and decreed that they should be banned from doing so during racing hours. A jockey revolt soon brought about the withdrawal of the edict.

298. RACE FIXING – BY THE FIXER

In a sensational admission, a bookmaker has revealed how he arranged an entirely pre-ordained outcome to a race, enlisting all but one of the jockeys involved to ensure the agreed result. Okay, it may have happened 146 years ago, but it is still a remarkable story.

Bookmaker and owner George Hodgman was the key instigator of the fix which took place in 1862 at Shrewsbury – and was arranged entirely to permit a number of his friends to win themselves a cache of cash.

It was the final meeting of the season at the course, taking place in the autumn and Hodgman justified his actions by pointing out that 'whatever took place was generally with an idea to help out some decent sportsmen who, at the finish of the season were hard up.'

The broke 'sportsmen' were Captains Little and Townley, George Eade and George Angell, with the last named approaching Hodgman 'with the idea of making up a small handicap for gentlemen riders.' Hodgman duly went to the course manager, John Frail and told him, 'There are four of the swells dead broke and we must get a race up for them.'

A notice was put up at the course, ostensibly inviting entries for the Welter Handicap over half a mile. But Hodgman told Frail the names of four horses which should be permitted to enter and that no others should be accepted.

However, Frail's son inadvertently accepted an additional entry, Mr Priestley's Tom Sayers.

Hodgman realised that they would now have to make sure this horse was the winner, although its form was abysmal.

Hodgman suggested to one of the top jockeys of the day, George Fordham that a Mr Priestley was looking for a rider for Tom Sayers, telling him 'I thought he might win.' Fordham was booked and other, compliant jockeys were arranged for the other four runners.

'Now, Angell, we must put a thousand pounds on Tom Sayers,' said Hodgman, who accepted the task of putting on the readies. Hodgman saw his 'putter-on', telling him – 'We've good men up. Nobody will know anything till they get to the post.'

As the horses arrived at the start, out of the hearing of Fordham, Captain Townley told the other three jockeys of the plot.

The starter set them off, but 'at the first attempt Tom Sayers refused to jump off, and the others obligingly came back; at the next 'go' he was soon allowed to take the rails.

The others allowed Fordham to poach a two length lead but as they approached the latter stages 'they were pressing Tom Sayers a bit too close.'

'Gentlemen' said Townley, 'let him get nearer home then we'll flutter.'

They 'fluttered' so astutely that while Tom Sayers crawled home by three quarters of a length, merely necks separated the others.'

After the race, Hodgman came clean to Fordham – 'and he roared with laughter – "I thought" he said "they were confoundedly kind to me. I ought to have been left on my beast a hundred yards".

Now Hodgman collected the winnings – 'The thousand laid out brought in 2500, which was cut up as follows; Capt Little 500; Mr Eade 500; Capt Townley 500; Jimmy Barber and Mr Dunne (owners) 250 each. Perry and Palmer (jockeys) had 150 between them and the remainder – 350 – George Angell and I shared.

The tale soon leaked out, and a considerable time elapsed before I was ceased to be asked; "Well, Tom Sayers, how are you going?"'

299. ARTHUR GETS FINGERED BY SHEILA

Jump jockey Arthur Thompson was captured in occupied France during the Second World War, but appropriately enough for a rider who loved to front-run, he escaped on a bicycle.

He was riding a rather more valuable and efficient conveyance when he landed the job as stable jockey to Capt Neville Crump for whom he twice won the Grand National – although after the first success on Sheila's Cottage in 1948 he found he wasn't quite the same man when he landed his second success on Teal in 1952 – as Sheila's, described by her trainer as 'an ornery old cow' lived up to her name and celebrated by biting the tip off of one of Arthur's fingers.

Ironically enough, when her stud career failed she was given to Arthur, clearly not a man to bear a grudge, who, when she died, buried her at the bottom of his garden in Wexford.

300. WHAT'S IT ALL ABOUT, CASH?

When Alfred Gibert's reins broke whilst he was riding Timely Column in Clairefontaine's Prix du Mont-Canisy in August 1989, the horse bolted, leaving the jockey in great peril and helpless to retrieve the situation.

Spotting what had happened, fellow jockey Cash Asmussen instantly forfeited his chance of winning the race on Glenelive to chase after Gibert, catching them and bringing the runaway horse under control, saving the jockey from probable serious injury.

Asmussen was honoured by a French TV station for 'the year's most sporting gesture.'

301. EXCESS BAGGAGE

Racegoers were baffled to see jockey Stephen Davis waving a yellow plastic bag during a hunter chase at Hereford in April 1995 in which he was partnering 10-year-old Arcticflow.

The horse finished 5th and the stewards hauled Davis in for a quiet word, fining him £75 despite being told that the object of the exercise was to persuade the horse to put his best foot forward. Instead, it seemed he succeeded only in making him a bag of nerves.

302. TURNING THE PAGE

Jockey Fred Page contested a chase at Birmingham's Henley-in-Arden course in April 1858 aboard talented but strong willed horse, Goldsmith. As the *Daily Post* later reported, 'He was mounted on Goldsmith, a fine horse, but a hard puller who completely overpowered Fred Page, and had treated that worthy with an extraordinary leap over a hay-stack, a bolt through a cabbage garden, and a visit to the kitchen of an antiquated dame in the town.'

303. NOTHING NEW

Controversy still rages over whether race meetings also featuring performances by bands like Status Quo, Jools Holland and the like really do much to promote the sport to new recruits.

But such things were going on over 40 years ago at Birmingham where, in 1964, they featured concerts by then chart-topping groups like the Swinging Blue Jeans – whose act was enlivened when course tipster, the Shilling Shocker, jumped up to join them for one number – and the Migil 5 at their Saturday evening fixtures.

They also offered free admission for ladies and created play areas for children.

The course closed down in June 1965.

304. THAT'S ALRIGHT, THEN, PAY US LATER

After stealing £10.3 million from his employers and others to fund his secret high-rolling racing and betting lifestyle, 58-year-old Graham Price, manager of the franchised Halifax Bank in Gowerton, South Wales, left an IOU in the safe – but only for £7 million!

The Swansea man, known locally as 'Mr Halifax', had embezzled millions from investors who had entrusted large amounts, including the life savings of some.

He was arrested in November 2004 when the IOU was discovered and admitted 43 separate counts of theft and deception – and asked for 263 similar offences to be taken into account.

'A lot of money went on horseracing, and it appears he was not very successful. He rarely went to a horse race, money was mostly put on through betting shops, over the phone or on the internet,' said Detective Constable Steve Daniels in November 2005.

Price reportedly handed over £1.7m to tipsters – who, confirmed police, would not be investigated. 'He'd told us he was at one stage getting 50 calls a day from tipsters,' said Det Sgt Hugh Rees. Price bought his own horse, Carte Diamond, for £69,000, spending £32,000 on training fees, and also ploughed £250,000 into syndicate horses.

Price was jailed for 12 years.

305. TIME OUT

It may have been the slowest first furlong of a race ever. Gordon Richards – with 163 winers for the season already under his belt, and later to be knighted, – on Ridge Wood, and Tommy Lowrey on Courier were the only two runners in Birmingham's 1m 5f, August 22,1949 Midland St Leger Trial Stakes.

Unbeknown to either jockey, both trainers – Noel Murless and Dick Perryman – had issued their jockeys with identical instructions – 'on no account make the running'.

Thus, as the shout 'they're off' went up, they were anything but. Courier actually turned round rather than take the lead, while Ridge Wood was virtually motionless.

Even a crack of the whip from the assistant starter couldn't spark them into action.

Eventually the two began to inch forward, covering the opening furlong in a reported 1 minute 24 seconds – the normal sort of time for an entire seven furlong race.

They kept up the go-slow for most of the distance before finally responding to the jeers of the crowd and beginning to race for the last quarter of a mile, with Richards and Ridge Wood prevailing in 5 minutes 14 seconds by three lengths.

The world record time for the distance was just under 2 minutes 40 seconds.

Inevitably, a stewards inquiry was called but the jockeys' explanations that they were following riding instructions was accepted.

306. ARCHER'S OLD DUTCH

The great champion jockey, Fred Archer didn't bet – no, he got someone to do that for him. Arthur Cooper was Archer's close friend and commissioner and the pair cleaned up when the maestro partnered 40/1 shot Dutch Oven to victory in the 1882 St Leger.

Rarely was a big race contender that sort of price when Archer was on board, but she had been beaten in her York prep race and not only had her odds drifted from 8/1, but Archer tried to get off of her and on to Geheimniss, the Oaks winner.

Much of the Dutch Oven money was already down and owner Lord Falmouth insisted Archer stay on board.

However, another of Archer's pals and hefty punter John Hammond never lost faith and went in to back her again. Archer rode like the champion he was to force Dutch Oven ahead of Geheimniss on the line.

Hammond collected £40,000 winnings and handed £10,000 to Archer as a 'present' while Cooper also cleaned up, to the tune of £20,000, of which Archer took £5,000.

In return, Hammond was handed Archer's whip, while Cooper received his saddle.

307. A LOAD OF BULL

When outsiders Watford made it into the Premiership at the end of the 2005/6 football season, they celebrated by touring the town in an open top bus.

When 40/1 outsider Caractacus won the Derby in 1862, landing trainer Bob Smith, based in Harpenden, just outside of Watford, winnings of £10,000 from his bets, a bullock was roasted whole in Watford market-place to celebrate the local triumph. Owner Mr Snewing, a publican, also 'entertained the poor of Watford to a gigantic fete'.

I don't think Hornet's fan, Elton John did likewise after the football team's promotion.

308. DREAMING OF A WHITE DERBY

The only time snow has fallen at Epsom on Derby day was in 1867 when the race was run on May 22.

Although some reports claim that the race was run in a blizzard, eyewitness accounts suggest otherwise, with racing writer Alexander Scott, who was present, declaring 'snow fell both before and after the race, but not during the time the horses were racing.'

309. CAP THAT

Jockey Paddy Merrigan was cautioned by the stewards for improper riding after a race at Cartmel on August 26, 2006, when he dropped his whip during the juvenile hurdle race, so whipped off his silk cap and used that instead as he finished 4th on Drawn Out.

310. GOING FEARS UNGROUNDED

Trainer George Margarson was eager to leave nothing to chance when his Woolfall Blue contested a maiden at Deauville in August 2006, so he walked the course to check out the state of the ground after some heavy rain.

Returning to the weighing room he called over jockey Olivier Peslier to advise him that the best ground was towards the stand side.

A baffled Peslier heard him out before pointing out that the race was actually being run on the course's new all-weather track.

311. THAT TAKS A LOT OF BEATING

Perhaps the most mysterious punter in Australian racing history was an Estonian – some say Yugoslavian – immigrant woman, Johanna Pauline Taks, who formed an attachment to a horse called Bernborough, backing him for increasing cash stakes as he ran up an unbeaten sequence of 15 races.

'She mainly wore a black dress and she used to wear a purple hat most of the time' recalled racing journalist Bill Whitaker of the lady who became universally known as the 'Woman In Black', although almost nothing else was known about her.

In spring 1946 Taks prepared to place her biggest wager yet on the horse who had won all over the country – in Queensland, in New South Wales and in Victoria. Always with Mulley on board, always showing the thrilling late winning surge to the line.

Now, on October 19, 1946, 107,167 racegoers had packed into Melbourne's Caulfield track for the 27 runner Caulfield Cup, on which Taks was staking a reported $A6,000 that the horse, the 2/1 favourite, could carry 10st 10lb to victory.

It was not going to be easy for the horse and his jockey Athol 'George' Murray – as some unscrupulous bookies were offering big money to anyone who could stop Bernborough.

As the race developed it was clear that, as race caller Jack Styring put it, 'there was a number of jockeys out there for one thing only and that was to beat Bernborough, and that was an absolute fact.'

The horse was trailing as they came into the straight: 'I was waiting for a run between two horses at the top of the straight and they came together and stopped him in his tracks' claimed Mulley, as the horse could do no better than 5th.

Some accused Mulley of pulling the horse and he was sacked by the horse's owner and trainer.

As for the Woman In Black, she told reporters: ' I'm going straight back to Sydney and I will retire as a punter. I backed Bernie because he looked so lovely, but he lost, and now I have the big headache', left the track, and was never heard of again.

Bernborough was brought out for another race, the Mackinnon Stakes at Flemington, partnered by new rider Billy Briscoe. He started favourite, but broke his leg during the race.

Rather than being destroyed, the horse was put in plaster and later sold to the stud of Hollywood mogul Louis B Mayer for some $A300,000.

Ms Taks' adventures had sparked memories of another legendary Aussie gambler, Canterbury-based Chinese market gardener Jimmy Ah Poon who, in 1905, had begun backing a horse called Poseidon in its first two wins as a three year old, staking just £10 on the first occasion.

The horse was trained by Ike Earnshaw, for whom Poon supplied carrots for his horses, getting to know Poseidon through visits to the stable.

Jimmy played up his winnings, backing the horse every time it won, but somehow avoiding his three runner-up outings.

Because of his limited English, when he approached bookies to back the horse he would ask 'Wha' price Possumum?' and his fame began to spread around the tracks.

When Poseidon won the AJC Derby at 7/1, Jimmy had made $A5,000 on the horse.

He now gave up the market garden and began to follow Poseidon round – he won the Eclipse Stakes at Caulfield at 7/4 with Jimmy betting $A1,000. Two days later he won the Caulfield Cup at 3/1, with Jimmy again on for a four figure stake.

Now a short-priced VRC Derby favourite, Poon went for a double in that race and the Melbourne Cup, taking a skinny 9/2 to some $A5,000. Poseidon skated up at 1/4 in the VRC – and promptly stormed to victory in the 1906 Melbourne Cup, at 4/1, leaving Poon a reported $A35,000 to the good – all from the one horse who had won 11 of his 14 starts.

Earnshaw had been concerned that Poon was gambling too much on his horse and had tried to dissuade him from risking so much – and he also turned down Poon's offer of free carrots for Poseidon for life after the Melbourne Cup win.

Now a wealthy man Jimmy quit the racing scene and headed back to his native China, where he reportedly lived a life of luxury on his winnings.

For years to come Earnshaw would receive through the post each Christmas from Hong Kong a parcel of Chinese delicacies.

312. HELL-O

Racegoers heading for the sports at Nottingham in the mid 19th century had to make their way to the track down Goldsmith Street, where they would pass a large sign on the wall of one of the houses, helpfully indicating, via a pointing finger; 'To the Races. The Way to Hell.'

313. GREED TAKES A KICKING

When trainer Tom Taaffe announced that his well-fancied contender for the 2005 Cheltenham Gold Cup had been working badly and he would almost certainly miss the race, his odds hurtled out from 7/1 to the 999/1 offered by nine layers on the Betfair betting exchange.

Several punters – particularly well informed or optimistic – decide to oblige each of these wannabe bookies to an average stake of £6 for each of them, presumably 'just in case' a miracle happened.

It did. The horse apparently amazed connections by improving rapidly to the point where he was reintroduced into serious contention for the race – leaving the nine greedy chancers who had believed they were taking a no-risk few bob by offering mugs the 999/1 odds, suddenly looking at the serious risk of shelling out a total of £53,946 to those clairvoyant punters.

Kicking King had become 7/2 favourite, leaving the 999/1 layers with no realistic way even of hedging themselves out of trouble.

With two fences remaining only Kicking King and 25/1 shot, Take The Stand, were possible winners, with the former proving too strong for the latter as he strode to the line ahead.

314. THAT NAME RINGS A BELL

In perhaps the only case on record of a footballer acquiring a racehorse-related nickname, Manchester City and 48-times capped England midfielder of the late 1960s and 1970s, Colin Bell, became universally known as 'Nijinsky' – whether in honour of the ballet dancer, or the 1970 triple crown-winning racehorse is unclear at this distance of time, although www.englandfc.com suggests the latter!

315. YOU'RE PULLING MY LEG

Jockey Tommy Hill was incredulous when battling down the stretch on Summer Fair in the

1961 AJC Derby at Sydney's Randwick, in a desperately close tussle against Blue Era-partnered Mel Schumacher, he felt Schumacher's hand grab his leg to impede his progress as they flashed past the post.

Blue Era got the narrow verdict but sensational film footage was to cost him the race after Hill protested to the stewards.

Brand new patrol camera technology had been in use for the final part of the race, even though the cameraman had failed to get it working until the very last stages of the contest. It was enough to show Schumacher's illegal action, though.

Schumacher, who had denied any such offence, couldn't believe it: 'I couldn't believe it. I couldn't believe they had one. It was just one of those things. You see bike riders do it, you see runners do it and it just, this time it just happened to be on film and we got caught. What can't speak can't lie.'

The stewards banned Schumacher for life, although the sentence was later commuted and he came back five and a half years later.

Racing journalist Max Presnell paid a strange tribute to Schumacher – 'Infamous though it was, foul ride though it was, that's the greatest ride I've ever seen.'

316. BOOKIES LOST FOR WORDS?

As a bell clanged to attract people's attention and a notice board displaying the word 'SILENCE' was hoisted, bookmakers at Auckland Park in South Africa's Rand district were officially struck dumb.

A meeting of local race-clubs had decreed that owners had complained that the continuous babble of voices at, around and by the on course bookmakers was making it 'impossible to have their commissions executed at a fair price' and that therefore they were introducing a rule forbidding the layers from calling the odds.

So, the ringing of the bell before the first race on January 31, 1925, plunged the course into a surreal, silent-movie-style environment in which bookies were only permitted to indicate or, presumably, whisper the prices they were offering.

317. BARELY BELIEVABLE

It was a racecourse commentator's dream: 'In the next race, Charlotte Kerton will be riding Knickerless.'

And on August 25, 2006, at Newmarket, the female apprentice very nearly was.

In actual fact, Charlotte was partnering a Nick Littmoden runner called, for reasons best known to owner Bill Hinge, Knickerless.

They may have been unfancied in the betting market, at 66/1, but Charlotte's booking certainly registered with those who knew her – "You wouldn't believe some of the texts I got before the race. One asked 'Are you going to be wearing any?" and another "Are you going to ride it like that, then?"'

The combination finished 9th of 15 and Charlotte, who rode using her pink saddle, felt she hadn't got to the, er, bottom of the horse – 'I'd like to ride her again,' she declared loyally.

318. THAT CORN-Y OLD CLAIM AGAIN!

Lt Col D M Baird, whose best achievement as an owner was to see his The Crofter finish 5th in the 1957 Grand National, had another, odder claim to fame.

Boasted the officer, born in 1898, 'Possibly I am the last person to have ridden the winner of a point-to-point without jumping a single fence – the East Cornwall, 1925.

'The jockey fell at the last fence, and I got up, mounted and weighed in over-weight. The rule was subsequently altered to the effect that the jockey who weighs out must also be the same at weighing in'. His record, then – unless you happen to know better.

319. SPECS APPEAL.

US owner and gambler, Colonel Edward Bradley thought he'd come up with a great idea when he fitted his short sighted racehorse with 'Equispecs', glasses for horses, at the turn of the 19th/20th century, only for the horse to throw its jockey and bolt – but at least it could see where it was bolting to!

320. GETTING THE BREAKS

Tommy Beasley was perhaps the greatest of the four Beasley boys – Harry, Willy and Johnny were the others – who all rode in the 1879 Grand National. Tommy won the great race on three occasions, was twice second and once third.

The eldest of the Irish family of amateur riders also boasted victory in the Irish Grand National, the Grand Steeplechase de Paris – oh, and he also won the Irish Derby on three occasions.

Yet his worst fall, in which he broke a leg, came when he was riding on the Curragh – to the Post Office!

321. LOCH NOT SO FINE

On the 50th anniversary of the sensational collapse on the Grand National run-in when well clear, Dick Francis, who was riding the Queen Mother's Devon Loch with the race at his mercy, insisted to me that it was the roar of the crowd which suddenly upset the horse, causing his dramatic reaction.

But over the years a top ten of possible reasons has been put forward: **Number 10** – that the horse had let rip with a giant fart. **Number 9** – 'a sudden, temporary, muscular seizure' suggested by writer Ivor Herbert. **Number 8** – the horse saw his reflection in the adjacent water jump and attempted to jump a non-existent, phantom fence. **Number 7** – fellow jockey Brian Marshall, who had also ridden Devon Loch, believed he broke a blood vessel. **Number 6** – a bizarre conspiracy theory had it that the horse was deliberately brought down by high-pitched whistles. **Number 5** – the horse suffered a minor coronary. **Number 4** – vet Dr Alastair Foster blamed an infestation of tiny worms which brought on iliac thrombosis. **Number 3** – it was cramp, declared an on-course Aintree vet. **Number 2** – 'the horse was electrocuted through an underground cable that shorted on the horse's racing plates.'

Number 1, though, is Dick's own theory which he explained to me, then aged 86, on March 28, 2006, 50 years to the day when it happened: 'No one could have done anything about it – other than fill the horse's ears with cotton wool. I had ridden for the Queen Mother before and got used to such receptions. But Devon Loch was a nervous horse and could not have known what the fantastic crescendo of cheering as the crowd welcomed a Royal winner would be like.

'When I watched the footage of the race I was convinced of what had happened. On the run-in, he pricked his ears and looked around at the water jump which he had jumped first time round, and as he did, so the noise hit him.'

And the Queen Mum's reaction? 'She said, 'well, that's racing.'

Francis later revealed, 'I've never really got over it. That evening I ended up walking beside the River Dee with (my wife) Mary and was tempted to throw myself in.'

322. THE ORIGINAL 'DEVON LOCH'

Probably because he was owned by the Queen Mother, there has always been a fascination with the Devon Loch incident and a general belief that it was unique.

But it was not. Something almost identical had occurred in the race before.

In 1903, the Grand National featured two almost identically named runners – Drumcree and Drumree. Both were up against a royal runner, Ambush II, owned by the King, Edward VII, in a field of 23 runners.

The King's horse looked all over the winner as he approached the final fence, only to fall. The King, like the Queen Mother 53 years later, was philosophical and asked immediately after the health of his jockey – 'I hope (Algy) Anthony is not hurt.'

But on the run between the second last and the final fence, Drumree, owned by the Duke of Westminster, looked to be going better than both Ambush II and Drumcree, and was set to take up the running when, as a contemporary report had it, 'Drumree stopped, ignored his jockey's urge, and fell with the staggers'.

An alarmed bookie who was obviously hoping 25/1 shot Drumree would save him a hefty payout over the similarly named 13/2 favourite, was heard to cry out 'He's gone! And they've all backed the other one.'

The equine ambulance rushed to the spot, but Drumree 'was got up and gently walked about'. Drumcree was eventually the winner of this eventful contest.

323. VIGILANT STEWARDS

The first horse officially warned off of racing for being 'a dangerous savage' was Vigilance, barred by the Stewards of the Jockey Club from being entered for any future races in 1912.

However, there is also a claim for that honour to be awarded to Lord Glanely's Quantock who, it was said in D W E Brock's *Racing Man's Weekend Book*, 'became so bad-tempered as to be dangerous to other horses, and in 1911 he was banned from race-tracks.'

324. NO WORD OF A LYE

Having won two races at Musselburgh's important Caledonian meeting in 1838, jockey Tommy Lye had to put his foot down to make it to Northallerton in Yorkshire where he partnered another winner the very next afternoon, having covered the 170 mile trip by stage coach and horse-back.

325. WATCH OUT

In 1866 Lord George Bentinck, then the turf's leading official, announced that 'The Clerk of the Course at York will regulate his watch by the clock of York Cathedral, and will be fined 5s (25p) for every minute he is behind time in the bell not ringing for the respective races.'

326. ELLINGTON'S WEIGHTING RACE

A seven pound allowance would come in handy for any horse contesting the Derby – and there are reasons to believe that the 1856 winner, Ellington, had just that.

How did his jockey, Thomas Aldcroft – a dandy of the day who allegedly introduced a fashion for peg-top trousers to the jockeys' room – manage such a feat? It was widely believed at the time that between the finish of the race and when he weighed in he managed to discard the almost weightless whip with which he had ridden and replace it with one weighing 7lbs, without which he would have been unable to make the weight.

Contemporary racing writer Col R F Meysey-Thompson declared: 'it was only by the help of that whip that he could draw his weight correctly' and also revealed another cunning subterfuge in common use at the time, 'a piece of metal shaped to go into a fob pocket and easily concealed in the palm of the hand, which was taken from jockeys after they had weighed out and handed back when they were dismounting preparatory to weighing in after the race.'

Adding weight to the theory that the unfancied 20/1 shot had a little weighty assistance en route to the victory, is the fact that he never managed to win another race.

Trainer Tom Dawson won £25,000 on the race and having collected his winnings in cash, stuffed the notes into a hat box which he then left on the train he caught home to Middleham.

Incredibly enough, the hat box was missing for a week, and one time apparently travelling as far as Aberdeen before it was reunited with Dawson, still carrying the cash.

*In August 2007, jockey Stephen Donohoe was fined £275 and banned for three days after being caught wearing boots with paper-thin soles as he weighed out, then changing them for the race and weighing in 3lbs overweight.

327. SNAP JUDGEMENT

Technology can make fools of us all as this section from noted racing figure and author John Fairfax-Blakeborough's 1927 work, *The Analysis of the Turf* demonstrated when it broached the subject of whether a photo-finish device would ever prove practical in racing. 'It is a debatable question if the camera would be any aid to accuracy in race judging. Apart from the delay which would follow in making the announcements – a delay which would be intolerable to a pent-up crowd – there would be the question of deciding the psychological moment to take the pictures.

The photographer who waited a fraction of a second too long, or pressed the button a fraction of a second too soon, would have quite a different result from that of the camera man who chose the identical second the first horse's nose reached the winning post. Probably no two photographs of the same finish would agree, and there would thus be more dissatisfaction and confusion than ever, even with operators long experienced and carefully trained to make the exposures.'

Being a confirmed Luddite, include me in with those who still don't see the point of a photo-finish camera. If the human eye can't split the runners what is the point of giving anything other than a dead-heat?

328. BARRED

In the mid 19th century many of the best American jockeys were black. Blacks were not, however, welcome at the races, as a report from the *New York Daily Tribune* of August 11, 1865, illustrates.

Describing the racing at Saratoga in that month, the paper reported: 'I should mention as a symptom of this era when the capacity of the human races are to be demurred, that half of the jockeys are the blackest Africans, and I have yet to learn that their color interferes with their fitness for this business. One of them, who passes by the soubriquet of Old Abe, is highly spoken of as a judicious jockey. The same democracy of feeling does not extend to the spectators' galleries, for an addendum to the Programme says: "Colored persons not admitted to the stand."'

329. SACRE BLEU

Towards the end of the 19th century the French racing authorities, concerned that English jockeys were dominating their scene, introduced a series of races to be ridden by jockeys of French parentage only, in an effort to provide more opportunities and experience for their indigenous riders.

However, 'the attempt has not been so successful as it might have been' revealed chronicler of French racing, Robert Black in 1899, adding that 'the secret of the comparative failure is stated by a "compatriot" to be that the French nature abhors an abdominal vacuum.'

330. PERFECT DAY

Despite some complaints about rowdy racegoers who have had a few too many and the odd punch-up spilling over into public areas, racing today is a fairly civilised affair with some of the more unsavoury elements of yesteryear banished to memory.

The memory of Harding Cox, an amateur rider on the flat and over the sticks, was sufficient in 1922 to offer a portrait of one of those less than appealing days.

He recalled 'a little meeting at Buntingford' at which the promoters 'had neglected to call in the aid of the police' as their course was patronised by the 'toffs' of the county, who flocked there 'bringing with them their womenkind, bedizened with a blaze of jewellery.

'The family plate was conspicuous, and when the luncheon interval arrived, at a given signal an attack was pressed home by the roughs. After having filled the silver bowls with the choicest vintages of their unwilling hosts, their health was drunk with acclamation to the very dregs, and then the trophies, plus forks, spoons and other utensils of sterling metal, were transferred to convenient sacks and dispatched to some melting furnace. Moreover, the ladies were urgently pressed to bestow souvenirs in the shape of diamonds and other precious stones and none dared to refuse.

After that, the gang devoted themselves to the real business of the day – viz racing.

The few bookies present were freely patronised, but the punters took no risks. They chose their own favourite and made sure of its "clicking" by the simple expedient of sending patrols to all the fences, to stop any horse and rider – except their own choice – who seemed to have the remotest chance of landing the stakes.

They did pretty well at this but decided the pencillers ought not to be allowed to depart without any superfluous dross remaining over – after the aforesaid operations – and acted accordingly.

To illuminate the end of a perfect day the exuberant lads set fire to all the fences and stands, and departed, drunken, but happy in a blaze of glory.'

331. CAL-AMITY

Carroll – known as Cal – Shilling, born in 1886, quickly showed himself to be one of the top jockeys in the States, clocking up 969 victories in 3,838 starts, an incredible winning percentage of 25%. In 1911 his rate was 36%.

But he was a hot-headed youngster and at the age of just 26, by which time he was widely regarded as America's best ever jockey, he had been implicated in a string of incidents and after getting involved in a fist fight with a rival rider during a race at Havre de Grace in Maryland, he was firstly suspended indefinitely and later permanently after being involved in a major scene at Pimlico in 1920 after efforts from various prominent racing figures to get him reinstated resulted in failure.

Shilling hit the bottle. In 1948 he was picked up on a vagrancy charge in Maryland, then in January 1950 his body was found lying under a van parked outside Belmont Park.

He had been laying there unnoticed for several days.

332. RINGING THE CHANGES

Doncaster steward, Lord Kelburne, had heard that the gathering of bookmakers in the main grandstand of the course to transact their business as was the tradition of the day had 'caused annoyance to the ladies' prior to an 1839 meeting.'

So he arranged for the bookies and their customers to be moved into a railed-off lawn area, or 'ring' as it soon became known. Other courses rapidly followed suit and the system has survived more or less in the same style until today.

333. GOING FOR THE JUGULAR

Noted equine 'character', Greenhills Gillie, was leading on the turn at Saratoga during a 1936 meeting when one of his rivals, Thorson, moved up to pass on his inside. Greenhills Gillie turned, lunged at his rival and tried to take a chunk out of his throat.

Greenhills Gillie was disqualified.

334. CALL THAT PROGRESS!

Not everyone is impressed with so called advances in the way in which racing is run.

American writer, Ed Hotaling, who chronicled the history of the sport at Saratoga in his 1995 book, *They're Off*, offered an alternative view when considering the state of play there in 1940 – 'It was the culmination of a decade that transformed the experience of America's first national sport. There was the huge, ugly (starting) gate, which for the first time blocked the public's view of the start; the photo finish, which basically told them to shut up; the scratchy, far-away sound of the radio broadcast, which added that they could stay home if they wanted to; and now there was the tote board and the betting machines at the windows, all but silencing any intercourse people might wish to have with those they were betting with.'

335. BEST OF A DOZEN?

The event at Independence racecourse in Iowa in 1891 was advertised as being 'best three of five' one mile heats for three-year-olds and under.

It didn't turn out that way, though.

Birchwood won the first two heats and it looked like the event would all be over quickly. However, Jessie L then won the next two heats. If either of these two managed to win the fifth heat everyone could go home.

It wasn't to be, as Maud M suddenly hit form and won the next two heats.

At that point they decided they'd had enough for one day and would come back the next to sort things out.

Next day they lined up for the seventh heat – which was won by Rahleta.

Ialene managed to win the eighth. Fred K the ninth, Dandy O the tenth.

Dandy O completed a double in the eleventh and finally closed the event out by also winning the twelfth and final heat.

336. HIGHLY STRUNG

It is recorded that in the 1860s a jockey on the Welsh jumping circuit known as 'Old Davies' would carry in his breeches pocket a ball of twine, which he would fasten to his horse's bit, so that in the event of a fall the line would pay out until Davies could right himself and pull his loose mount back in order to re-mount.

337. TAIL END

To commemorate Red Gauntlet, the chestnut gelding winner of the first race ever run at South Australia's Morphettville course on September 23, 1875, the tail hair from Sir Thomas Elder's runner was plaited in the shape of Scotch thistles and inserted into a small silver cup to be used as a trophy for future events at the track.

Not only did Red Gauntlet win the first race – he did so having bolted twice before the race. Afterwards his rider, J McCann could not pull him up until he had completed another circuit, but he then came out later in the afternoon to win again.

338. HOWARD'S WAY

Former Conservative leader Michael Howard, a man noted for his tough stance on crime found himself a victim at the races, revealed his wife Sandra.

Referring to her husband's 'passion' for racing she commented in *Stella* magazine in September 2006, 'racing is enjoyably social, as well as being a chance to dress up'.

And Michael apparently enjoys following racing's dress code, too.

'Michael has a replacement Panama, the smart type that squashes flat for holiday travel. His original, which I bought at exorbitant cost, didn't return one year from Glorious Goodwood, where it had been hung alongside a row of others. He had come back wearing a Panama, but a stiff, unbendable affair with a chain-store label. It's been a source of endless gramophone record recriminations on my part, fuelled by resentment that someone else, who had probably won on every race as well, went home with such a headgear trophy.'

339. DON'T TAKE A FENCE

Esposito's Tavern, which borders the stable area at US track, Belmont Park, traditionally has its picket fence painted in the colours of the winning owner after each running of the Triple Crown race, the Belmont Stakes – whose winner also receives a blanket of carnations – traditional flower of the race – which takes ten man hours to put together as between three and four hundred flowers are glued on to a green velveteen spread.

The race also boasts its own musical theme – 'Sidewalks of New York', written in 1894 by vaudevillian Charles Lawlor and hat salesman James W Blake.

340. GRAND STAND

A tower in Lancashire's Leasowe Castle, from which Ferdinando, fifth Earl of Derby, '2nd Heir to the English throne', watched horse racing taking place on the nearby Meols Sands in 1593, is believed to be the oldest existing racing 'grandstand'. It can be visited today by racing enthusiasts who book into what is now the Leasowe Castle Hotel.

341. HOW COOLE IS THAT?

Only one racegoer fancied the chances of Coole in a 34-runner race at Haydock in November 1929 sufficiently to back the beast on the tote. The horse won and a lady from Liverpool was duly paid out at record win odds of 3410/1.

342. THE WILD NORTH WEST

The wild west came to Manchester's New Barns course in 1888 when legendary Colonel 'Buffalo Bill' Cody staged his rodeo-style travelling show there.

Racegoers were also able to watch a unique race between English jockey Johnny Latham and a Mexican rider called Escovita in which the former partnered 20 thoroughbreds and the latter American broncos. Each horse was ridden for four furlongs before the jockey switched to the next in line.

At the end of the race the Mexican had prevailed by some 300 hundred yards – not so much because of the speed of his mounts, which were often outpaced by the thoroughbreds, but because his rodeo dismounts saw Escovita switching between horses much more quickly than his rival.

343. QUESTIONS ASKED IN THE HOUSE

The controversial name of a racehorse was brought up in the Canberra House of Representatives in October 2006 when Adelaide member, Kate Ellis described the name of the thoroughbred, General Yamashita as a 'deep affront' to war veterans.

The Japanese military man in question was hung in 1946 for war crimes.

Although the horse, trained at Camperdown, ran and finished runner-up at Victoria under that name on October 17, it was reported that owner David Allan would be changing it, although he reportedly described the name as 'fairly innocent', explaining that the colt had been known as Tiger at the stables, while the General had been known as the Tiger of Malaya. Other members of the same thoroughbred family had been given militarily related names.

'Innocent' was not perhaps the description relatives of the 100,000 Filipino citizens slaughtered in the crimes in which Yamashita was implicated, might have chosen.

344. COLD WAR ON BOOKIES

Three Russian computer 'hackers' were sentenced to eight years in prison each in October, 2006, after being found guilty of extorting over $4million from British and Irish online bookmakers.

Their method of operation was to launch 'distributed denial of service' (DDOS) attacks on the company websites, demanding a 'ransom' before ceasing to block the targeted sites which were unable to operate normally whilst under attack.

Ivan Maksakov, 20, from Balakovo, Alexander Petrov from Astrakhan and Denis

Stepanov from St Petersburg were tried in the Saratov region some 500 miles south-east of Moscow after being detained in an operation involving Britain's National High Tech Crime Unit, Interpol, the FBI and Russia's Interior Ministry.

All major British bookmakers, including William Hill, Coral and Totesport, denied paying over any ransom money.

345. ATTY EVER AFTER?

Apprentices may feel they have a tough life – but they should think themselves lucky they weren't around 60-odd years ago, if the views of top trainer from those days, Classic-winning Stockbridge-based H T Persse, universally known as 'Atty', are anything to go by.

In 1940, Atty, whose stable star was the unbeaten grey spotted speedster, The Tetrarch, outlined his views of apprentices.

'For the first two years they are almost useless, but afterwards they may become very useful indeed. They get well fed, well clothed and have a fine outdoor life. And it is extraordinary how they put on weight, the one thing they should not do.

In selecting an apprentice I like to see his parents, for then I can estimate from their size what the boy's future proportions are likely to be.

Boys are the very devil, the bugbear of a trainer, needing to be watched all the time. Smoking in a stable cannot, of course, be tolerated. What owner or trainer wants to see his precious possessions roasted alive?

None of my apprentices is allowed off unless he is given special permission. They have their own club on the premises, where they can buy very cheaply anything they need. By paying a nominal subscription each boy is entitled to read a variety of papers.

Though at first their pay is very small, it is not unknown for one suddenly to become possessed of a brand new bicycle. Since no one would dream of thinking that someone, seeking stable information, had bribed him, the trainer is forced to conclude that the boy has suddenly discovered some rich relations.

The treatment of boys in stables is no harder than that of the average public school boy, usually not so hard; and so he need not complain of the rigours of his lot.'

346. WEB DOUBLES

Many racing figures have their own websites, but logging on to look at them can be fraught with problems if you don't know their web address you could end up viewing someone other than who you were seeking.

Jumps trainer Kim Bailey, for example. Did you know that he is 5'8" tall, with a 26" waist and 34B bust? Oh sorry, no, now I look a little more closely, this is the website of a shapely Geordie lass called Kim Bailey who, she tells me 'is interested in working up to implied nude.' Now, do you really think that the jumps trainer of that name would resort to those lengths? Probably not – which is perhaps why he has of late been unable to replicate the form which saw his stable send out the winners of the Gold Cup and Champion Hurdle only years ago.

If you can drag yourself away from Ms Bailey, and find the 'wrong' Barry Hills you could find yourself reading about an American landscape painter of the same name.

And Jamie Osborne could be confused with James Osborne, who has racing connections of his own. The late – died 1992 – James, who recently had a Brighton omnibus named in his honour sculpted bronzes of the legendary Eclipse and the Queen's horse Burmese.

Paul Nicholls, you may be unaware, also appears to have an interesting sideline – he 'is one of Britain's best young actors and one of the best looking'. What's more he has appeared in Eastenders. So when does he get the chance to look after his horses, I wonder?

And you may have thought that David Pipe would have his hands full taking over the reins from Dad, Martin, but it seems he is doing a bit of moonlighting – playing for Bristol Rovers Football Club!

Now, Michael Stoute is not the sort of person I would have had down as offering advice about 'how to make her chase you'. But on his wesbite, on which he describes himself as being '27 years old, male, crazy, New Jersey', it soon becomes apparent he is talking about a different type of filly from the ones he normally associated with.

Can you imagine Tony McCoy as a James Earl Jones 'sexy, cool' soundaliko? That's what he must be getting up to during his injury stints if the Antonio McCoy website, tonymacvoice.com is to be believed.

Have a rummage around the www.google.com site and I'm sure you'll come across some interesting examples of web doubles for yourself.

347. DOUBLE BED

American jockey Kent Desormeaux was involved in a spill at Hollywood Park in 1990 when he was kicked in the head by a following horse. He fractured his skull in several places and was suffering from internal bleeding.

Taken to hospital to recuperate he found himself in the same ward as his wife, Sonia, while she gave birth to their son, Joshua.

348. MINTED

Sydney racehorse owner Ernie Williams was at the 1950 Easter sales when he spotted trainer Ted Hush sucking on a Mintie sweet. Williams asked Hush for one of his sweets, but was told 'Why should I give you one, you only buy horses for (rival trainer) T J Smith?'

Amused, Williams shot back – 'Okay, you buy a horse for me.'

Hush found a horse for Williams for the then hefty price of 3,200 guineas.

Once over the shock of the cost Williams wanted to name the horse Minties in honour of the sweet without which he would never have been purchased, but thought better of it and named him Hydrogen, under which name, between 1950 and 1955 he won all but £60,000 in stake money – passing the immortal Phar Lap's record total along the way and winning 26 times.

349. 'AM I OUT OF MY MIND?'

Top Australian racecourse commentator Joe Brown, who called 31 Melbourne Cups, questioned his own sanity whilst calling the 1971 Chairman's Handicap at Caulfield, prior to which he had been informed that Magic Gold had been scratched, which he duly announced to the crowd.

As the race unfolded, Brown was running through the horses' positions when he thought he spotted Magic Gold's colours, but told himself he had to be mistaken.

On the second circuit he looked closely and realised that they were, indeed Magic Gold's silks. 'Ladies and gentlemen' said Brown during his commentary, 'I don't know whether I'm going out of my mind, but the scratched horse Magic Gold is running fourth.'

There were shouts and hoots of laughter from the crowd as Brown called the final stages of the race with Magic Gold amongst the front-runners as they swept past the post.

After the race, Brown was relieved to discover that he was neither hallucinating nor losing his mind, but Magic Gold had been scratched when his trainer W Hewitt, realised that he had sent him down to the start without some of the weight he was set to carry. However, as there was no way of communicating with the starter by then, it was decided to let the horse run, regardless – one of the very few official non runners ever to run!

350. STRINGING US ALONG?

A *Racing Post* reader believes he may have hit on a previously unconsidered way in which infections can be spread amongst runners from different stables.

'When horses are loaded into starting stalls, handlers use a rope – or similar – to thread through the bridle to lead them to the stall,' wrote John Bushby from Cumbria in October 2006. 'This rope is then used on another horse and so on. As these ropes are in such close proximity to the mouths of horses any infections may be passed on.'

He suggested that the ropes should be regularly disinfected or changed.

351. VIRTUALLY UNBELIEVABLE

A punter who didn't back a 50/1 shot in a 'virtual' race shown in a Coral branch, because the winner was never quoted in any betting shows was nonetheless paid out as though he had staked £1 on the selection.

Swansea punter, Terry Rogers, 48, was compensated when Coral realised their error and accepted that had he known the outsider was in the August 2007 Steepledown contest he would have backed it as he always followed outsiders.

They blamed a 'technical error' for their failure to display odds for the 'runner'.

352. DEAD LOSS

South Australia's gambling watchdog was called into action after a punter, Tom Hunt, staked five Aussie dollars on a horse called Chicakaloo in late September 2006, at odds of 200/1 for the Epsom Handicap, to be run on October 7.

The odds were long, but not that generous – considering that the horse had been put down on September 9, over a fortnight earlier, after breaking a leg.

Hunt had made the bet, well aware that the horse was dead, but interested to know whether the bet would be taken by the Totalisator Agency Board, which later indicated that it had been unaware of the animal's death,

Generously, the TAB indicated that 'any punter who backed this horse after its death will receive a refund.' Always assuming that they had been told about it and become aware of the fact, in order to apply for the refund, of course.

'I was concerned to read that a bet was still being taken for a horse that died almost three weeks ago. An investigation was immediately put in train by the office of the Liquor and Gambling Commission' declared state gambling minister, Paul Caica.'

There was no indication of how many other punters had backed the dead cert.

353. RED FACED BOOKIE

Bookie Harry Ball was dismissive when punter Frank Waite offered to bet 2/6^d (12½ p) on 8/1 shot Gold Meter at Pontefract in October 1931; 'If that wins I'll give you £5 a week for life,' declared Bradford-based Ball in a manner he later referred to as 'jocular.' Gold Meter won. Waite demanded his fivers for life. Bull refused. Tattersall's Committee sat in judgement – and ruled in 31-year-old Waite's favour.

354. NOT SCOT FREE

Dual Derby winning trainer Jack Jarvis recalled one of his most humiliating moments in his posthumous 1969 autobiography.

It was when he felt his horse Fearless Fox had been deliberately 'roughed up' by a jockey in the 1937 Ascot Gold Cup. Extremely upset, Jarvis who confessed to 'possessing a temper, the combustion point of which is fairly low,' confronted the jockey, swearing at him in the process. He ended up being fined £25 by the stewards for his outburst, and having to settle out of court when the aggrieved rider took him to court for slander.

Jarvis was suitably contrite about one part of his insulting rant:

'I certainly should not have used the expression "Irish bastard'."

Well, that's true enough.

'Particularly as the jockey in question was born in Scotland.'

When Jarvis, who trained from 1914-68, won his second Derby in 1944, with Ocean Swell, owner Lord Rosebery was away in Scotland 'while my wife and I were both unwell and in bed at home'

Not THAT unwell, though, as 'I had a nice bet on Ocean Swell just before the off.' At 28/1. The celebrations that night were unconventional, as Jarvis hosted what in these days might be presented as some kind of an orgy – 'That evening, Lady Rosebery and her step-daughter Lady Helen Smith, came up to our bedroom and told us the details of Ocean Swell's triumph.'

Knighted in 1967 for services to racing, he died in 1968.

355. NOT THE BOOKIES' FAVOURITE

'The Remembrancer colt', owned by Lord Darlington and partnered by top jockey of the day, Sam Chifney, was well fancied for the 2000 Guineas in 1812.

Just prior to the off, Chifney paraded around on the un-named colt while his owner's second string, the unfancied dark horse, Cwrw was plodding round with a stable lad on his back. Unbeknown to most, although Lord Darlington himself had been backing The Remembrancer to win him £20,000 in public, in private his agents had been lumping on the apparent no-hoper, Cwrw.

As the runners and riders headed for the start, Chifney suddenly dismounted from The Remembrancer colt, who was announced as a non-runner, and jumped up on Cwrw.

Pandemonium as bookies realised what was happening and slashed Cwrw to favouritism. But the damage had been done, the money was down – Cwrw (however that was pronounced) came home clear of his rivals.

356. CLAREFUL CHOICE

Clare Balding, revealed the *Daily Mail* on September 19, 2006, 'has made an honest woman of her actress girlfriend Alice Arnold.'

It seems certain that BBC TV commentator and member of the famous racing family, Clare, 35, was the first major racing figure to take part in a civil partnership ceremony.

Dress code for the occasion, followed by a reception for 120 guests was described as 'glamorous but fun'.

357. VOTE FOR EMILY

In September 2006, the *Guardian* newspaper backed a campaign to persuade Epsom racecourse to 'honour' the memory of the militant suffragette Emily Wilding Davison who in 1913 threw herself under King George V's runner Anmer during the Derby, suffering fatal injuries.

Discussing the newly redeveloped Queen's Stand at the course, Tristram Hunt wrote 'There is no recognition of Davison, her role within the suffragette cause, or the significance of her sacrifice.'

Campaigners want a plaque placed on the course with the inscription from her gravestone: 'Deeds not words.'

358. OH, SHOOT!

Ruthless was one of the best horses to race in the US during the late 1860s, a filly who racked up 11 top quality wins – including the first ever Belmont Stakes in 1867 – during her career.

She was retired to stud at Francis Morris' Saratoga farm, close to which one day a party of hunters found themselves. One of the hunters spotted an animal moving about at a distance, took aim, and fired – shooting dead Ruthless, perhaps the only thoroughbred shot when mistaken for game.

359. A CRYING SHAME

Top jockey George Fordham was convinced he won the 1863 Derby, run in dreadful weather, on Lord St Vincent's 4/1 favourite, Lord Clifden. But Mr Clark, the Judge, ruled that he had been beaten on the line by 10/1 chance Macaroni.

Fordham did not take the defeat well. He had arranged to dine with friends at Carshalton that night and set off there with a jump jockey friend of his, Stait.

Stait was recognised en route by a racegoer, a Mr Oldaker, clerk of the course at Harpenden who told him, unaware of the identity of his companion, that he had seen the Derby and that Lord Clifden had been deliberately pulled.

Fordham grabbed the man, threw him into a furze bush, then 'mercilessly thrashed with his whip the man' said a contemporary report, which revealed that 'by the time he reached Carshalton, Fordham was so upset that he would neither have any dinner nor enter the dining room, but sat on the stairs outside and shed bitter tears.'

360. DOUBLE RESULT

In his book, *The Analysis of the Turf*, published in 1927, renowned racing writer and course official, John Fairfax-Blakeborough, told of the time when, acting as Judge, he gave two official results in the one race.

It happened at Perth. 'A race described on the card as being two miles was really over a distance of three miles. The jockeys, or some of them, were guided by the card and rode a desperate finish when they had gone two miles.

'I judged them, put up the numbers, left the box, and was making towards the weighing-room when I saw that the horses were still running. So I returned to my post of duty and ultimately gave another decision.

'Of course the stewards asked me for an explanation and I pointed to the race card. They suggested – very kindly – that that was not the guide the Judge should take, but the official Racing Calendar.'

361. EARLY WHISPERER

Racing fans have always been intrigued by talk of 'horse whisperers' – those people who seem to have an affinity with often troubled or uncontrollable problem horses.

They are not a modern phenomenon and in the late 1860s, one Colonel Westenra, later to become Lord Rossmore, had a promising racehorse, Rainbow, who was proving very awkward to control and had to be withdrawn from a scheduled race at the Curragh.

A friend of Westenra, Lord Doneraile told him he knew a man who would 'cure the brute' but Westenra refused to believe it and offered to bet Doneraile £1,000 to that effect.

Doneraile took on the wager and brought over a man from Cork who lived near Dublin, Con Sullivan, known as The Whisperer, 'due to the supposition that he whispered into horses' ears.'

Sullivan went in to Rainbow's box on his own and shut the door behind him.

For 15 minutes nothing was heard. Then, 'those outside rushed in – and found the horse on his back, playing like a kitten with The Whisperer, who was sitting by him. Both appeared exhausted' said a contemporary report, 'particularly the man, to whom it was necessary to administer brandy.'

The Colonel paid up.

362. LONG SHOT

Climbing on to the winners' podium after his sensational victory in the 1986 Arc de Triomphe, Pat Eddery was shocked to find himself shaking hands for no apparent reason with the legendary J.R.Ewing of tv's Dallas and his screen wife Sue Ellen – alias actor Larry Hagman and actress Linda Gray. Photos of the occasion show trainer Guy Harwood looking equally baffled. Still, no one got shot.

363. SEE FOR YOURSELF

Maybe it's just me, but I thought it was strange to see the following advertisement in *The Irish Field* weekly newspaper which catalogues Irish racing and equestrianism, in its edition of September 9, 2006:

'HORSES WANTED for slaughter. Owner can see them put down. Cash paid on collection. Contact Michael.086...'

364. BOB'S JOB, INDEED

Bob 'The Baron' Skelton (1882-1959) was a renowned punter on the Australian circuit in the 1920s and 1930s – a Sydney paper dubbed him 'the greatest and gamest punter in the world.'

Skelton always looked for an edge over the bookies. He once ran a horse at the Kensington track, where his jockey was named as J Nugent – a name unfamiliar to every racegoer at the course.

Skelton toured the bookies, backing his runner for fortunes and shortening his price in to favouritism.

The horse duly obliged, partnered by Nugent who, it was soon noted, bore a remarkable resemblance to crack rider of the day, Mick Hayes.

The bookies were in uproar, believing they had been had and demanding an enquiry, to which the stewards agreed and called Nugent and Skelton in for questioning.

Once in the stewards room, Nugent produced official documents showing that he had legally changed his name by deed poll from Mick Hayes.

The stewards had no option but to signal the all clear.

365. JUMPING POWDER

Although the final placing of his horse is not recorded, owner Mr Patrick, whose bay mare Lazy Bet was being partnered by jockey Bill Wright of Uppingham in the 1829 Leicestershire Steeplechases, was confident that the rider was perfectly prepared for the mount:

'He drank three parts of a bottle of Port Wine, and then had two glasses of brandy and a pipe. This may be termed Jumping Powder; but I must do Mr Wright the justice to say that it was the opinion of all that he performed like a workman, and spurned the idea of reconnoitring the ground. "Damn the ground" said he, Mr Patrick told *The Sporting Magazine* in April 1829.

366. SPIRITED PERFORMANCE

Top gentleman rider of his day in the late 18th century, Garry Moore, was running a horse in a race at The Curragh. Racegoer and acquaintance of Moore, Fred Russell, was enjoying a brandy and soda prior to watching the race, when he 'noticed Garry do the same, and then saw him have a soda water bottle filled with some of the finest Old Jameson whisky.'

Russell followed Moore when he left and saw him pouring the liquor down his mare's throat.

'This made him fly back to the ring, when he backed her for all he could get on recorded author Charles Adolph Voight in his book, *Famous Gentleman Riders*. Russell was asked why he'd backed the horse, and he described what he had seen, adding 'I know Garry wouldn't waste a pint of Old Jameson on a mare that was not trying!'

367. UNSEATED RIDER

When Irish jump jockey Danny Morgan, who had won the Cheltenham Gold Cup, the Champion Hurdle, the Welsh and Scottish Grand Nationals and the Champion Chase, decided to enlist as the Second World War began, he signed up for the Royal Horse Guards.

He failed his recruit's riding test – so asked for, and was granted, leave to attend racing at Newbury that afternoon – where he rode two winners.

368. POIGNANT PUNTER'S SUICIDAL FINAL GAMBLE

Australian-born Hugh Rowan was a massive gambler of the 1930s and 1940s. He would bet up to £100,000 a day, reacting impassively, win or lose.

Described as 'an eccentric who lived by his wits' by racing journalist Norman Pegg, who also suggested that he 'must have made lots out of confidence tricks on rich and gullible people', Rowan had something of the Howard Hughes about him – he would pay his West End hotel bill two years ahead and 'was such a believer in absolute cleanliness that he would have three baths a day and otherwise wash himself another four or five times. He riled hotel staff by slinging any soiled clothing like socks and shirts out of his room and had his belongings packed in a clean white pillowcase because dirt, he said, could not collect in the corners.'

Rowan pretended no knowledge of racing form – 'did not know how to read form, did not carry field-glasses, rarely indeed watched a race at all, even when he invested £50,000 on a horse'.

Eventually the tide turned against him and in 1947 the Royal Ascot meeting left him £90,000 in debt. Within a day or two he settled £60,000 of the debt to various bookies, but it seems he had no means of meeting the rest of the debt, so he opted for drastic measures.

Some years earlier after losing a similarly large sum he had threatened suicide and disappeared from the scene for a while, leading many to believe he was dead – until he burst back on the scene.

This time he retired to his hotel where, recalls Pegg, 'he decided to end it all. He was around 80 years of age, his powers had declined and his money and credit were gone. He sent a note to a friend saying he was going to commit suicide, and he told the night porter he was to be called in five minutes time. And would the porter bring something with him with which to untie knots?

'When his bedroom door was forced open, Hughie Rowan was dead. But not death from his own hand. There was a rope nearby but a postmortem examination showed he had died of heart failure. He had sat there waiting to hang himself when Providence had stepped in to thwart the gambler's last throw.'

369. HITTING THE WALL

A race took place at Ballyshannon in Ireland on November 3, 1792. It was 'a sweepstakes of 10gns each, three mile heats and to leap a six-foot-and-a-half wall the second round.'

There were four runners lined up, owned by Mr Jones, carrying a featherweight, a Mr Raferty, Mr Fawcitt and Mr Dixon respectively.

There was a controversial element to the race as the *Sporting Magazine* described: 'One of the horses was only to carry a feather and was rode by a boy. The first from the post was the horse carrying the feather. When he came to the wall he was stopped by the boy who, with great dexterity, alighted, turned the horse over, climbed the wall himself to the other side, mounted again, and came in first to the winning post.

Another horse and his rider leapt clearly over, and the two other horses baulked at the wall. It is now contended that the horse rode by the boy has lost, because the latter dismounted at the wall.'

The case was referred to the Irish Turf Club to be decided – and they duly gave it 'in favour of the horse rode by the boy, alledging (sic) that, there being a saddle on the horse's back when he leaped the wall, it was sufficient as a featherweight.'

370. BALLS

Trainers and owners concerned about the health of their racehorses had a limited amount of medical assistance available to them towards the end of the 18th century – but William Radley, Druggist and Chymist of No 27 Near Gray's-Inn-Gate, Holborn, was there for them, with his patented Horse Balls.

The Balls, 'by the King's Royal Letters Patent', were described in loving detail in a notice distributed by Mr Radley – 'The Purging Balls contain, in a small compass, all the essential qualities of a stomachic purge. They do not cloy a horse's stomach as most purges do, but without the least griping scour a horse well and make him stale urinate plentifully.

'Horses, after being badly or irregularly fed or coming from grass into a stable, are apt on change of diet to have humours flying about them which, settling on the lungs, legs or blood vessels, cause either an obstinate cough grease or farcy, which might be prevented by a few doses of physic, and therefore highly necessary for horses newly purchased. Price 2s each, parcel containing three doses.'

371. DUEL PURPOSE

Not best known for his racecourse honesty, the Earl of March, later the Duke of Queensberry, universally known as 'Old Q' in 1751 raced his horse Bajazet against Irishman Sir Ralph Gore's Black And All Black at the Curragh for a reported stake of 10,000 guineas.

Bajazet was beaten despite his jockey managing to get rid of some excess weight en route in an effort to swing the balance his way.

This ploy was spotted by Gore, with the result that Old Q found himself challenged to a duel at 5a.m. the next morning.

When March arrived, recorded a contemporary report, 'The Irishman's retinue was increased by a polished oak coffin which, sans ceremonie, he deposited on the ground, end up, with its lid facing Lord March and his party. Surprise, however, gave place to terror when his lordship read the inscription plate engraved with his own name and title, and the date and year of his demise, which was the actual day as yet scarcely warm.'

Lord March reconsidered his position immediately when informed by Sir Ralph that 'My dear fellow, you are of course aware that I never miss my man.'

March issued a humiliating apology and escaped with his life.

372. TOURMENTED

Tourment started 7/10 favourite to win the 1947 Arc de Triomphe – but it was a minor miracle the horse was even alive to race.

When the Germans were fleeing France at the end of the War, the Nazis were not too concerned about how they treated mares and foals in studs which they had commandeered during the occupation.

A mare called Fragment and her foal were in the charge of a retreating soldier, who was intercepted by staff from the Haras de Varaville stud who were desperately trying to track down their animals.

The soldier was asked how much he would accept in return for the horses – and parted company with them for 1000 francs each – about two guineas.

The foal was Tourment – who eventually finished 5th in the Arc.

373. NAME AND SHAME

An owner refused permission by the US Jockey Club to run a filly in the name of Sally Hemings, a colonial era slave reputed to be a mistress of the 3rd president of the USA, Thomas Jefferson, sued in the courts in September 2005, arguing that 'the denial deprived him of his rights under the US Constitution.'

US District Senior Judge, Karl Forester dismissed the lawsuit, but owner Garrett Redmond insisted that the name was a natural for a horse whose mother is named Jefferson's Secret and sire, Colonial Affair.

The Jockey Club rules say that 'names considered in poor taste or names that may be offensive to religious, political or ethnic groups' will not be approved.

374. ROD FOR HIS OWN BACKERS?

Trainer Rod Simpson who seems to have left and returned to the game more times than any other handler – in September 2006 he was in his 14th yard – has had more than his fair share of strangeness during his life. He was named after a ship his Dad once served on, HMS Rodney; was engaged to a former Pan's People dancer; worked behind the scenes on TV programmes like Dad's Army and Morecambe& Wise; is renowned for a flamboyant fashion sense, and once said he liked 'to wear yellow suits, pink suits, black and red striped trousers.'

Simpson has admitted to the odd spot of smuggling when a travelling lad – 'you learned how many wristwatches you could get around one horse's leg and then cover with a bandage, how many bottles of perfume you could get in the hay net without them rattling.'

He broke his leg in four places playing football; his jockey career consisted of five beaten rides.

As a trainer he won the 1983 Cesarewitch with Bajan Sunshine but one of his horses, Dollar Pocket, failed a dope test – after he apparently put some of his baby's teething gel on the horse's testicles. He was fined £350.

He ran a horse in the Derby which he backed to finish last at 2/1, 'but the bast*rd went and beat one' and he once had to wear a bullet-proof vest in the parade ring at Cheltenham when death threats were made against his wealthy owner, Terry Ramsden.

Simpson remembers Ramsden once calling him 15 minutes before the off of a race to ask him 'How's that horse?' Simpson told him it was fine: 'It had better be, I've just had a million quid on it.'

375. LONGCHAMP TRAGEDY

Seven racegoers were killed when an air-raid by the Americans hit Longchamp racecourse in occupied France at its first meeting of the season in April 1943. Runners were going down for the first race, just after 2pm when American bombers struck, despite the efforts of German ack-ack batteries stationed in the centre of the course to bring them down.

The planes rained 14 bombs on to the course, from the windmill, across the track, to the Petit Bois. Fortunately, none hit the crowded stands but the five minute attack caused death, devastation and destruction.

However, the decision was taken to go ahead with the meeting and emergency repairs were put into operation which enabled the first race to be run at 3.30, even though the tote had been damaged and didn't work until the final two events of the day.

The stewards were criticised by the collaborationist media the next day but Parisian 'turfistes' supported their actions and particularly their donation of half a million francs to the victims and their dependants.

376. TOO FAR FOR KSAR

Australian jockey Frank Bullock won two of the first three runnings of the Arc de Triomphe in 1920 and 1922; Ksar won the second and third runnings, on both occasions beating Flechois into second place.

But when Ksar took on Flechois again it was 'for some unknown reason' according to Arc historian Arthur Fitzgerald, in the 3 mile 7 furlong – extraordinarily, over twice the distance of the 2400 metre Arc – Prix Gladiateur, again at Longchamp, in which Flechois, a proven stayer, gained his revenge.

Ksar never raced again.

377. WOULD IT STAND UP IN COURT?

A German court ordered that Viagra should be given to a stallion, after the horse's new owner complained that he was impotent, and refused to pay the full sale price.

The purchaser of Vedor handed over just ten per cent of the agreed €4000 fee, claiming that the horse had only one testicle and was not rising to the occasion with his female partners.

However, in March 2006 the court heard that when the Viagra was administered Vedor seemed 'fully functional' and the buyer was required to make the full payment.

378. WOOD YOU BELIEVE IT?

Despite a lengthy career in the music business during which he has been part of The Faces and The Rolling Stones, and enjoyed considerable acclaim as a serious artist, guitarist Ronnie Wood declared that it was 'his proudest moment' when he was honoured by the Irish Thoroughbred Breeders Association as 1998's Best Small Breeder. His 75 acre stud is in Naas, County Kildare.

Amongst Wood's racehorses are Joleah – named after wife Jo and, yes, daughter, Leah – and Flip The Switch.

He said the award 'meant as much to me as being inducted into the Rock n Roll Hall of Fame.'

Wood has owned horses since at least 1989 and it is said that he chose his racing colours of white with a red sash to match those of his favourite beer, Red Stripe.

379. ON THE BRIDAL

Philip Mitchell-trained Sylvan Twister's jockey stood out as she rode the horse across Epsom Downs in August 2006.

For Jackie Talbot was wearing a wedding dress and veil as she partnered her mount as part of her contribution to National Wedding Dress Day and in the process raised a four figure sum for her nominated charity, the McCrod Oesophageal Cancer Fund.

380. WATERY GRAVES

Doug and Eph Smith were the 20th century's most successful jockey brothers. Doug, clocking up 3,112 career winners, was a five times champion while Eph didn't manage that but did ride a Derby winner – Blue Peter in 1939 – amongst his three Classic triumphs and 2,310 other winners. Eph, born 1915, was found dead in a brook near Newmarket in 1972 while Doug, born 1917, was found dead in his Newmarket swimming pool in 1989.

381. NEWS TO ME

Standard practice now, but the first national newspaper to publish starting prices was the *Evening News* in 1883. Editor Frank Harris trebled the paper's circulation three-fold within three months as a result.

382. EYE, EYE

The winner of the 1843 Governor's Purse run on South Africa's Cape of Good Hope, delighted in the strangely strange name of Here-I-Go-With-My-Eye-Out, for reasons lost in the mists of time.

383. ON THE BALL AT THE RACES

When Premiership football club Charlton Athletic signed a new defender, 27-year-old Senegalese, Soulemayne Diawara, in August 2006, they decided to announce the £3.7m player's arrival at Lingfield Park.

The Times observed somewhat snobbishly, 'British football has moved away from the old dogtrack and bookmakers' image in recent years, but Charlton Athletic stepped back in time yesterday.'

384. ROCKING AND ROLLING AT THE RACES

Popular rock n roller turned actor, Tommy Steele made an early impression on the racing world, he revealed in his 2006 autobiography, *Bermondsey Boy*.

He recalled the summer of 1946 when, he said, his father took him to Goodwood races.

Tommy's Dad was a racecourse tipster who would use his wits to convince racegoers that he could do them a favour by imparting information derived from his mysterious sources which could enrich them. A small fee would invariably change hands, or he would persuade them to 'put a bit of silver on for me'.

He had set up a scam which involved young Tommy, nine-years-old at the time, sneaking into the paddock and pretending to be stable lad to one of the next race runners, so that his Dad could point him out to his mug as a genuine insider.

All went well until Tommy got so close to one horse that when he saw his Dad looking his way and 'raised my cap and gave an enormous wave', he startled the horse so much that he reared up, tossing his jockey into the air, and bolting, causing a chain reaction – 'there were horses everywhere and people dashing about all over the place.'

Tommy fled the chaotic scene and made himself scarce, fearing recriminations from his irate parent, but 'in spite of the events of the day our horse won by six lengths and we were going home with a bit of silver in our pockets.'

385. RACE MEATING

Perhaps the strangest race run at Nottingham's Forest racecourse took place in the summer of 1801 following the same-day wedding ceremonies of four butchers from the town.

They held a well attended wedding picnic in the shadow of the racecourse grandstand, and decided to use the facilities of the course to stage a donkey race, each ridden by one of the grooms.

A contemporary report records that the race was run over 'half the racecourse' and that the winner would receive 'the expenses of his wedding day from the other three'.

'The four benign looking steeds were bedecked with mascots from the wardrobes of the ladies. One was neckerchiefed with a pair of long stockings; another had a pair of stays attached to his tail with a bow of green ribbon; the third was saddled with a night-gown; and the fourth wore a voluminous pair of ladies "nether-garments". Needless to say, this animal finished last; the one adorned with the stays proved an easy winner.'

386. PUNTERS LEFT STANDING

When betting shops first opened their doors legally in May, 1961 the law was intended to discourage people from lingering in them for any length of time.

Not all Licensing authorities were as keen on implementing the rules quite as sternly as Basil Aldous, chairman of the Newington Betting Licensing Committee, covering London boroughs like Camberwell, Lambeth, Southwark and Bermondsey.

In April 1963 he announced that he would be inspecting all 181 betting shops in the area and would cancel the licences of any premises he found encouraging people to 'loaf about' as he put it.

He told the *Sporting Life*, 'In the committee's view it is quite wrong, and contrary to the public policy, that those who elect to enter an office to place a bet should hang about there after their business has been concluded.

'A person who buys a packet of tea in a shop does not hang about afterwards' he declared pompously and somewhat irrelevantly, 'and we regard placing a bet as comparable. We hope that licensees will discourage the practice and, in particular, will refrain from encouraging members of the public by providing them with chairs and the like.'

Mr Aldous added that 'we regard the loafing about in betting shops by members of the public, many for hour after hour, as thoroughly undesirable'

He even suggested that no more licences would be issued 'until we are convinced that real efforts are being made to discourage loafers.'

In July 1964 an application for the first betting shop to provide a 'lady gamblers only' section was turned down by the same licensing authority

387. TWO, AND A PUNTER, TO JUMP IN THE NATIONAL

Jockey Jimmy Frost was beginning to dream of Grand National glory during the 1989 running of the race when with just a couple of fences to run he could tell that his mount, Little Polveir 'was still very easy and responsive.'

As the pair turned for home, though, 'it was then that a lager lout jumped out in front of me. He was hopping up and down. I saw him and thought I'd better go round him, but he was on the bend and to go round would have meant we were on the wrong leg, and to have changed legs going round the bend would have been awkward.

'I recall thinking, "sod it, if he wants to stand there, I'll hit him", which was a silly idea because that could have brought me down. I wouldn't have gone straight over the top of him but I'd have winged him. Luckily, he lost his bottle and ducked back under the rails at the last second'.

A relieved Frost drove Little Polveir on and over the final two jumps for a 28/1 triumph – probably not celebrated with a pint of lager.

388. PUBLIC STEWARDS INQUIRY

The rights and wrongs of holding stewards' inquiries in public have been debated long and loud over the years.

But it is a little known item of turf-trivia that as long ago as 1919 a stewards inquiry did take place in public – and it even involved the champion jockey, Steve Donoghue, who had somehow managed to lose on the hot favourite Diadem, in the five-runner King George Stakes at Goodwood, after meeting trouble at the start and effectively being left.

When he brought the horse in after the race there were boos and jeers – 'the very dregs of humanity seemed to be gathered round, hurling insults and threats at me' recalled the rider, adding, 'I was openly accused of having deliberately pulled my mount to prevent her from winning.' One particularly virulent accuser was later revealed to have been warned off the Australian turf.

A contemporary report by Donoghue himself explained, 'The stewards questioned me and I was told there must be an enquiry. A few minutes afterwards I was called, and was making my way to the stewards' room, the proper – and customary – place for an enquiry to be held, when I was astounded to learn that this one was to take place on the open verandah outside, in full view of the public.

'Why is this?' I asked myself. 'For the special edification of my cut-throat friends?'

'I could think of no other reason, but heart-broken as I was at the disaster to my little favourite, I was able to endure this ordeal with stony indifference, and for 25 happy, howling minutes, the roughest 'toughs' in the crowd thoroughly enjoyed themselves! No one concerned in the enquiry could hear a word that was being said about the accident, but we carried on amidst what seemed to be a perfect bear-garden and my special well-wisher, the Australian crook, raved, stormed, yelled and swore to his heart's content.

'I should not think that the experiment was considered to be so successful as to warrant its being established as a precedent for any more open-air enquiries.

'Of course, I was eventually exonerated for any blame and the incident was officially closed.'

389. RACE BREAKS OUT DURING PUNCH UP

'No less than one hundred and fifty six carriages' of the nobility and gentry were amongst the hordes who turned out to see the first day of the 1714 York Summer Meeting in the July of that year.

And they were treated to an extraordinary race for Her Majesty's Gold Cup.

It was for six year olds carrying 12st and was run in four mile heats.

In the third heat, Mr Childers' brown mare Duchess, ridden by Robert Hesseltine, 'ran a very severe and punishing race' with Mr Peirson's brown horse Foxhunter, ridden by Stephen Jefferson.

Admittedly the rules about what jockeys could and could not do were rather less strict than today and jostling and whipping were commonplace.

On this occasion, recalled racing writer of the 19th century, 'Thormanby': 'Robert Hesseltine made Duchess run Foxhunter so near the cords that his jockey was obliged to whip over the horse's shoulder. Duchess was thus enabled to gain the judge's fiat by a length.

'But no sooner had Hesseltine pulled up than Jefferson rode alongside of him and struck him across the face with his whip. Hesseltine returned the compliment and they cut away at one another amidst the cheers of the bystanders till the blood was streaming down their faces, and dyeing their jackets and breeches crimson.'

Then the owners got involved, both claiming the race.

A committee of 'Tryers' was empanelled to consider the matter – and awarded the race to Foxhunter.

That sparked a heated row between the owners which almost resulted in a duel before calmer heads intervened and suggested a re-run – won clearly by Duchess.

Both owners again claimed victory – 'there were mutual charges of foul riding and a challenge passed between the owners while the two jockeys had another set-to, this time on foot, which ended in the discomfiture of Hesseltine.'

The matter then went to a court of law – 'the decision of the Court was a curious one. It was that all the horses that had been placed in the different heats had an equal right to the prize, which must therefore be divided between them.'

390. NEXT TIME YOU ARE IN ASHKHABAD IN APRIL …

… pop along to the annual Day of Turkmenian Racing Horse, held on the last Sunday of that month, a national holiday.

Traditional horse races are held to mark the occasion. Horses are held in great esteem in Turkmenistan where a huge equine centre was recently created near the capital, equipped for breeding, racing and training and with a 'special building to accommodate a Jockey Club.'

391. PICKPOCKET POLICEMAN

Arrested during the 1790 Enfield Races, infamous pickpocket George Borough was transported to Australia, where he eventually became Chief of Police in Paramatta and unrepentantly declared that he and others like him were 'True patriots all, for, be it understood; We left our country for our country's good.'

392. THE PUNTING PHILANTHROPIST

Wealthy German-born Baron Maurice de Hirsch made his cash in the mid 19th century by investing in the creation of the Oriental Railway, which ran from Constantinople to Europe.

The Jewish entrepreneur became involved in racing, raising eyebrows when he declared that all his horses would run for charity and that he would give their winnings and his own gambling profits to a charity for London hospitals and a Canadian fund for helping immigrants, which he did right up until his death in 1896, aged 65.

In 1891 alone he gave £3m 'for the relief of suffering', still having enough left to leave his wife £8m when he died.

Not all racing folk welcomed the Baron, and turf writer W A C Blew claimed in his 1900 work, *Racing*, 'As is well known there has been in Paris a very hostile feeling towards Jews, and owing to this animosity, Baron Hirsch was blackballed from the French Jockey Club. He bided his time, however, and in due course, as money was no object to him, he contrived to buy the ground on which the Club stands, and having given the members thereof to clearly understand that they were merely tenants at will, turned his back on French racing, became a patron of the English Turf, carried out great philanthropic schemes for the benefit of his co-religionists, and distributed among our English hospitals the sums won on the Turf by his horses.'

His best horse was La Fleche, for which he paid the then enormous sum of 5500gns as a yearling. She won all four races as a two year old, then the 1000 Guineas in 1892, and started 11/10 favourite for the Derby in which she was beaten by a 40/1 outsider, only to reappear two days later and win the Oaks and then the St Leger.

La Fleche was controversially sold to leading racing figure Sir Tatton Sykes in the year that Hirsch died, who had neglected to put a ceiling on what he was prepared to pay and ended up having to fork out 12,600gns – but not before leaving the horse to fend for itself at Sledmere Station where it had been sent to him.

While the row raged about the cost of the great horse, the local station-master had to feed the deserted animal who would otherwise have perished but eventually produced offspring who never threatened to match her own achievements.

393. IF AT FIRST

The four runners for the Thirlmere Selling Hurdle at Carlisle on September 27, 1980 all refused at the first fence – at least twice!

Eventually they all managed to negotiate the obstacle – Keep Skyhigh refused for a third time – and Jonjo O'Neill's 2/1 joint favourite Seek Him Here finally made it round to win the race. Oddly enough there were no bids for him afterwards.

394. BETTING ON A 'SACROSANCT' RACE?
BLASPHEMY!

It is a horse race which has attracted double dealing, cheating, foul play, skulduggery and rule manipulation on a grand scale. Yet when it was suggested that betting might be permitted on the outcome of Italy's famous and colourful twice-yearly 'Palio' in the Tuscan city of Siena, gasps of outraged horror rent the air.

'It's not just a horse race, this is a way of life for us. You would never bet on your life,' spluttered local author Dario Castagno, presumably unaware that some people have certainly bet on their lives – in fact I currently have on my books a bet from a man in Glamorgan that he will outlive Lester Piggott, but that's another story.

The Monopoli di Stato, the regulator of gambling in Italy, had suggested that perhaps the time had come to permit commercial wagers to be placed on the Palio, which dates from the 13th century and in which, on July 2 and August 16, jockeys wearing medieval costume, from 10 of the city's 17 contrade or districts, compete for a silk flag during a race round the main square of Siena, the Piazza del Campo, which lasts for under two minutes and which has only one rule.

Spectators might think that one rule is that there are no rules, but it is that the jockeys may not grab the reins of their rivals.

Crashing into opposition horses, hitting them, whipping them, knocking jockeys off of their horses – all seem to be permitted, positively encouraged, even.

First round the square three times is the winner. Apparently, horses can even win if they cross the line minus their jockey.

So why not bet on the outcome? Well, unofficial bets have been placed for centuries, and foreign 'outsiders' are now betting on it, too. But resistance to official, commercial wagering was remaining implacable in August 2006 when the Consorzio per la Tutela del Palio, 'protectors' of the race turned the idea down flat.

Even Italy's biggest betting company, SNAI, was not interested: 'We accept bets on many races and festivals, but we would consider it blasphemous to bet on the Palio.'

Author, Castagno, added, 'The idea of going into a betting office and putting money on the Palio is distasteful.'

Siena's Mayor said that he was not happy about even betting organisations from foreign countries permitting betting on the Palio, but 'the important thing is, that it's not going to happen here.'

I wouldn't bet against it, signor.

395. SMELL OF SUCCESS

Canadian born (in 1878), Elizabeth Arden, whose US-based cosmetics empire made her a wealthy woman, got into racehorses in a big way, buying her first horse in 1941, becoming the leading money winner in 1945 and landing the Kentucky Derby with Jet Pilot in 1947. She died in 1966 and was inducted into the Canadian Racing Hall of Fame in 2003.

Ms Arden, who operated from Lexington in Kentucky, had her own ideas about the running of a racing stable – hers was painted in her racing colours of cherry pink, white and blue. Plants were hung over the stalls, soothing music was piped into them and the horses were gently sprayed with her Blue Grass perfume – named in their honour, and which became a huge seller for her. Whether because people liked the idea of smelling like horses or because it was a great fragrance, remains open to debate.

Her methods led one of her trainers to comment that 'my mother used to say only horses sweat, people perspire. That is not true in our stable, where it is the horses who perspire and the people who sweat.'

Ms Arden once said cryptically, 'Treat a horse like a woman and a woman like a horse – and they'll both win for you.'

She once did try to treat one of her horses like a human and rang the world famous

Mayo Clinic where she spoke to a specialist who refused to offer up a diagnosis for a horse. 'So, what would you do if he were a baby?' asked Ms Arden.

'I wouldn't enter him in the Santa Anita Handicap' said the doctor, and hung up.

396. SHOCKING, BUT I CAN SEE THE LIGHT

A dispute had broken out between an anonymous owner and a trainer over the purchase of a horse which one had bought from the other 'by supplying electrical equipment, including two chandeliers' reported the *Racing Post's* Howard Wright in August 2006, adding that it 'is a perfect case of why the mandatory payment of training fees through Weatherbys is not a straightforward matter.'

397. NONE DUNNE FASTER

The word around the track was that jockey Jimmy Dunne would not be 'off' on board Soldier Lad at the Springsure country track in Queensland, in 1915.

Chief Steward Frank McGill had heard the rumours and made a point of telling the jockey he would be keeping a close eye on him during the race.

He did better than that – he found a horse which he rode over to the start of the 5f event. Off they went, and before long, off came Dunne, tumbling from his horse.

Over rode McGill and as Dunne rose to his feet he was informed that he had just been suspended for a year!

398. A REAL RUM DO

The first ever race meeting in Melbourne, took place in March 1838 with bullock carts used as a makeshift grandstand, butcher's implements used for the weigh in, and a discarded clothes prop for the winning post. Bets were laid and paid in bottles of rum and one celebrating winning punter imbibed so deeply of his spoils that he staggered woozily into the River Yarra and drowned.

399. STRUCK DOWN

Suave Dancer, the 1991 Arc de Triomphe winner, was sent on secondment from the National Stud to stand in Australia.

He never returned – he was struck by lightning in 1998 whilst in Melbourne.

400. ON HIS TOD

The commonplace phrase 'on your tod' can be traced back to the start of the 20th century when American jockey Tod Sloan arrived in the country to revolutionise riding styles here by bringing with him the 'monkey-on-a-stick' style which helped him land 108 wins in 345 rides during his first full season.

Tod's style also featured front-running tactics, so he was often out in front on his own.

Sloan was eventually thrown out of British racing because of his gambling propensities.

He wasn't the first US jockey to ride here, though – Afro-American Willie Simms won four races from 19 rides when he appeared in 1895.

401. WINNING STREAK

Horse racing was first targeted by the now ubiquitous shameless exhibitionists known as streakers on an Australian course, where they do at least have the climate for it, back in 1974. Two apparently unremarkable racegoers at the Doncaster Cup, run at Sydney's Randwick track, stationed themselves by the furlong pole.

No one gave the man and woman, clad in raincoats and sandshoes a second glance, but as the field entered the straight, the unidentified pair threw off their outer wear, to reveal absolutely nothing underneath, and sprinted straight across the track in full view of jockeys, horses and spectators.

In the same year, the final day of the Cheltenham Festival saw a mass streak of six young men, who tackled the final fence – with Peter O'Sullevan adding a commentary to their exploits.

Well known British streaker, serial offender and Southend grandfather Tony Buckmaster, hit the tabloid headlines in June 1988 when he streaked at Epsom in full view of the Royal party on Derby day. He was fined £50. In 2003, Liverpudlian Mark Roberts scaled a fence at Ascot on Ladies Day and ran down the course with 'Lady Muck' written on his chest.

402. REVVING UP

It seemed impossible to discover precisely why, but the announcement in June 2006 that controversial, high profile American public figure and civil rights campaigner, the Reverend Jesse Jackson had been appointed to manage the Jockeys' Guild, was notable for its incongruousness.

He made an instant impression by describing jockeys as 'semi-indentured servants'

As US racing expert Dan Farley commented, 'Stay tuned. This could be one rough ride.'

403. SORRY?

Culture Secretary Tessa Jowell was asked by an *Independent* reader, Peter Blythe, from Kent, 'are you a gambler?' in July 2006, and she answered: 'No, but I did have a bet at Ascot this year, and won £30 which I gave to charity.'

So, Tessa, unless the stake money was given to you, you must be a gambler. If not, would you have donated the stake money had you lost?

404. AND THAT'S NO JOKE

The late, controversial comedian Bernard Manning liked a bet – starting with a one shilling winning bet on a horse called Wayside Inn at 14/1 when he was just 14.

His biggest win was £25,000 when he doubled up on 11/1 winner Dallas, with Dancing Brave in the Arc de Triomphe, but he was ultra-critical of Dancing Brave's Derby defeat – 'I'll never forget that one as long as I live. He came from 18th to finish second and even when I put the video on now I still think he's going to win. The way (Greville) Starkey rode that horse, like a bleeding amateur, cost me £2,000.'

405. STEWARDS ENQUIRY – INTO STEWARD

Officiating at the 1938 running of the Galway Plate, on July 27 of that year, one of the stewards, Lieutentant-Colonel S S Hill-Dillon, DSO, watched the unfancied 20/1 shot, six year old Symaethis, partnered by Don Butchers, romp home in the 23 runner race.

Unhappy at the running and handicapping of the horse, Lieutenant-Colonel Dillon requested that the stewards should hold an enquiry into Symaethis' much improved performance.

Slightly odd, this, as the horse was owned by Lieutenant-Colonel S S Hill-Dillon.

The stewards duly enquired and reported that they were 'entirely satisfied with the explanations given, and considered that the improvement in the form of Symaethis was due to the not abnormal improvement in a young mare, the much altered conditions of the going, and to the extremely able manner in which she was ridden.'

406. DERBY WINNER TAKES ON OAKS WINNER – IN A SELLER!

It was one of the greatest showdowns in racing – the Derby winner lined up against the Oaks winner – in a selling race.

Astonishingly, it really happened – Blue Gown, winner of the 1868 Derby and Ascot Gold Cup; Formosa, winner of the 1868 1000 Guineas, Oaks and St Leger – and Vespasian, the winner-to-be of the Chesterfield Cup.

All three lined up, alongside four other runners for the 1m Epsom 1869 Spring Meeting Trial Stakes – an 'optional selling race', conditions of which were:

'5 sovs each, with £100 added; winner to be sold for £500; if for £200, allowed 5lb; if not to be sold, to carry 9lb extra.'

Racing enthusiast Alexander Scott was there to witness this 'remarkable incident', declaring, 'one might search racing history in vain to find a field of such grand quality contesting an unambitious event like this one. What a field to contest a selling race!'

The race was won by Blue Gown, with Formosa second and Vespasian third.

407. MAN, O MAN

Man O' War, winner of 20 of his 21 races, was perhaps America's greatest ever equine hero. 'Big Red' was retired in 1920, yet was still attracting crowds to his retirement home of Faraway Farm in Kentucky, when he died in 1947.

His owner, Samuel Riddle, arranged to have the horse fully embalmed and placed into a giant casket, lined with his racing colours of black and yellow. He was buried at Faraway, and the entire funeral was broadcast live on national radio.

In 1976 the grave and the magnificent 3000lb bronze sculpture of the horse by renowned Herbert Hasseltine, were moved to the Kentucky Horse Park.

408. SILENT REVOLUTION

The racecourse commentary originated in Mexico.

Racing official George Schilling, was watching the filming of a silent movie, Sunset Derby, taking place in 1927 at the track where he worked, Tijuana in Mexico, when he had a brainwave.

Director of the movie, Albert Rogell, had set up a system of loudspeakers and microphones to enable him to speak to actors and extras during shooting.

Schilling 'got to wondering that if he could instruct the crowd, why couldn't I use it to tell the people where the horses were during the running of a race.'

Schilling had the system extended up to the stewards' stand and demonstrated his brainwave during the running of a race.

Course owner James Coffroth was so impressed by the effect of the set-up and the commentary that he immediately told Schilling: 'Get one of those outfits tomorrow'.

The days of the silent racecourse were over.

409. AHEAD OF THEIR TIME

The daughter of Hyperion and Rockfoil, racing as a three-year-old in 1946 was called Rock Goddess – best part of 30 years before the likes of Debbie Harry and Madonna hit the stage. The 1789 Derby was won by Skyscraper, in the days when I am reasonably sure there weren't any, while the 1797 Oaks won by a filly wearing horseshoes rather than trainers, I would wager, was named Nike.

One wonders where racegoers eager to watch the 1808 Oaks would have stayed – certainly not in the namesake hostelries of the winning filly, Motel.

And I cannot believe that The Locomotion was the hit of the day when Little Eva landed the 1901 Lincoln.

Although they would have used many methods to arrive for the 1833 Oaks few would have turned up on a Vespa – which was the name of the triumphant filly.

Argos could have opened no branches when the horse of that name won the 1915 Middle Park while the 1917 Derby winner Gay Crusader, owned, oddly enough by Aussie A W Cox who raced under the assumed name of 'Mr Fairie', may have had connotations scarcely dreamed of in those more innocent days.

It seems that TV executives at a loss for programme titles and characters over the years may well have delved back into racing history for such names as Panorama, the 1938 Coventry Stakes winner; Blue Peter, who won the 1939 Derby; and Baldric who had a cunning plan to win the 1964 2000 Guineas.

410. PADDLE SAVED SINKING BOOKIES

Eleven horses set off from Sydney on the ship SS City of Melbourne, bound for the 1876 Spring Carnival in Melbourne.

Several of the horses were well fancied contenders for big races, but they never reached their destination. A gale struck and several horses were washed overboard and drowned, others were crushed.

Only two horses survived. One, rescued by his jockey Joe Morrison, who revived him with gin and beer, was called Robinson Crusoe – and some reports made great play of this fact, as it seemed so appropriate. However, it appears that the name was bestowed after, rather than before the incident. The horse went on to win the AJC Derby. One horse named after a famous figure did perish, though, and that was Robin Hood.

The equine tragedy saved Melbourne bookies, who were harbouring large liabilities on the horses – particularly on the aforementioned Robin Hood – from a potentially ruinous payout so they were delighted at what had happened. In a gesture designed to show that all the legends about the granite from which bookies' hearts are carved are undoubtedly true, they banded together to present the skipper of SS City of Melbourne, one Captain Paddle, with a purse as a token of their gratitude. Aaah, bless!

411. STONED

Racing at Oswestry's little known track in the early 19th century was not always an entirely safe undertaking. At an 1832 meeting, reported the *Shrewsbury Chronicle*, 'a fellow threw a stone and struck Lear, the jockey, a violent blow on the head when riding up the course; he was immediately apprehended and given into custody by the Hon Thomas Kenyon, who also committed some of the numerous light-fingered gentry to prison.'

Nine years earlier, 'Mr Edwards' horse, Jack Spigot bolted while running the third heat, and in making over the rope, he fell upon the rider, Gamble, and killed him.'

412. SENSATION-AL JUMP

The first meeting, taking place in November 1867, held at a new course in Croydon, at Stroud Green, Woodside, introduced the racing world to perhaps the most controversial individual fence in the sport at the time – the 'Sensation' Water Jump.

This fence was 15ft wide – further than the one used for the Grand National – and some 5ft high, with water, according to one estimate, 3ft 6in deep.

It was an accident waiting to happen and despite being a crowd-pleaser, duly produced a fatality in only the second race run at the new track as Voightlander fell and broke his back, landing on top of the legs and thighs of his rider, Mr Crawshaw, who could only be moved from under the animal through the exertions of 'several policemen and bystanders'.

Another horse, Reporter, fell also and after the race the height of the fence was reduced by cutting a portion off of the top.

In the fourth race, despite the reduction in size, two more runners fell.

The meeting was brought to the attention of the press, with the *Pall Mall Gazette* unhappy at the 'cruelty being inflicted' on the runners.

The RSPCA got involved and issued a summons against Voightlander's owner-rider Mr Crawshaw, accusing him of 'cruelly ill-treating and torturing his horse at Croydon races' when they may have been better advised to prosecute the Race Committee.

There was a lively court case which resulted in the dismissal of the prosecution after veterinary evidence revealed that Voightlander was suffering from a complaint which could have caused his death at any time. It is likely, though, that the case did not do a great deal to promote a positive image of the sport.

413. BEST SOLUTION ALL ROUND

After unscrupulous Betfair customers attempted to make a profit by laying triple Gold Cup winner Best Mate for the 2006 Cheltenham Gold Cup even as the horse lay dying at Exeter in November, 2005, the exchange was forced to change its rules.

Despite a vote amongst customers which revealed that 46% favoured maintaining the 'buyer beware status quo' Betfair's Tony Calvin said in December 2005 'We will suspend an ante-post market on receiving reliable information that a horse is dead.'

414. STANDING UP VIAGRA CASE

Two vets and a pharmacist were arrested by police in Naples in February 2006 as part of an on-going investigation into the running of illegal race meetings where runners were allegedly given Viagra to boost their chances of winning.

Apparently, crooks had been organising meetings on public racecourses after hours and staging meetings at their own, secret tracks – one of which was discovered at Marigliano, equipped with its own grandstand, betting kiosks and punters' car park.

Stolen horses were often used in the races and in 2005 officers investigating the network, confiscated 80 horses and shut down one of the illegal tracks.

During the investigation, evidence had reportedly been uncovered that Viagra was also being used to dope horses running at legal meetings.

415. MONEIGH MAKERS

The racegoers at Deauville in August 2006 for the Prix du Haras de Fresnay-Le-Buffard Jacques le Marois day were intrigued by the colourful painting on the cover of the racecard.

And even more so when discovering that it was painted by former top French racehorse Kingmambo, winner of the Poule d'Eassai des Poulains and the St James's Palace Stakes and now standing as a stallion at Will Farish's Lane's End stud in Kentucky. Here he put nose, lips and tail to canvas to create his 'Moneigh' as such paintings by thoroughbreds are known when they are sold to benefit the Kentucky-based charity, Rerun, set up in 1976 to help find second careers for former racehorses. Kingmamabo's first, and only, painting was bought for $350 by Maria Niarchos-Gouaze, who arranged for it to be used on the racecard.

Other horses whose artistic talents have been captured on canvas include Cigar, John Henry, Tiznow and Smarty Jones.

416. THE DERBY WITH THREE 'WINNERS'

The record books say quite clearly that 20/1 shot Blink Bonny won the Derby in 1857.

But even 150 years down the line there are those who will disagree with the official verdict and make a case that the actual winner was … well, depending on which camp you support, a 200/1 no-hoper, Black Tommy, or the Birmingham-trained 12/1 chance Adamas.

Blink Bonny was an intriguing enough 'winner' on her own. Having run 11 times as a two year old and been winter favourite for the race, her price drifted when she suffered dental trouble and it seemed unlikely that she would go to post, her price lengthening to 33/1 only to contract rapidly when she did make it to the line. Having 'won' the Derby she completed a notable double a couple of days later by winning the Oaks as well. She should have won the Leger but was deliberately stopped in the final Classic.

Blink Bonny, Black Tommy, Adamas and Strathnaver went past the post in the Derby in a blanket finish of four, all spread out across the course.

No one knew who had won, even though many were convinced that their particular favourite had done so.

First to claim victory, though, were connections of Adamas. That horse's trainer, John Escott, would claim some 40 years later: 'I can see 'em finish now, all of a cluster. A sheet would have covered the lot. Mine had lost a lot of ground at the start (there had been an hour's delay getting the race started with horses and jockeys – four of whom were later fined for disobedience to the starter – delaying the 'off'), but had made it up after.'

Escott always claimed that Adamas' number initially went up into the frame as winner – 'When I saw my number 13 go up I never had such a feeling in my life. I turned round to wave my hand to someone who was standing at the back of me, and when I moved my eyes again to the number board I was dumbfounded to see my 'oss's number shifted and Blink Bonny's in its place. Instead of first they put him third'

Escott, whose memories were tracked down by noted racing historian Chris Pitt, said that his jockey John 'Tiny' Wells supported his contention, telling him, 'I don't care where they've placed me. I know I've won'

So frustrated were the pair that 'he burst out crying with vexation and so did I' according to Escott. Wells would win the next two runnings of the Derby, Escott never got close again and 35 years later was working as a casual labourer at Birmingham's Sutton Park, where he had trained Adamas, telling anyone who would listen that he was a Derby winning trainer.

But there is a third claim to victory in this extraordinary tale.

A Mr Drinkald owned Black Tommy, dismissed by bookies as a no-hoper, but quietly fancied by Drinkald who had backed him to win a fortune – persuading one layer to offer him the bizarre wager of £20,000 to a coat, waistcoat and hat.

As the Derby runners flashed past the post Drinkald, too, was convinced he'd pulled off the greatest shock result ever – 'Thank God I've won the Derby' he was heard to shout, adding a tad selfishly, 'And not a soul is on but myself!'

It is recorded by a friend that when Blink Bonny got the nod, Drinkald 'turned green and gasped as if he had been struck a heavy blow just below the heart.'

Author and observer of the racing scene, Alexander Scott, later wrote, 'Some of the inner history of Black Tommy's defeat was later revealed to me by a man named Taylor, who acted as valet and confidential man to Mr Drinkald. Both master and man were heavy gamblers, and knowing Black Tommy to be in grand trim and possessing a great chance of winning, they staked practically everything on the horse. To further ensure that no one would be in the paddock to talk about the horse Taylor, the valet, actually saddled the Derby colt himself.

'All their dreams of fortune were frustrated by Blink Bonny ... both owner and man were ruined.'

417. PRACTICAL JOKE – 1825 STYLE

Newmarket's Craven meeting took place from April 6 in 1825 and on the final day of the meeting, 'a ludicrous trick was played off on the landlord of the Wellington. A wag, for whom he had drawn many a cork, observing him absorbed in the business going on, extricated the lynch-pin of his buggy; so that when he applied his whip with an intention of moving to another part of the Heath to have a better view of the Newmarket Stakes, the wheels separated from the body of the chaise, and Boniface was upset, occasioning considerable mirth to the spectators'

Works every time, that one!

418. SCRUB THAT IDEA

London was set to acquire a brand new racecourse in August 1817. The good folk of the parishes of Fulham and Hammersmith had raised money and actually commenced operations for the track at Wormwood Scrubs – site today of the infamous prison.

With the course ready to begin racing on August 20 'the whole concern was suddenly and imperiously put to a stop' recorded a contemporary account – 'by the following communication': 'Sir – I do hereby give you notice not to come upon or trespass, or commit any trespass in or upon a certain place called Wormholt Wood, otherwise Wormwood Scrubs, in the parish of Fulham and county of Middlesex; and that in case you do so, after this notice, you will be considered a wilful trespasser, and an action at law will be forthwith commenced against you for the same.'

The correspondence was dated August 14 and by 'the Solicitor, in behalf of the Deputy-Assistant Quarter-Master-General'.

The Army had shot down the racecourse.

419. RACING TO TOP OF CHARTS

When highly praised 'folk chanteuse', Isobel Campbell won a nomination for the prestigious Mercury Music Prize, the 'Oscars' of the music world, in 2006, she was quick to refer back to her earlier days when she worked in a Glasgow betting shop for Coral.

Her album 'Ballad of the Broken Seas', recorded with rocker Mark Lanegan from the band Queens of the Stone Age, was a great success, and Isobel recalled that when she worked in the betting shop for a summer, 'There were a lot of real characters around. People's wives used to drag them out by their hair. Having led a sheltered life, it was like being thrown in at the deep end. But I loved it.'

And she still recalls the customers, some of whom must have made it into her songs.'This drunk old man came in once and he made such an impression on me because he was trying to lose, but he kept on winning loads of money. He kept saying, "Take it, blondie, take it, just have it." I was tempted because I was an impoverished student.'

Eighteen years old at the time, Campbell soon moved on to greater glories, but recognises the debt she owes that job – 'Working at the bookies was intense and hard going, but that's how I'm finding music right now. I'm ready to go away and grow vegetables.'

This story reminded me of another female icon of the music business. The Adverts were one of the successful early punk bands, who cracked the charts with their big hit, 'Gary Gilmore's Eyes' a song about an infamous murderer. On bass the group featured a very photogenic, leather-clad girl, Gaye Advert, whose poster graced many an adolescent lad's bedroom wall.

A few years ago I discovered she was working in a William Hill branch in North London. I rushed round there, ostensibly to interview her for the company newspaper, but really to get her signature on my copy of the Adverts' album, 'Crossing The Red Sea'. Any offers for it?

420. PLUS ÇA CHANGE

As this book was being written, the arguments over horses being laid to lose races and then not being permitted to run on their merits, were raging.

But there is very little new under the sun and I came across a fascinating exchange – sorry about the pun – dating from 1844 when Captain, later Admiral, Rous, the supreme administrator of racing in this country was being quizzed by a House of Commons Gaming Committee, a member of which asked:

'Suppose a person to have backed a particular horse, and to have reason to believe that

that horse could have won the race had he been allowed to do so, but that the owner of the horse, from reasons best known to himself, had by some arrangement with others as to the other horses and so on, had not allowed the horse to win, would you think that a person losing under such circumstances had a claim to recover the money back again?'

Came the reply, 'Not in that instance. In the first place, if you choose to back another man's horse, you do it at your own risk. I have hardly ever known any instance of gentlemen losing their money on the Turf, especially those not much on the Turf, when they do not conceive that they have lost their money rather from roguery of others than from their own stupidity; they had always much sooner make out the rest of the world to be rogues than that they themselves are fools.'

421. CHINA CRISIS

William Hill were delighted with their plan to launch an internet betting site in Mandarin just in time to attract Chinese customers for the 2001 Grand National which was being screened in that country for the first time.

'Gambling is illegal there but there's still a huge passion for it' said Hill's pr man, David Hood. 'In the 48 hours before the race we opened somewhere in the region of 2000 new accounts'.

Delight all round – except that noone seemed to have anticipated the consequences of the fact that many Chinese gamblers like to follow local superstitions and traditions – 'It was just unfortunate that red is the lucky colour in China. To a man they all backed Red Marauder, the winner, at 33/1, and what should have been a sparkling result for us was horrific.'

422. BERTIE'S UNFAIR COP

Marlborough-educated Bertie Short, born in 1849, set his sights on a job with the Indian police back in the days of the Raj.

Using his connections and pushing his luck a little he duly made it into the force in a place called Dehra Dun where, as he was well aware, there was an active racing scene.

And Bertie was a racing man – so much so that he started to ride at the meetings there with some success. 'His police duties appear to have occupied a bare minimum of his time and though money was short, he managed to keep a few horses and to get round all the meetings' contemporary accounts record.

In 1873 Bertie fancied his best horse, War Eagle, to land something of a gamble. But he decided to pull a few strings to ensure that the good thing became a certainty.

Bertie duly pulled in a couple of his best cops for extra duties, which involved stationing themselves alongside each fence so that in the event that either Bertie or War Eagle came to grief they would be in place to catch the horse so that Bertie could remount.

He also arranged with a well known professional jockey, Dignum, that he should also be stationed in the middle of the course on a hack so that in the event of Bertie taking a tumble from his horse, Dignum could take over. This was apparently permitted by the rules.

The race began and Bertie was going well on War Eagle, with one of his main rivals, ridden by the top amateur of the day, David Papillon falling at the second. The rider called to the policemen standing by the fence to catch his mount – only to be greeted by blank expressions and lack of movement.

Bertie duly came home clear on War Eagle, to land the gamble, leaving Papillon to write a letter to the media on the subject of 'the tax payer being required to maintain an expensive police force apparently solely engaged in furthering the extra mural activities of junior officers.'

Bertie Short's luck was out when he injured his hand very badly when he was mauled by a horse which turned savage. His hand was amputated. The resourceful Short had 'a leather bucket made to cover the stump with a steel hook in the end. He used to have his reins sewn into loops into which he hooked his hook and thus he continued to ride in races, and claimed that he was actually better off as, if he fell off, he could never let go of his horse.'

Eventually the police force ran out of patience with Bertie's lack of application and fired him. He died in 1894.

423. SOMETHING SNAPPED

Australian jockey Noel Callow was puffing a crafty cigarette at Caulfield racecourse near Melbourne on Easter Monday, 2006, when one of the course chefs objected to him doing so, saying he was too close to the kitchen.

The chef, Eddie Dumaresq, used his mobile phone to take a photo of the offending and, to him, offensive rider, but Callow objected and demanded the phone so that he could delete the picture. Dumaresq, somewhat heftier at 6ft and 80kg than the pint size, 54kg jockey refused to comply – whereupon he apparently got a wallop for his troubles.

Callow was fined A$750 – just over £300 – for his negative actions which had caused the trouble to develop in a flash.

424. PUMPKIN HEAD

Aussie owner/bookie/gambler, Humphrey Oxenham had to pay 2,000 guineas to buy back his racehorse Acrasia after losing her to a Mr John Mayo in a poker game two weeks before the 1904 Melbourne Cup, for which she was entered.

Mayo was the owner of Lord Cardigan, the 1903 Melbourne Cup winner.

Oxenham raised the cash to get her back and she rewarded him by winning the big race, giving him even greater satisfaction by beating Lord Cardigan, who tragically died within four days of the Cup.

Oxenham, born in 1854, first got into betting when he was offered, accepted and won a bet of £200 to 6d that he could not walk the two miles from Bathurst where he was born, to Kelso in a specified time – oh, and he had to balance a pumpkin on his head at the same time. He did it.

425. ATTY TRICK

These days no one bats an eyelid when the likes of Jenny Pitman, John Francome or Richard Pitman pens another racing-themed novel. They are simply following in the footsteps of Dick Francis, the first noted racing professional to put his on course experiences to profitable use.

Well, they are – in as far as it goes – but their real fore-runner is now long forgotten.

Henry Seymour – better known as Atty – Persse was, for some 50 years at the top of the training profession. Born in 1869, he lived until he was 91, started training in Ireland in 1902 and moved to Britain in 1906. The best known horse in his charge was undoubtedly the The Tetrarch, a grey with curious white markings who became known as The Spotted Wonder, was never beaten in seven outings, and is still regarded by racing historians as perhaps the fastest horse ever to grace the British turf.

A master of his art and, above all, of training two year olds, Persse insisted , 'the great thing in training a two year old is to keep its speed, and if it loses it, it must be rested at once.'

A severe disciplinarian and a spikey character who did not begin to mellow until his latter years few would have suspected that he had literary talents, and it may well be that he didn't – however, in 1924, he produced probably the first novel with a racing theme written by a member of the racing establishment – published by an imprint noted for its romantic fiction, Mills & Boon. '*Trainer and Temptress*' was penned in conjunction with A J Russell – who couldn't have been the well known northern jockey of that name, who was born in 1918 – and dedicated to 'the whole of the vast and picturesque community of the Turf'.

Was it any good? If you'd like to find out, keep an eye out on ebay – a copy sold there for £12.50 in August 2006.

426. GUNNING FOR THE WHIP

The Fulham Hurdle at Flemington in Melbourne in February 1966 was slightly delayed when the starter was distracted from his task by the sight of Walter Hoysted waving a shotgun in his general direction.

And Hoysted, eldest son of one Australia's best known trainers, Fred, was not just there to discuss the prospects of the runners, he was making a serious protest against the whipping of horses during races

Just to emphasise his point, Hoysted discharged his shotgun – fortunately without hitting anyone, human or equine.

At this point a promise was made that whips would not be used in the imminent race.

That was rescinded once Hoysted gave himself up to the constabulary.

Despite arguing that 'I would not have hurt anyone', Hoysted was jailed for a month and fined for being armed with a shotgun, for firing the weapon 'without authority' and for assaulting a policeman.

427. SHIRLEY NOT

Jockey Sam Shirley, a rider on the American north west circuit, did the rounds of local bars in Spokane in August 1994 when he was set to ride a horse called Why Dilly Dally at local track Playfair.

Sam told bar owners and drinkers in a large number of establishments that his wife had been in the bar a few days previously with friends with whom she was getting a lift home.

However, she decided to leave early and had the barman call her a cab in which she left. When the other couple left, their car crashed and they were killed.

Sam's wife therefore felt that the barman had saved her life and he wanted everyone to know how grateful he was by telling them that the horse he was riding in the sprint race that afternoon would win.

The horse had little form and opened up in the on-track betting at odds of 20/1, but as the area-wide gamble kicked in those odds plunged to 9/5 favourite.

The horse finished last and after the race jockey Sam Shirley denied all knowledge of having visited any local bars or tipped the horse to anyone at all.

428. STAR STRUCK

A new service for owners was introduced in early 2006 when former silversmith and publisher, John Puxty, launched a scheme offering to help owners name their horses, improve their performances, and help identify other prospective purchases for them – via astrology.

Puxty's tariff offered 'Improving performance: includes visit to assess horse and astrological analysis – £486'.

Puxty is far from the first to endeavour to show a connection between astrology and racing. I own a book published almost one hundred years ago by Foulsham and Co in London, written by 'Sepharial', and titled 'The Silver Key'.

Explained Sepharial, 'The Silver Key is an attempt, along scientific lines, to answer the general question as to the possibilities of Astrology, Numbers, Colours and Symbolism, in connection with the successful forecasting of Racing results.'

Astrology has its enthusiasts, amongst them 'Mystic Meg' of *The Sun*, who once missed witnessing her horse Optimist win a race at Yarmouth after she unexpectedly became stuck in a traffic jam..

429. DOWN PAYMENT

When racing was abandoned at Northern Ireland's Down Royal meeting on November 5, 2005, due to a bomb scare, the 8,000 racegoers present were handed a £5 free bet to use at the next meeting on December 26.

Arriving at Down Royal for the Boxing Day meeting with their free bet vouchers, racegoers were frustrated when they were evacuated following a bomb scare, and the meeting was again abandoned.

430. ENGLAND SKIPPER LIKES A PUNT, SHOCK.

Chelsea star John Terry, appointed England captain by Steve McClaren in August 2006, has always enjoyed a flutter – newspaper reports suggested he was staking £5,000 a week on horse and dog races in December 2005.

However, his club boss Jose Mourinho was not at all worried about his millionaire defender's gambling – because he is English.

Mourinho said at a press conference, 'In every street I find a minimum of three bookmakers shops. That's your country, your culture, that's what you love, that's what you do. So for me, an Englishman going to the bookmaker or being at home and using computers to bet is normal.'

Had Terry been Portuguese, though, it may have been different – 'If a Portuguese player goes to a bookmakers I am worried, because our fathers since we were kids have said to us 'Not one coin, not one single coin in bets, playing cards, casinos.' We have this in every family, not one single coin. This is our culture, this is your culture.

'So, for me, John Terry betting is normal. I can guess that £1,000 for John Terry will be £20 for you. I don't know, £20 or £50? If you bet £50 a week, does it become a drama for the organisation of your economic life? I don't think so. John is English and I can do nothing.'

431. TRAGIC END TO CHINESE EXPERIMENT

Up to 600 racehorses and mares were believed to have been slaughtered when a bid to launch racing in China failed in late 2005.

Racing at Tongshun racecourse near Beijing stopped abruptly in October as the government refused to sanction gambling and the man behind the scheme, Hong Kong-based businessman Y P Cheng, believed to have ploughed £58m into it, pulled the plug.

Trainers, mostly expats, were stood down and workers at the track dismissed.

The course had opened in 2002 and racegoers were 'rewarded' for picking winners in a 'guessing game', in an effort to get round the strict no-gambling rules. That practice was clamped down on by the authorities in 2004.

Englishman Nigel Smith was the only British trainer amongst the 16 licensed to train in Beijing, others came from Ireland, France, S Africa, New Zealand and Australia.

'This was virtually the first time I'd ever been out of Worcestershire but I love it here' said Smith, 'I have been asked to take an extended holiday and told that we might restart in 18 months.'

They didn't.

432. STALLION LOST IN THE POST

A bizarre mix-up when a transport company collected a stallion from Newmarket to be delivered to Western Australia resulted in the wrong horse taking the trip and being prepared for stud duties for some six months before the case of mistaken identity was revealed.

Dubai Excellence – half brother to Dubai Millennium – was the stallion bought by the chairman of Western Australia's Turf Club, Ted van Heemst for £160,000. But when the horse arrived in February 2005, unbeknown to all concerned, he was actually an inferior Irish bred horse called Samood.

The error was only spotted days before the start of the Australian breeding season in September, by which time the real Dubai Excellence had been delivered to Ukraine where, presumably, Samood should have ended up.

'It seems that the mix-up occurred when both stallions shared a paddock near Newmarket' explained Michael Ford, keeper of the Australian Stud Book. 'The wrong stallion left for Europe instead of going into quarantine for his trip to Australia.'

433. RED CARDIS

Hippolyte Cardis finally cracked it by landing a bet worth €257,685 with the PMU in August 2005.

Recovering from an illness, the 72-year-old was delighted and took his ticket for payout – only to be told that he was a week late presenting the ticket.

The PMU has a 15 day limit for collecting bets, otherwise the money is forfeited into a pension fund for those who work for racecourse companies and the Pari-Mutuel.

Cardis wasn't over concerned as he could produce a medical certificate showing that he could not have collected the ticket as he had been in hospital, but he was refused payment and his winnings went into the fund, part of the €50 million unclaimed during the year.

434. TIPSTER TOM YOURS FOR PRETTY PENNY

After giving colleagues in the office a couple of losing tips, *Sunday Mirror* racing writer Tom Reilly was put up for sale on ebay by his fellow hacks in April 2006 – with bids invited from a mere penny. Reilly hit the headlines as a freelancer when he wrote a story for *The Sun* exposing a breach in Grand National security when he got himself 'within doping distance of joint favourite Hedgehunter.'

But he also made the mistake of advising the *Sunday Mirror* hacks to invest their hard earned cash on the horse – which was beaten into second place.

Then 'Tom Reilly, Ace of Lies' as he was described in the ebay sale details, 'insisted he had a 'great tip' on Rohaani, 3/1 favourite in the 3.15 at Kempton. It came in second.'

That was the final straw for the admittedly short-on-patience *Sunday Mirror* staffers, who offered ebay surfers 'Yours for a fair price, one Tom Reilly, slightly dog-eared, unable to either dope or pick a nag. Except to come second.'

But maybe Reilly redeemed himself with a winner – the auction was halted before a buyer could be found.

435. POST HASTE FOR ROMANCE

Advertisements in the *Racing Post* are usually placed by bookmakers looking for punters, but a most unusual type of ad appeared in the paper on December 3, 2005, which put the racing world in a spin wondering who might have placed it.

'Wanted' it said in bold, black capital letters – 'Romantic Male for L.T.R.'

Now, being an innocent I have no idea what an L.T.R. may be, but the 'young looking and at heart 55yrs 'Mare' looking for her 'Motivator' to share fun and more in the paddock' quite clearly did.

She outlined the 'Pedigree required' from respondents to her ad – 'Love, passion, fun, respect, racing, travel, sun, excitement, happiness, good living. Someone to be proud of' and definitely also to have 'no ex's lingering in the stalls'.

And what would he – presumably he – be offered in return? Well, 'All the above, plus blonde, sparkling blue eyes, well groomed, good temperament, doesn't bite or kick!' (well, there's always a down side, isn't there?) '5ft 9in medium healthy build. Needs honesty, love, cuddles and more in return for happy life together.'

And that was it – no further clues – just a box number to write to.

The ad didn't reappear, so one hopes that this lonely heart managed to get that L.T.R.

436. LONG SHOT IS ODDS ON FAVOURITE

The Long Shot Trophy is run annually to this day at Caymanas Park in Kingston, Jamaica, the course where racing first took place in 1959 and where, in 1969 hugely popular local equine celebrity, Long Shot, collapsed and died just before the finishing post during what was reportedly his 202nd race.

Jamaican reggae group, The Pioneers, had already celebrated the horse in a 1968 single called 'Long Shot (Bus' Me Bet)' which told how jockey Marcus 'lick 'im, whip 'im; lash 'im' but couldn't get him past Chagga Warrior, the winner. It was a local hit.

Now, though, they came up with a tribute to the horse and its tragic final appearance, 'Long Shot Kick De Bucket', singing of the 'weepin' and wailin' which went on when the horse fell and expired and how 'Long Shot fell, all we money gone a-hell'.

As expected the single, complete with its opening racecourse fanfare and its jaunty chorus, and namechecks for several of the other runners in the race, was a big hit in Jamaica, but it then took off around the world, reaching number 21 in Britain in late 1969.

The band called their subsequent album 'Long Shot' and continued to be very successful. In 1980 the track suddenly bounced back into the limelight when The Specials included it on a live record which soared to number one, prompting the reissue and second chart entry of the original.

Not even Arkle, Best Mate, Desert Orchid, Red Rum, Sea Biscuit or Secretariat have ever inspired a number one single!

In 2006, legendary West Indian fast bowler Michael Holding, a great racing and betting man, revealed that his first experience of both was some 40 years ago at Caymanas Park where presumably, he bet on or against Long Shot.

437. CHERIE BLAIR'S DAD'S DEAD WIFE'S TIP

Actor Tony Booth, father of Tony Blair's wife, Cherie, believes he backed a 40/1 winner after his dead second wife, Coronation Street actress Pat Phoenix told him to.

Booth and Phoenix – who played the fiery character Elsie Tanner – married in 1986, days before she died of lung cancer.

He says that shortly after she died, she appeared to him while he was at home in bed.

'She said, "Do you want to ask me anything?"' he told an interviewer for a December 2005 Independent on Sunday article. 'I said "Yes. What's going to win the Cesarewitch on Saturday?" I am totally serious. She said "Number 23 at 40/1."'

Racing fan Booth told his sceptical interviewer, 'Look it up. I had £20 each-way and it won.'

'£20 sounds cautious' says the interviewer – although, of course, the bet was £40 in total.

'Absolutely' replies Booth, 'Why didn't I bet more? And of course, I could have asked her anything. Did you meet God? Is there an afterlife?'

**Orange Hill won the 1986 Cesarewitch, returning a starting price of 20/1.

438. REVVED UP FOR RACING

Satellite TV broadcaster Racing UK thought they had identified a pub which was paying under the going rate to receive the live feed of racing, as it was being charged only the domestic rate, about one fifth of the commercial subscription.

Enforcement staff at the channel duly interrupted transmission, shortly before the 2006 Cheltenham Festival.

The subscriber was devilishly upset and kicked up an unholy row – pointing out that the name of his home was entirely appropriate to his profession and heaven only knew why they should have cut him off.

Staff duly amended their records to reflect the fact that 'Immaculate Conception' was the address of a vicar rather than the name of a hostelry.

439. DIDDY DIDN'T

When rapper P Diddy attended the 2002 Kentucky Derby he came up with two bizarre reasons for deciding which horses to back.

He reportedly first selected a runner whose colours matched those of his tie, before opting for another runner in the next race, which he believed had smiled at him.

Both were beaten, costing him several thousand dollars.

His efforts to encourage his horses also caused comment, with one racegoer saying, 'He was jumping up and down on tables, shouting and waving his cash around.'

440. EVEN MORE MAGNIFICENT THAN FRANKIE

Frankie Dettori quite rightly took the plaudits for his astonishing September, 1996 seven-timer at Ascot which relieved the bookmaking industry of up to £50m, but jockey Eddie Castro eclipsed even that performance when, at Calder in Florida in June, 2005, he became the first rider to win nine races on a single card.

He was also equalling the record of nine winners in one day, set by Chris Antley in 1987 when he rode four at Aqueduct in the afternoon and five more at Meadowlands in the evening.

441. MONEY TO BURN?

American firefighter Chris Hertzog really hit the jackpot when his $1 ticket for the trifecta at Turf Paradise, near Phoenix Arizona in May 2005, landed a $864,253 jackpot (approx £463,000).

But he couldn't find his ticket, so faced losing his payout.

Next day, pari mutuel clerk at the track, Brenda Reagan discovered a couple of tickets lying alongside her machine which she idly checked before intending to discard them.

One of them was Hertzog's trifecta.

She remembered that 'when I punched out Chris's tickets – 50 exactas and 50 trifectas-there were so many that they bunched up and these two must have fallen to the side.'

Hertzog, who had completed a divorce just a week before, must have been tempted to propose to Reagan when he was reunited with the ticket, but contented himself with handing her an appropriate, but not revealed, reward, and said, 'This ain't changing my life, I'm going back to the firehouse.'

442. WISDOM OF SOLOMONS?

Jockey Scobie Breasley drove a moderate horse called Buoyancy home to a 6/1 victory in the 7.5f Berkeley Welter race at Ascot, Melbourne in December 1939. But even as he was taking the horse into the winners' enclosure, listeners to the radio station 3XY were still being told by racing commentator, Harry Solomons, that the race was poised to start.

For the race was the subject of a daring plot, which involved cutting the radio broadcast cables of every station connected to the track, except for 3XY.

Once the links were cut, Solomons was indicating to his accomplices across the country which horse had won the race, so that they could place 'after-time' bets.

He then began a 'phantom' broadcast of the already completed race.

Sadly for Solomons, though, the link to one station, 2GB, in Sydney, had stayed in place.

Very quickly, suspicions about the 'coincidental' loss of signal to the other stations were voiced and some bookies refused to pay out on bets accepted close to 'off' time, although it was later alleged that up to £20,000 was paid out.

Solomons was initially suspended, and then dismissed.

He fled to Fiji as the net tightened, but was arrested there and brought back to stand trial. Solomons was sentenced to six months jail in August 1940.

443. NOT SO ANGELIC

American amateur jockey Angel Jacobs made a big impression as he rode a series of winners to run up a lead in the Bollinger Champagne Series of races, taking a convincing lead in the 1998 competition.

He had arrived in the UK in September 1997 and landed his first winner, Bold Faith, at Newbury in June 1998, quickly adding three more victories to that total. He claimed to be a godson of US racing legend, Angel Cordero and told how childhood poverty had meant he rode ponies on a beach with bridles made from shoelaces.

However, his 'unusually compact and efficient style' had raised suspicions that maybe he was rather more experienced than he was letting on.

In August 1998, after he had landed his fifth winner within three months, the Jockey

Club looked a little more closely at the 29-year-old, and it emerged that he was actually Puerto Rican-born Angel Monserrate, a professional jockey in the US who had been banned from racing there after failing a drugs test in 1995.

The next year he had ridden under the alias of Carlos Castro, but was exposed and arrested after winning a race in the US, then being charged with forgery, criminal trespass and 'tampering with a sporting event'.

'Jacobs/Monserrate/Castro' was given a ten year ban by the Jockey Club, and said, 'I'll definitely miss the racing game. It's my life and they have taken it away.'

But he was nothing if not persistent, and in April 2003, racing journalist Lydia Hislop revealed that he was back in Newmarket, riding out for trainer Phil McEntee, and pointed out that he was banned from being 'employed in any racing stable' or 'dealing in any capacity with a racehorse.'

Commented Hislop, 'There is no evidence that he profited from betting when posing as an amateur. Quite simply, riding is his particular talent and he thrived from the attention it brought him. He couldn't stop then and he can't now.'

444. BEST, ER, MANE?

Desert Orchid was as much the focal point of the occasion as bride Frankie Burridge when she wed property developer Bill Younger in Nottinghamshire in August 2006.

The horse, a member of the Burridge family since being foaled in 1979, wore a floral wreath and led the guests and happy couple from the church to the reception.

*In June 1988 when Terry Lee Griffith wed Kathleen Boutin at Delaware Park racecourse, best man to 44-year-old trainer Griffith was his 6yo racehorse, The Maltese Cat, clad in a tuxedo.

445. DIVING IN

Racing writer Lee Mottershead wrote a profile of Auteuil jumping course in a *Pacemaker* article in July 2006, in which he revealed of 'Auteuil's signature fence, the Riviere des Tribunes', a water jump consisting of a metre-high fence overlooking 5.5 metres of water, that 'the French swimming squad use it every other Thursday for diving practice'.

Wow, what a story, I'll put that in the book, I thought and looked around the web for further details of the fence. I found none mentioning its alternative use, so rang Lee, who confessed that he had made it up entirely! Slightly miffed that I had literally dived straight into Lee's little joke, I almost immediately received a phone call from self-styled 'betting guru' Derek McGovern, formerly of the *Racing Post*, currently with the *Mirror*, telling me that he was about to write a review of my book, *The Magnificent Seven*, about Frankie Dettori's 1996 clean sweep of all the races at Ascot. He asked me one or two questions and then suddenly said, 'Can you name all seven of his winners?'

I got to five and went blank. McGovern was over the moon – 'you can't even remember them and you wrote a whole book about them. I'm putting that in my review' he laughed.

Oh well, it's a fair cop, I'd been done twice in a row – but can YOU name the seven?

446. STAMP OF GREATNESS

Aussie jockey legend Darby Munro received that rarest of accolades – his likeness on a postage stamp – in 1981 on the Australian 22 cent variety.

Mind you, the triple Melbourne Cup winner – 1934/44/46 – who was known as The Demon Darb – had to wait until 15 years after his death to get the honour, by which time he was beyond the reach of even a first class stamp.

447. STONED

Former sailor Dennis Collins was at Ascot races in 1832 when he spotted King William IV.

Collins was not the greatest fan of His Majesty and made that rather obvious by chucking a stone at the monarch. Mistake.

He was grabbed by racecourse security, or whatever passed for such a thing back then, charged with high treason, found guilty and sentenced to be 'hanged, decapitated and quartered'. Not much margin for error, there, then.

However, the King was unhappy with this punishment, clearly he didn't think this would cause Collins sufficient suffering, so he intervened and on the pretence that he was offering him a reprieve, declared that he would instead have him transported to Australia.

Don't forget, this was before barbies, Fosters and, just, the Ashes.

Oddly, Collins opted for this alternative but, had there been telephones, might well have rung home asking for the hanging, decapitating and quartering, once he set foot in Sydney and discovered they hadn't even got round to building the Opera House or Bridge yet.

448. IS THIS A RECORD? NO, IT'S A HORSE

Unless you know better, the career of South African horse, Darius, who finished racing at the age of 19 in 1929, having raced for 17 consecutive years in a total of 236 races, clocking up 42 wins, 38 seconds and 29 thirds, must be some kind of record.

Well, it may be a South African record, but in the early 1920s, US geldings George de Mar and Seth's Hope were said to have raced 333 and 327 times respectively, winning 60 and 62 of them.

449. TRAINING TIP

Here's a handy hint for any trainer trying to get into the mind of a wilful or stubborn racehorse – try hypnotising him.

In 1900, a Professor de Villiers appeared on stage at the Opera House in Port Elizabeth in his native South Africa, explaining how 'to control and make completely amenable any intractable horse by hypnotism.'

Details of the Prof's methods seem to be lost in time, but I'm sure Derren Brown or Paul McKenna may know the gist of the type of thing he would have been suggesting.

'Look into my eyes, you are getting coltish ...'

450. WORST TURNED OUT

When Maid of Honour won one of South Africa's most important races, the Metropolitan Handicap, in 1888, she was in no condition to have won any 'Best Turned Out' award, had there been any such thing in those days. Mr Hilton Barber's horse had apparently 'nearly hanged herself with her halter during the night' and 'went to post looking quite gruesome with her jaws terribly swollen and her left eye hanging right out of its socket.'

451. NAP OF THE DAY

When Napoleon Bonaparte was sent to be exiled on the island of St Helena in 1815 he moved into a house called Longwood.

Captain – later Admiral – Rous, who was later to become Chairman of the Jockey Club back in England later in the century, organised horse racing in the grounds of Longwood, with runners imported from South Africa's Cape Colony.

The racing continued there until Napoleon's death in 1821.

452. WORST RACE EVER?

Hereford's February Novice Selling Hurdle, run on the 29th of that month in 1992 has very strong claims to be considered the worst quality jump race ever.

The 2m3f event attracted 13 runners – none of whom had ever managed to finish in the first three of any race they had contested.

Nine of them failed to get round. Six were pulled up; two fell; one unseated rider.

The last of the four to finish, Northern Glint, was tailed off. The 3rd, a 50/1 shot, finished 'at one pace'; the runner-up, 20/1, found 'no extra on the flat' and the winner, Arr Eff Bee, whose form figures were PPPB, went off virtually unbacked at 50/1, ridden by Ian Lawrence, trained by Peter Smith, and took 5 minutes 12.4 seconds to complete the course – 29.8 seconds slower than the average time.

The horse attracted no bids after the race.

453. COMING TO A HEAD – NO MORE FOR OLIVIER

Disputes and disagreements between jockeys and trainers tend to be couched in diplomatic language – but not in early August 2006 when top French trainer Criquette Head-Maarek laid into Olivier Peslier after he rode her Quiet Royal into fifth place in Deauville's Prix Maurice de Gheest:

'He rode a stinker and I'm fed up. Quiet Royal should have won but my orders were simply not followed, as usual. The race was a disgrace.'

After the race all the horses owned by Alain and Gerard Wertheimer, which are partnered by Peslier, were removed from her stable – 'I don't want to work with Peslier any more. I phoned the owners and they decided to stay with their jockey and not me.'

It is to be hoped that the breakdown of relations between them does not result in the kind of confrontation which occurred on April 21, 1990 when Jenny Pitman was fined £200 by stewards at Ayr after striking jockey Jamie Osborne in the face after her horse Run To Form collided with the rails, and Jenny blamed Jamie who was partnering Dwadme.

454. ONLY HERE FOR THE EL GOLEA

One of the top horses in Australia during the mid 1930s, and early 1940s, El Golea was the unfortunate victim of a bizarre plot which saw a pair of villains breaking into the stables of 1940 Melbourne Cup favourite Beau Vite. They fired two gunshots at what they believed to be the fancied horse only to hit El Golea who nonetheless recovered to race again.

His turf record is now obscure but his popularity at the time led to his name entering the language as rhyming slang for beer.

455. THE ACCOMPLISHED JOCKEY – 1840 STYLE

In his seminal work, *History of the British Turf*, published in 1840, author J B Whyte attempted to list the 'most essential points necessary to form an accomplished jockey'

Size? 'The jockey should be rather under the middle size, say about five feet, five inches, and although light, should possess a compact, muscular and active frame. He should be, in fact, a pocket Hercules.'

Character? 'He should be of a shrewd and calculating disposition, and neglect no opportunity of improving his judgment by observation and practice in his profession. Above all, he must be a perfect master of his temper, accustomed to keep a constant check upon his tongue, possess much personal intrepidity, be honest to his employers, and of temperate habits.'

Mm – up-bringing? 'In order to obtain a good seat, hands, a knowledge of pace and confidence, it is absolutely requisite that he should have been reared, from his earliest years, in a racing stable, and been accustomed to ride constantly horses of all forms, shapes and tempers.'

Fitness? 'By constant exercise, and by the practice of athletic games, he should endeavour to acquire as much as possible that pliability about the arms, shoulders and back, which adds so much to his power and ease when in the saddle.'

Appearance ? 'He should habituate himself to be scrupulously attentive to cleanliness in his person, and to the neat fitting of his clothes, especially when in the appropriate costume of his calling.'

Anything else? 'The important item of economy – the practice of which will not only, by rendering him independent, place him beyond the temptation of bribery.'

Remind you of anyone, yet?

456. HOW THE ACCOMPLISHED JOCKEY CAN KEEP DOWN HIS NATURAL WEIGHT BY TRAINING

J B Whyte, having described the archetypal 'accomplished jockey' then proceeded to purvey the training schedule by which he could keep himself in peak condition:

'Strong walking exercises with abstemiousness at table should be preferred by the jockey to excessive use of medicine; being certainly not as injurious to his health.

'The sweaters or cloths to be worn by the jockey in his walking exercise must be regulated as to quantity, by the state of the weather, and the temperament of the wearer. The clothes generally used for this purpose consist of from four to six waistcoats, some of them with sleeves, two or three pairs of drawers, with a suit of loose common clothes over all. These drawers and waistcoats, we believe, can only be procured at Newmarket, and are made from a flannel which does not shrink, and which combines a pleasant softness with considerable strength.

'Duly equipped in this dress, the jockey starts early in the morning for his walk, having previously partaken of some slight refreshment. He commences at a moderate pace, which he increases as he proceeds, and having gone a distance of about four miles, he may indulge himself with a little rest in a convenient place, and at the same time partake of a little warm negus (sic), or cyder with some ginger grated in.

'Being refreshed, he starts to return home, and this time he should come at a good smart pace the whole way, so as to enter the house in a state of profuse perspiration, and having taken a cup of tea or some weak negus, he should repose for an hour or so on the bed, being well covered with blankets, and be careful not to take off the sweaters till the perspiration has somewhat subsided.

'He should then strip and place his feet in warm water, at the same time sponging his body all over previous to re-dressing; being careful to wear flannel next to his skin, and to clothe himself sufficiently warm; for, from the pores being open, he is in danger of catching severe colds, and the many complaints which too often take their rise from these causes, and from inattention to which caution, jockeys have, on more than one occasion, lost their lives.

'By strictly pursuing this system, a man may reduce himself from twelve to sixteen pounds in a fortnight.'

457. BREAK A LEG

The oft-used phrase 'break a leg' to signify wishing someone good luck, would have rung hollow to northern-based jockey Benjamin Smith who was kicked on the leg by opponent, Brilliante, prior to the start of a race at York in August, 1786 in which he partnered the grey, Ironsides for Lord Archibald Hamilton.

Smith rode Ironsides to victory in the four mile race but almost fainted in the saddle afterwards and had to be carried to the scales, where medical assistance was called, revealing that he had ridden with a broken leg.

458. A TOUGH TUSK

Stewards of the Western Australian Turf Club had little alternative but to ban Perth trainer George Way for 20 years in 1987 when he was found guilty of doping two of his horses, Brash Son and Hollydoll Girl – the latter, embarrassingly owned by WATC chairman, John Roberts – with 'elephant juice' – nickname of the drug etorphine, said to be able to tranquillise even that animal.

459. THE RACECOURSE SACRIFICED BY HITLER

When Germany was planning a spectacular stadium in which to stage the 1936 Olympics, they began redeveloping an existing one ten miles from the centre of Berlin.

Hitler visited the site to check on the progress of the work and was told that it was proving difficult to expand the stadium to incorporate thousands more seats required because the Berlin Horseracing Association were refusing to permit works which would impact on the adjacent Grunewald racecourse.

According to writer Guy Walters' book, *Berlin Games*, Hitler demanded to know, 'Is the racecourse necessary?'

Who was likely to stand up and say that it was? No one, of course. Berlin did boast two other tracks, both in a better financial condition than Grunewald.

'The stadium must be demolished. A new one must be built in its place, capable of seating 100,000 people'.

That was the death-warrant for Grunewald racecourse which, having hosted Germany's prestigious 12f Grosser Preis Von Berlin between 1909-33, duly disappeared under the new stadium buildings.

460. BANKS OF SCOTLAND

Flamboyant bookie John Banks, who died aged 68 in 2003, was credited with the description of betting shops – which opened in Britain in May 1961 – as 'a licence to print money'.

Glaswegian Banks (born John Boyle in August 1934) was the Barry Dennis of his day, a larger than life, widely recognised character who transcended his chosen profession. He wore a huge, black fedora hat, drove a yellow Rolls Royce and had an aeroplane painted in his racing colours of purple-white cap with purple spots.

After a row with Ladbrokes boss Cyril Stein, Banks was prevented by the authorities from naming one of his horses 'Greenwich Mean Stein' and had to settle for the sarcastic Adorable Cyril.

His first betting shop was opened near Hampden Park and he expanded to a 34 strong chain before selling out to Mecca.

In 1978 Banks' career suffered a huge setback when one of his horses, Stopped, favourite for the Imperial Cup at Sandown, finished only third after being hampered in running. Jockey, John Francome, with whom Banks had become friendly, was cautioned by the stewards for riding an 'ill-judged' race.

A Jockey Club inquiry later found both Banks and Francome guilty of 'conduct likely to cause serious damage to the interests of horseracing' although no 'stopping' of horses was alleged. Banks was warned off of racecourses for three years and fined £2,500 while Francome was fined £750 and suspended for the remainder of the season – 'much more than I had bargained for.'

Francome persistently denied any wrong-doing and in his 1985 autobiography, *Born Lucky*, commented, 'Now that I have retired I am looking forward to renewing my friendship with him (Banks).'

461. JOCKEY ON FIRE

Irish jump jockey Paul Carberry was given a two month jail sentence by District Court Judge Patrick Brady after being found guilty of a breach of the peace on an Aer Lingus flight from Malaga to Dublin in October, 2005.

Carberry, for reasons best known to himself, set fire to a newspaper whilst returning from a break with friends. He was not even under the influence of alcohol at the time but protested that it had been 'a pure accident with no harm to anyone ever intended.'

*Jump Jockey Timmy Murphy was sentenced to six months jail in 2002 after drunken antics on board a flight from Tokyo to London earlier that year. He no longer drinks but said in his autobiography, *Riding The Storm*, 'The demons are still there, on my back, on my shoulder, in my saddlebag.'

462. ECLIPSED

Racing was interrupted for an hour at the appropriately named Moonee Valley track in Australia on October 23, 1976 – in order to allow an eclipse of the sun to take place.

463. NO INQUIRY NECESSARY

Stewards can deliberate at length over controversial incidents during races before deciding how to dispense justice.

There was a time when such decisions were taken and implemented literally on the hoof. Sixteen went to post for the 1818 Derby in which Prince Paul was 11/5 favourite but became more and more unsettled during the ten false starts before they finally got underway in a cloud of dust kicked up on the hard going.

As the runners came to the business end of the race with Prince Paul going on only to be challenged and passed by 7/2 winner Sam and runner-up Raby, a 'dandy', 'either through ignorance or want of accomplishment in the equestrian art' according to a contemporary report, 'got directly in the way of the horses as they were stretching away neck and neck in order to reach the goal first for this important prize, by which one of the horses was entirely thrown out of the race, and many of the others much jostled'.

The dandy, it appears, decided to make himself scarce and, digging his spurs into his mount, made a dash for it.

Immediately, though , 'many of those present, including the deputy stewards and some others, gave immediate chace (sic) and overtaking him, administered as he fled a most outrageous horsewhipping, which was not desisted from till he was clear of the course.'

Now, that's what I call a Stewards Inquiry!

464. BROLLY TOUGH

The 1921 Grand National was a quite extraordinary affair in which only one horse, the winner, 100/9 shot, Shaun Spadah, and his jockey Fred Brychan Rees, got round unscathed.

The race contained amongst its competitors a quite extraordinary cast list of characters.

Of the 35 who set out, only four eventually finished. 9/1 favourite, The Bore, fell at the last but one fence, breaking jockey Harry Brown's collar bone in the process. Undaunted, Brown remounted and, with his arm swinging uselessly at his side, somehow got over the last to finish a remote second.

Third place went to All White, who was remounted by rider R Chadwick, having come down once. This was an improvement on his fate the previous year when he had failed to finish having fallen, and somewhat more straightforward than 1919's eventful attempt – when he finished 5th, partnered by a Frenchman, T Williams, the only jockey available who could do 9st 10lbs, when usual rider Chadwick had been injured. Williams and All White had been going easily on the second circuit, only to be pulled over to permit his jockey to lean over to be violently sick. A pre-race snack of sea-food had come back to haunt him.

All White was also owned by Colonel William Hall-Walker, a man who when breeding, would match his mares and stallions according to their astrological zodiac signs.

Having finished 4th, after his horse, Turkey Buzzard, had fallen on three occasions, rider Captain O H 'Tuppy' Bennett (who would win the race on Sergeant Murphy in 1923, only to be killed on December 27 of that year after falling from Ardeen at Wolverhampton in an incident which would lead to the introduction of compulsory crash helmets) sought out owner Mrs Hollins, looking for congratulations. She chased him around the paddock, aiming blows at him with her umbrella for daring to submit her beloved horse to such stresses and strains.

It was a good job she was not aware that American jockey, Morgan de Witt Blair, (apparently known as 'Bam' after his habit of uttering that exclamation when injecting himself with who knew what, prior to races) desperately trying to win a substantial wager by getting his own veteran and complete no-hoper, 13-year-old Bonnie Charlie round, had remounted after no fewer than four separate falls. The pairing didn't complete, but in 1925 he tried again – this time still smarting from a fresh, raw scar from an appendix operation carried out just two weeks previously, and having had to lose 18lbs in the previous 48 hours to do the weight of 10 stone to partner 40/1 chance Jack Horner – on which he managed to finish in 7th place.

465. BARBOUROUS

Owner/trainer/rider Frank Barbour, whose Koko won the 1926 Cheltenham Gold Cup, had replicas of several well known fences – including some of Aintree's – laid out at his County Meath stables.

He once rode in a Members Race, took a tumble, got up, left the course, hitched a lift to Dublin, and sailed for America – still clad in his riding gear.

466. FIFTEEN YEARS AND A LENGTH IN IT AFTER 14 MILES

'They write from Lincoln,' declared the *Westminster Journal* of June 23, 1744, 'that on Thursday seven night, there was a very extraordinary horse race on the course of that City, between a six year old horse belonging to Southcote Parker, of Bliber, in that county, Esq., and one aged twenty one years belonging to Gilbert Colecut, of Lincoln, Esq.; they ran 14 miles round the said course, and performed it in 39 minutes, for 100 guineas, which were won by the former by only a horse's length. There were great wagers laid, and the greatest concourse of people ever seen there on such an occasion.'

467. TAILED OFF

When Arthur Yates, who was at his peak as a jockey in the 1870s performed a remarkable recovery when falling at Croydon's water jump only to grab his mount's tail and leap back into the saddle over its quarters, before riding on to victory, one of the popular prints of the day immortalised him in verse:

'In racing reports it is oft-times said,

A jockey has cleverly won by a head

But Yates has performed when all other arts fail,

A more wonderful feat, for he won by a tail.'

Yates later trained at Bishop's Sutton, Alresford in Hampshire where the inmates worked alongside a menagerie of rare birds, deer and zebra.

468. WATER JUMPER

The 1884 Grand National winner Voluptuary never jumped a fence in public before that race, and never jumped another fence on a racecourse afterwards – but he did so nightly at a theatre in Drury Lane where he leaped a water jump on stage in the Grand National scene incorporated in the play, The Prodigal Daughter. His stage jockey, Len Boyne, would earn five shillings bonus if he fell off during the performance.

469. INTENT ON THE TOTE

When the Tote operated for the first time, at Carlisle and Newmarket on July 2, 1929, the staff were housed in tents. Although no one cut the ropes, as had been feared, the telephone wires from the Newmarket set-up were sabotaged.

470. DIVINE SIGNIFICANCE

Love Divine won the Oaks at Epsom in the year 2000 – 22 punters who bet on the contest, placed 63 bets between them via a new operation called Betfair which was making a market on a race for the first time.

471. WHAT A COCK-UP

'Starter cocked it up – Aintree cocked it up – Jockey Club cocked it up' That was the verdict of *The Sun* on the day in 1993 when what national heroine Jenny Pitman ('the only reason she banks with Lloyds is because of the black horse on their logo' according to writer Sue Mott) dubbed a piece of 'knicker elastic' malfunctioned, leaving some of the Grand National runners heading off round the course believing that they were really racing, despite a surreal racecourse announcement declaring, 'This race is not actually taking place', and many others milling about waiting for a recall which never came.

Starter Keith Brown was dubbed 'Captain Cock Up' for his mishandling of the affair, despite pleading, 'It was bound to happen some time and it just happened that I had to be in charge at the time'.

Jenny Pitman's Esha Ness 'won' the non race. She had tried to stop it half way through, charging into the weighing room to demand, 'You must stop this race. What are you doing? My bloody horse has already gone one circuit. I don't want to win the National like this.' She didn't.

Tearful 'winning' jockey John White explained why he had raced all the way – 'I could see there were only a few horses round, but I thought the others had fallen or something.'

No one was paid out by bookies – to the mild annoyance of punter Alan Ruddock, whose tricast on Esha Ness, Cahervillahow and Romany King to finish in that order might otherwise have made him £3,000 richer. Judy Halling wasn't overjoyed, either. She had had a premonition that something might go wrong and went in to see her local bookie in Tring, Richard Halling, to ask for a bet to that effect. 'I wouldn't rob you of your money, love,' he told her kindly.

The race was declared void, to Mrs P's rage. Mr Pitman – jockey turned TV pundit, Richard, reportedly called it 'the worst thing to happen in the sport since the suffragette

Emily Davison was killed throwing herself in front of the King's horse, Aboyeur in the 1907 Derby' (close enough – it was 1913, the King's colt was Anmer, and Aboyeur the 100/1 winner) even though no one actually died. Trainer Charlie Brooks put it into perspective, 'It wasn't a disaster. Two young boys getting killed in Warrington was a disaster.'

A 34 page report was produced by a subsequent inquiry but all it really came up with was the suggestion of a second recall man further down the course.

To add insult to injury, they wouldn't even let Jenny Pitman have the 'Grand National Winner' horse blanket.

472. NOT A LEG TO STAND ON

Jockey Levi Barlingume fell and broke his leg during a race at Stafford, Kansas in a 1932 meeting. Nothing unusual about that, except that he was 80 years old at the time...three years younger than Harry Beasley whose final mount, Mollie, was unplaced at Baldoyle, Dublin in June 1935, but 71 years older than the age at which Aussie, Frank Wootton rode his first winner in South Africa.

473. FRANKLY STRANGE YEAR

Dettori turned up for racing at Newmarket after Italy won the 2006 World Cup, with that country's flag painted on his cheeks ... days later he reported for duty almost bald – wife Catherine had slipped with the equipment whilst attempting to give him a DIY haircut, necessitating a drastic scalping all over ... Dettori finished 4th with 8.2% of the votes in a June 2006 vote to find Britain's best-dressed celebrity dad ... later in the year he appeared in a TV advertisement for Tesco supermarkets ten years on from his September 1996 'Magnificent Seven' – Frankie scored a 'famous five' from seven rides at Goodwood on June 10, a 779/1 accumulator ... a number of Frankie's favourite racing trophies and his MBE were stolen in an August burglary at his home ... he acted as an interpreter for non English speaking Italian jockey Edmondo Botti at a York stewards inquiry in August..in the same month he became a DJ at York's popular Gallery nightclub ... September saw Frankie ready to mount up to partner Mick Channon's So Sweet at the Curragh when he was told by officials that he could not ride – wife Catherine owned a half share of another runner in the race, St Anna Aresi – which put Frankie out because of the Irish Turf Club rule which states jockeys cannot have a potential conflict of interest – a rule introduced some three years previously, of which official Cliff Noone commented, 'Frankie should have known – it was brought in on the jockeys' insistence'... September 28, 2006, was the tenth anniversary of the famous Magnificent Seven day when he rode all seven winners at Ascot. Frankie recalled to Sue Mott in the *Daily Telegraph* how that night after he changed racing history, 'Catherine (his wife) had me sucked into going to one of her ex-boyfriends' parties. I didn't want to go and we ended up on the greatest day of my career going to bed, not talking and sleeping back to back' ... a few days earlier he was engulfed in controversy when he cried 'foul play' after claiming his mount Librettist, 6th in the Queen Elizabeth Stakes at Ascot, was 'deliberately' run wide by Coolmore second string jockey Seamus Heffernan as their first string, George Washington went on to win. Aidan O'Brien hit back that Dettori 'threw the toys out of the pram like a spoilt child'. Heffernan was suspended for 14 days.

474. THAT REALLY TAKES THE BISCUIT

Celebrated US horse Seabiscuit, subject of an award winning book by Laura Hillenbrand which landed the William Hill Sports Book of the Year, and was subsequently made into an Oscar-nominated movie, took part in probably the roughest match race ever staged in the States.

In August 1938 Seabiscuit, hailed as the American champion, took on South American star Ligaroti, owned by superstar crooner, Bing Crosby – who was also one of the founders of Del Mar racecourse in Southern California, where the $25,000 winner-take-all race was run.

It took place on August 12, over nine furlongs, with Seabiscuit carrying 130lbs and Ligaroti 115.

Public interest in the event was extraordinarily high and 20,000 fans turned out to see the race which had been hyped up by the media.

George Woolf rode Seabiscuit who was racing on the rail side, allowing his opponent, partnered by Noel Richardson, to poach a narrow lead for the first half mile. 'Down the backstretch, Seabiscuit managed to gain a slight lead, but they entered the stretch almost nose and nose' reported writer Robert F Kelley in his *'Racing In America 1937-59'* – 'All down the stretch, with the crowd roaring, they fought each other, and Ligaroti, which had the reputation of bearing in, was laying over on Seabiscuit. But George Woolf, instead of taking back, lashed at Noel Richardson, and they were literally locked together as they crossed the finish line.'

Seabiscuit won by a nose, taking four seconds off the track record and the stewards considered their options before announcing that the result would stand.

However, both jockeys were suspended for foul riding – on the home stretch, in an illegal attempt to hinder Seabiscuit, Richardson had grabbed at Woolf's saddle cloth and then his bridle-rein, while in retaliation Woolf used his whip on Richardson.

Seabiscuit secured fame and fortune and is remembered to this day, while Ligaroti went to stud, was a failure, and collapsed and died while covering a mare – whose foal, a colt, was named Last Bang!

Almost 59 years to the day at Del Mar on August 3, 1997, echoes of the jockey joust were stirred as Corey Nakatani hit apprentice jockey Ryan Barber, knocking him from his mount, leading to Nakatani's suspension.

475. GETTING UNDER THE SKIN

Equine artist George Stubbs, perhaps the greatest of all painters of thoroughbreds, who died aged 81 in 1806, studied horse cadavers to acquire his unprecedented knowledge of the interior workings of the animals.

Explained writer Jane Clinton, 'He would suspend the huge carcasses from the ceiling to get the most natural stance of a horse he could before bleeding the horse by the jugular vein and injecting them with liquefied tallow or wax.'

Stubbs, who painted the early champion racehorse, Eclipse, would remove muscle layer by layer, making drawings as he went.

His best known work is the huge 1762 painting of the prancing horse, Whistlejacket.

476. JAZZY CELEBRATION

'I remember raiding the mini bar in my room, popping the cork on a half bottle of champagne, and then sitting in the Jacuzzi for two hours with my necklace on.'

But Emily Jones' delight at winning the Ladies Diamond race at Ascot in 2000 didn't last long. The Welsh lass flogged the De Beers diamond necklace she won after riding Peter's Imp to victory: 'An owner gave me £5,000 for it, and at the time it was very welcome because it helped me pay a few big bills and got the bank manager off my back.'

But Emily, then 28, regretted the sale for ever more and in July 2006 confessed to the *Daily Telegraph's* Jim McGrath that if she was ever fortunate enough to win the race and necklace again 'I think I'll call it a day. I'll probably retire from riding on the spot. And I'd keep the diamond this time – even if they came to evict me.'

477. SHERGAR SHAMBLES?

The Sun of March 28, 1991 ran as its front page lead story the exclusive, stunning, news that Derby winning equine superstar, Shergar, kidnapped after his record breaking 1981 triumph in the world's greatest flat race and subsequently the subject of a huge man-, sorry, horse-hunt – had been found alive.

Alive, and grazing in a field in Jersey in the Channel Islands.

Needless to say, he wasn't, and the story, suggesting that a group of bounty hunters were seeking a third of a million pounds finder's fee for revealing the whereabouts of the horse to insurance chiefs, was soon shown to be a non-runner, just like the 1989 *Psychic News* 'scoop' which revealed Shergar to be 'alive and well and has been on English soil.'

On a more serious note, Irish police, who frequently receive reports that horses' remains have been discovered and have yet to close the Shergar case, are said to believe that his remains were buried in Leitrim and the horse's groom, Jim Fitzgerald says, 'A horse like Shergar would usually have a grave with a plaque but he's lying in some field somewhere, and no one knows where he is.'

478. LUCKY TOSSER

Motormouth bookie Barry Dennis was a little surprised when a punter at Windsor in July, 2006, asked him which horse he should back.

The man was 'a sharp suited geezer' who had just put £1,000 on a 9/4 favourite and was collecting his returns of £3,250 when he asked Dennis, known for tipping losers in his 'Bismarck' slot on Channel 4's Morning Line programme, 'Which should I back, Barry, number five, or the two horse?'.

Already a little disgruntled at being over two grand down to the man, Dairy explained that 'he picked the horses, I grudgingly paid him out if he won'.

The man leaned over and picked up a £1 coin from Dennis's tray and said: 'Heads, it's number five; tails, number two.'

Heads won – and he backed the 2/1 favourite, putting his whole £3,250 on the runner – which duly won

When the punter came back he took £9,000 and handed back the extra £750 for Dennis to spend on 'a drink'.

Said the bookie, 'What a lucky tosser.'

479. KEEP ON IN RUNNING

Sir Peter O'Sullevan, already informing the nation on radio and TV, was invited to become the first racecourse commentator by explaining proceedings and calling the runners over the public address system at Goodwood in 1954 – a first for the track, and for Britain   'Until then, there was no commentary on British racecourses of any sort.' And O'Sullevan revealed why he was not best pleased by the innovation, introduced by clerk of the course, Ralph Hubbard. 'It was regarded by some as being an absurd intrusion, and by others – myself among them – as an intrusion on the fact one could bet in running. I was one of only a handful who knew what was going on.'

480. REMIND ME, JUST WHO
IS ON STRIKE HERE?

A July, 1981 meeting at Down Royal started innocuously enough with the Gate Handicap Hurdle in which 20/1 shot Adirondack trained by Frank Stewart and owned by Cahil Fergus, beat the heavily backed 6/4 favourite Tilbury, who had been gambled down from 5/1, trained by Peter Russell, and owned by, er, Cahil Fergus.

Punters were far from happy as the gambled on good thing had been turned over by his owner's supposed second string. Winning jockey Gerry McEnhill then somehow managed to forget to weigh in.

The stewards duly held an inquiry, before relegating Adirondack to last place and awarded first place to the favourite, Tilbury.

Now the bookies were far from happy, suspecting that McEnhill's amnesia might have a suspicious cause. So unhappy were the layers that they declared they would not pay out. They stormed into the secretary's office to emphasise their annoyance.

After a period of wrangling the bookies were persuaded to pay up. But their price for so doing was to announce that they were withdrawing their services for the remainder of the afternoon.

Now the racegoers got nasty. With no tote system in operation they now had no way of gambling on the remainder of the races. Once again the secretary's office was inundated, this time by disgruntled spectators and wannabe punters demanding their admission money back.

They were refused a refund – so decided that in that case there would be no more racing. Fifty of them charged on to the track, refusing to move and delaying the start of the next race. Police arrived and dispersed the mutinous crowd.

So, racing could resume? Well, not exactly. Now the chief sponsor of the NEXT day's card, Barney Eastwood, a bookmaker, withdrew his financial support – while his colleagues escalated their strike by insisting they would not be bet on the next day, either.

The meeting was abandoned.

481. BREAST OF LUCK

When 33-year-old Hull woman Julie Bovill won £500 from a day at Wetherby races in 1998 she had the front to spend the money on having her breasts enlarged from 34A to 34DD.

482. MARK MY WORDS!

The 1954 7/1 Ebor winner was By Thunder! One of very few horses whose names have boasted an exclamation mark. The only other one I have located is Wake Up!

483. KEEPING UP APPEARANCES

Maintaining standards earned a rider in the 1939 Essex Union point-to-point meeting the approval of traditionalists, but did little for his chances of winning the race he was contesting, as the *Horse and Hound* report indicated – 'In the Members' Heavyweight event the Hon Secretary Major V S Laurie, was, as usual, the only rider correctly dressed in 'hunting' costume, his top hat, however, being a bit of a liability in the high wind.'

The galloping Major finished last of four.

484. NO GOOD?

Owner Mr T Tracton must have caused some confusion in 1897/8 when he was running his horses No a winner at Hexham – and the gelding Yes ... these were far from the shortest named horses to grace a racecourse. AZ was running in Australia at the turn of the 19th/20th centuries – Oh won the Lincoln in season 1906/7. 'He' lifted the 1918 Coronation Cup ... A20 won the 1958 Queen Mary Stakes ... H20 was a 1928 winner while C.C. was around the circuit at the same time ... WA Stephenson's first winner, in 1946, was named T.O.D. ... E.S.B won the 1956 Grand National ... while US won in

Belgium in 1927... Boo was a 50/1 third in the 2006 John Smiths Magnet Cup at York. However, you'll have to search hard to find a shorter named runner than the Argentinian born colt racing in 1930 under the name: I.

485. HAND IT TO THE LAGS

What would be the reaction if Ascot or Newmarket races decided to donate a proportion of their income to the prison service? Unlikely, I grant you, but if they ever decided to take such action they could justify it by pointing to a precedent set by a northern racecourse in 1775 when, reported the *Newcastle Journal*, 'the Stewards of Morpeth Races, desirous that all ranks of people might partake of the general satisfaction, so apparent at the meeting, humanely ordered five pounds of the subscription money to be distributed amongst the prisoners in the jail, an example worthy of imitation.'

486. YEAR WE GO

Yearling races first took place at Newmarket's Houghton meeting in 1791. They struggled for popularity and almost died out, but in 1821 a race for yearlings was introduced at Middleham with the winner of that event carrying 8st 4lbs. Horses then took their ages from May 1, and the winner, Bedlamite was nearly two. In 1856 yearling racing was again revived, at Shrewsbury in November, run over a two furlong course. In 1859, a year after all horse's birthdays were stipulated to be on January 1, however, the Jockey Club banned the practice.

487. SOUNDS GOOD TO ME

It is to be wondered whether the good folk of Airdrie would, today, react in the same way as their forbears of almost 150 years ago did if it were decided to stage a local race meeting in the town. For on August 3, 1861, in a story lamenting the fact that the annual race fixture was imminent, the *Aurdrie & Coatbridge Advertiser* called for the banning of the event as it brought only 'fast youths, fancy men, gamblers, blacklegs and women of easy virtue' to the area. Yes, and the problem was …?

488. LADIES FIRST

The 1927 Medway Challenge Cup, run over one and a quarter miles at Hawick in Scotland's St Leonard's racecourse, was notable for the victory of Rufus – not only because the horse had already finished second that afternoon when odds-on favourite for the 6½ furlong Vertish Stakes – but because in the second race he was ridden by owner Miss Marjorie Haddon. It was extremely rare for a woman to ride in, let alone win races. She was the first female ever to ride there, and the *Newcastle Journal* reported, 'Miss Haddon rode Rufus herself and was received with a great outburst of cheering when she returned to weigh in.' Rufus returned even money.

However, ladies were racing much earlier than this, as an edition of the *Newcastle Courant* of August 28, 1725 reveals, advertising that 'on Tuesday the 14th, the Ladies Plate of £15 value, by any horse. WOMEN to be the riders, each to pay one guinea entrance, three heats, and twice about the common for a heat'. Sadly, there is no record of the outcome of the race.

489. WE ARE SAILING

A unique race took place at Hartlepool races in September 1857 when for the only time recorded in the annals of the turf, a race called The Mariners' Stakes took place, with the stipulation 'to be ridden by captains of vessels'. Three skippers floated along, with Captain Thomson sailing home to collect the £10 prize money, on Phoenix, which duly sunk its two opponents, partnered by captains Ling and Parsell.

490. RACING IN SACKS FOR GARTERS

The meeting advertised in a handbill headed Guisborough Races, 1784, described what racegoers might enjoy on the day – 'A match between Sir Wm Foulis's colt Turkey Nab and Mr Chaloner's colt Sturdy. The last comer in to win. Changes of jockeys, crossing, jostling and kicking.

A Purse of Silver to be run for by men in sacks. Crossing and jostling. Ladies' Plate. A shift to be run for by ladies. No lady to enter who has more than one shift. A pair of cotton stockings for the second and a pair of garters for the third. After the races a soap-tail'd pig will be turn'd out, and whosoever throws him over his shoulder by the tail is to have him for his own property' Certainly beats bouncy castles and hog-roasts!

491. DISTEMPER DISASTER

'Direful distemper attending the horned cattle' was the reason given for the abandonment of racing in the north of England in 1744 at tracks including Durham, Newcastle, Stockton, Morpeth, Carlisle, Chester-le-Street and Bishop Auckland, in what sounds like an early variant of foot-and-mouth disease which would strike the sport hard in the 20th century – costing 110 fixtures in all during the winter of 1967/8.

It returned in 2001 when it cost Istabraq the chance of a fourth consecutive Champion Hurdle victory as the whole of the Cheltenham Festival was scrapped as part of a total of over 120 racing days to fall victim to the outbreak.

492. LAST RITES

When trainer and jockey Adam Scott, whose Jazz Band won the 1924 Northumberland Plate died in a fall from his own horse Command in a chase at Kelso in March, 1925, he was buried in his racing colours of light blue and maroon cap ... an argument between Northumbrian sporting rake William 'Bowrie' Charlton and Henry Widdrington of nearby Buteland, at Bellingham races on February 21, 1709, resulted in a duel, fought with swords, at the end of which, 'Bowrie sorrowfully threw his cloak as a pall over the man he had slain' … on December 4, 1636 at Durham races, 'John Trollop the younger, of Thornley in a sudden quarrel, fought with William Selby of Newcastle and slew him on the spot' … jockey George Herring, who rode Hollandaise to win the first St Leger, met his end at Hull races on July 27, 1796 when, despite being thrown twice by a mare called Gipsy, he insisted on getting back on, only to be unseated again and killed as a result.

493. YE OLDE STEWARDES ENQUIRIE

Aberdeen, where horse racing had been taking place on the seashore since 1661, was the scene of an eventful contest in 1787, according to the *Aberdeen Gazette*, which recorded that 'On Thursday last the Magistrates fined two young gentlemen of fortune and rank in 10 guineas each, for profanation of Sunday by riding a race for a bet on the sands, and afterwards galloping on the streets in a manner which endangered the lives of some of the citizens.'

494. ONLY ONE HUNDRED AND NINETEEN TO JUMP

Chasers of today don't realise how cushy they have it. When steeplechasing was in its infancy a testing course really meant just that – witness this account of a race from April 23, 1821, run over ten miles and featuring 120 jumps.

'A steeple race for 100gs, between a mare belonging to T Grant esq, rode by Mr Thos Clitherow, and a mare of Mr Stevenson's, rode by Mr Cartwright, was run from Sturton Church, near Horncastle, to Wickerby Church, a distance of 10 miles, over a very heavy country, with upwards of 120 leaps. After a well contested race, which was run in 45 minutes, Mr Stevenson's mare won by about half a minute.'

At this stage races of this type were commonly run between two churches and became known as 'steeple-races'.

495. RACING TO THE BALLOT BOX

In 1840, racing decided the outcome of an election when, after the Liberal council running the city/town of Lancaster passed a motion to abolish the local race meeting, electors rose up and voted the legislators out of office.

Lancaster's first meeting had taken place in 1698, but despite the vote in its favour it did not survive beyond 1857.

496. HAT'S UNLUCKY

George Stevens' record of riding Grand National winners is unsurpassed – you'd have to take your hat off to a man who won the race five times – on Freetrader in 1856; Emblem in 1863; on Emblematic in 1864 and then twice on The Colonel in 1869 and 70.So, maybe the Cheltenham-born ace was reliving one of these occasions in his mind's eye in June 1871 as he hacked down Cheltenham's Cleeve Hill on a placid cob.

Perhaps he was visualising the hats being hurled triumphantly skywards by his delighted backers, as he headed towards the post on yet another National winner – just as a rogue gust of wind blew his own hat off, causing his mount to shy and whip round, hurling Stevens off his back and into a violent collision with a rock.

Stevens came off worst and died from his injuries.

497. PIG IGNORANT

In 2004, ace marathon runner Huw Lobb collected £25,000 from the sponsor when he became the first two legged competitor to out-run the first horse and rider home in the gruelling 22 mile William Hill Man versus Horse Marathon, held in Mid Wales.

But almost 200 years earlier, the first – and, as yet only, recorded occasion on which a pig outran a thoroughbred in a race was taking place.

In 1816 a wager was made by the Marquess of Queensbury and a farmer on whose land the Dumfries racecourse in Scotland was situated. The farmer bet he could train a pig to outrun a racehorse.

The bet was struck and the pig put into training at Tinwald Downs Farm. On a daily basis the farmer cum pig trainer would take the porker the three quarters of a mile along the unfenced farm road which was to be the 'racecourse', to Houston Cottage, where the winning post was to be – and where the pig would be fed with his favourite food.

This happened for some weeks, at the end of which the pig was fully fit and well aware of what awaited him at the end of the course.

Sure enough, declared contemporary reports, 'On the day of the race it (the pig) got a flying start and beat the racehorse.'

Recording the event, racing historian John Fairfax-Blakeborough declared 'So far as I know this is the only instance on record of a contest between a pig and a Thoroughbred.'

And perhaps there have been similarly few occasions on which a racing greyhound has taken on a Thoroughbred. It happened in October 1986 at Copenhagen's Klampenborg when five-year-old sprinter Miami Prince lined up against Danish Greyhound Derby winner Irish Jackpot for a 450 metre contest won by a diminishing 8 lengths by the dog.

In December 1800 at Doncaster 'a mare was started, and after she had gone a distance of about a mile, a greyhound bitch was let loose from the side of the course, and ran with her nearly head to head to the distance post where five to four was laid on the greyhound; at the stand it was even betting, but the mare eventually won by little more than a head,' reported a contemporary account.

498. JACK IT IN

75 year old Jack Lee's luck seemed to be in at long last as his Scoop 6 selections and accumulator bet placed on Saturday, October 30, 2004 all won to set him up with a total payout of £957,714 for less than three quid stake money.

But one of his winners, Babodana at Newmarket, was disqualified and placed second. Jack's virtual million was wiped out completely as a result.

The philosophical Geordie, who had been betting for 55 years without a big win, commented: 'That's gambling for you.'

As a result of that disqualification the Scoop 6 pool was carried over and next week Manchester punter Stuart Bolland cashed in on Jack's misfortune by winning the enhanced Scoop6 worth £1,132,657.

Bolland had heard of Jack's misfortune, though, and announced that he would hand over £15,000 to the Newcastle man at a presentation on Wednesday, November 18.

On Tuesday, November 17, Jack Lee died.

499. GHOST OF A CHANCE

1876 Derby winner Kisber is still in action over 130 years after his big race triumph. For the 4/1 Classic winner was later exported to Germany where he was stabled at Parhassy Castle, dying there at the age of 18 – and loving the place so much that he haunted it forever more and has frequently been seen, partnered by a jockey clad in his Derby winning colours of crimson, emerald and white, hurtling along, flat out, presumably intent on recreating his piece of equine history ... Frankie Dettori's Stetchworth home is said to be haunted by a ghost called the 'Blue Lady' ... early champion jockey Fred Archer's ghost haunts Newmarket Heath, and as recently as 1993 his spirit was reportedly present when a séance was held at his former Pegasus Stables by stable lads ... six time Queen Alexandra Stakes winner at Ascot in the 1920s, Brown Jack has been seen galloping across the nearby Mill Ride Golf Club ... when racing was scheduled for Macao in 1828 local magistrates vetoed the plan for fear that it would interfere with Chinese burials at local tombs..readers of downmarket tabloid *The Sport* have been offered tips from beyond the grave, courtesy of a deceased jockey ... top Aussie jockey Jimmy Duncan ignored the spooky warning from his father in 1946 that he had dreamed of his death in a particular race. Duncan rode anyway and was thrown and killed ... in 1996 Epsom racecourse's course sales manager, Marilyn Watkinson was haunted by a 'lady in black' in 'the 1914 building which used to be a hospital during the 2nd World War. I really was rather scared'.

500. COCK-UPS

Owners of racehorse turned stallion, Bonfield, sued a veterinary practice for $A1m in 1987 when treatment for an injured mouth resulted in an adverse SIDE EFFECT which left the horse with an 'idiosyncratic reaction' – so idiosyncratic that it caused the horse's penis to remain erect for 30 days.

Eventually the owners withdrew the complaint – obviously believing that, unlike the horse, they couldn't make it stand up in court.

STRANGE RACING NUMBERS

- **007** number worn on training saddlecloths of all New York trainer Harold James Bond's string.

- **4** furlong races were run under Jockey Club Rules until May 27, 1912.

- **7** letters in Lady Beaverbrook's horse's names, amongst them Bustino, Relkino, Niniski, Boldboy.

- **9** screws and the plate which held jockey turned trainer Jonjo O'Neill's right leg together after a fearsome fall are on display at Cheltenham's NH Hall of Fame.

- **13** of July, 1951 was when England's first evening meeting was staged at now defunct Manchester.

- **17** Group race winners – sent out at odds of 20/1 or bigger since the pattern was established by Clive Brittain – including Terrimon, 500/1 Derby runner up in 1989.

- **23** victories in one season – a record for Fisherman in 1856.

- **24** per cent of races in the UK were matches in 1807 – down to 7% by 1843.

- **30** *Tons A Day* was the title of Bill Veek's, operator of Suffolk Downs in Bostons' book which referred to the amount of manure/straw which had to be cleared from the track stables each day.

- **51** years over which permit trainer William Francis tried unsuccessfully to win his own point-to-point Members' Race.

- **54** pounds – the weight of jockey George Fordham when he rode in the 1852 Cambridgeshire.

- **58** ran in Britain's biggest ever field, the 1948 Lincoln won by Commisar.

- **59** the average number of thoroughbreds racing in France between 1833 and 1840.

- **60** at least – the age of John Forth, oldest Derby winning jockey, when he rode Frederick in 1829

- **79** wins in 176 races was the record of Catherina, foaled in 1830, who raced from 1832-41.

- **103** races without a single win – but Quixall Crossett did have his own fan club by the time he retired in 2001.

- **187**: number of Japanese media representatives officially accredited to cover their national hero Deep Impact's 2006 Arc de Triomphe bid.

- **201** 'I always thought there were 200 ways you could lose a racehorse. This was 201' said owner Virginia Kraft Payson in 1990 when her Uptown Swell drowned whilst swimming after being stung by a bee.

- **234**: record number of mares covered by Spread Eagle (1795 Derby winner) in 1801.

- **1,022** thoroughbred foals were born in the UK in 1999 – of which only 347 were ever entered for a race.

- **1,085**: the record number of losing rides by a jockey in one season, held by Frankie Dettori in 1994.

- **4,775**: number of wins clocked by Nebraska owner, Marion H. Van Berg (1896-1971).

- **10,000**: winners bred by Kentucky based John E. Mudden (1856-1929).

- **15,000** gathered at Cambridge to see racehorse poisoner Daniel Dawson hanged in 1811.

- **54,813** was the record number of horses who contested 62,272 races in the States in 1973.

- **100,000**th recorded race run in Ireland was, according to *The Sweeney Guide to the Irish Turf*, The Clara Maiden Plate at Gowran Park on August 11, 1969, won by Strawberry Belle, trained by John Oxx.

BIBLIOGRAPHY

Adair, Garry, *Great Tales of Sport 1838-1864*, MW Publications (date unkown)

Ahern, Bill, *A Century of Winners,* Boolarong, 1982

Anonymous, *Horse Racing,* Saunders, Otley & Co, 1863

Beavis, Jim, *The Croydon Races,* Local History Publications, 1999

Black, Robert, *Horse Racing In France,* Sampson Low, 1899

Brazil, Alan with Parry, Mike, *There's An Awful Lot of Bubbly in Brazil,* Highdown, 2006

Brock, D W E, *The Racing Man's Week-End Book,* Seeley Service, 1949

Brown, Capt T H, *A History of the English Turf*, Virtue, 1931

Buckingham, John, *Tales From The Weighing Room,* Pelham, 1976

Cavanough, Maurice, *The Melbourne Cup,* Jack Pollard, 1976

Church, Michael, *The Derby Stakes; The Complete History 1780-2006*, Raceform, 2006

Clower, Michael, *Champion Charlie*, Mainstream 1997

Costello, John, Finnegan, Pat. *Tapestry of Turf,* Moa, 1988

Cox, Harding *Chasing And Racing,* The Bodley Head, 1922

D'Arcy, Fergus, *Horses, Lords and Racing Men,* The Turf Club, 1991

Davies, Grenville, *A Touch of Colwick*, Pride of Place, 1994

Fairfax-Blakeborough, J, *Northern Turf History, Vols 1,II,III,IV*, J A Allen

Fairfax-Blakeborough, J, *Paddock Personalities,* Hutchinson

Fairfax-Blakeborough, *Noel.J.F-B,* Allen, 1978

Fitzgerald, Arthur; Seth-Smith, Michael, *Prix de l'Arc de Triomphe 1920-48*, J A Allen, 1980

Fletcher, J S, *The History of the St Leger Stakes*, Hutchinson 1902

Francome, J, *Born Lucky,* Pelham, 1985

Frith, W G C, *The Royal Calcutta Turf Club,* RCTC 1976

Gale, Joan, *The Blaydon Races,* Oriel Press, 1970

Good, Meyrick & Betts, John, *Winners For 1946,* Good & Betts, 1946

Harewood, Lord and 'Many Authorities'. The Lonsdale Library : Flat Racing Seeley Service 1940

Hickle, David, *Gentlemen of the Australian Turf*, Angus and Robertson, 1986

Hodgman, George, *Sixty Years on the Turf,* Grant Richards, 1901

Huggins, Mike, *Flat Racing & British Society, 1790-1914*, Cass, 2000

Hollingsworth, Kent, *The Archjockey of Canterbury*, The Blood-Horse, 1986

Hotaling, Edward, *They're Off! Horse Racing at Saratoga,* Syracuse, 1995

Hunter, Avalyn, *American Classic Pedigrees 1914-2002*, Eclipse Press, 2003

Huxley, Dennis (Editor), *Millers Guide 2006/7*, Miller Form, 2006

Jaffee, Jean, *They Raced To Win,* Struik, 1980

Jarvis, Jack, *They're Off,* Michael Joseph, 1969

Knight, Henrietta, *Best Mate; Triple Gold,* Highdown, 2004

Krone, Julie; Richardson, Nancy Ann, *Riding For My Life*, Little, Brown, 1995

Lee, Alan *Cheltenham Racecourse*, Pelham Books, 1985

Logan, Guy B H, *The Classic Races of the Turf*, Stanley Paul 1928

Longrigg, Roger, *The History of Horseracing*, Macmillan 1972

Lucas, Pat, *Fifty Years of Racing at Chepstow*, H G Walters Ltd, 1976

McGuigan, John, *A Trainer's Memories,* Heath Cranton, 1946

Mortimer, Roger; Onslow, Richard; Willet, Peter, *Biographical Encyclopaedia of British Flat Racing,* MacDonald and Janes, 1978

Mortimer, Roger, *The Encyclopaedia of Flat Racing,* Hale, 1971

Mortimer, Roger, *The History of the Derby Stakes,* Michael Joseph, 1973

Nichols, Peter, *Guinness Sports Yearbook 1994,* Guinness, 1993

Noud, Keith, *Course for Horses,* Boolarong Publications 1989

Pegg, Norman, *Focus On Racing*, Robert Hale, 1963

Pierce, Peter, *From Go To Whoa*, Crossbow, 1994

Pitt, Chris & Hammond, Chas, *When Birmingham Went Racing*, C C Publishing, 2005

Prior C M, *The History of the Racing Calendar and Stud Book*, The Sporting Life 1926

Randall, David, *Great Sporting Eccentrics*, Guild Publishing 1985

Rees, Tom, *Racing Reminiscences,* Cwmnedd Press, date unknown, c1922

Rickaby, Fred, *Are Your Horses Trying?*, Allen 1967

Roberts, Michael; Tanner, Michael, *Champion's Story,* Headline, 1994

Rouge et Noir, *The Gambling World,* Hutchinson & Co, 1898

Ruckley, Harry, *Oswestry Racecourse*, Shropshire Books, c1985

Scott, Alexander, *Turf Memories of Sixty Years*, Hutchinson, undated – early 20thC

Smyly, Patricia, *Encyclopaedia of Steeplechasing,* Hale, 1979

Staff of Blood-Horse Publications, *Horse Racing's Top 100 Moments,* Blood-Horse Publications, 2006

Stokes, Penelope, *Free Rein – Racing in Berkshire and Beyond, 1700-1905,* Penelope Stokes 2005

Sweeney, Tony & Annie, *The Sweeney Guide to the Irish Turf, 1501-2001*, De Burca, 2002

Thompson, Phil, *On The Turf,* Quarry Publications, 1991

Thormanby, *Famous Racing Men*, James Hogg, 1882

Tomlinson, Jenny, *Born Winners Born Losers*, Reeve Books 1990

Tyrrel, John, *Running Racing*, Quiller Press 1997

Vamplew, Wray/Kay, Joyce, *Encyclopaedia of British Horseracing,* Routledge, 2005

Veeck, Bill; Linn, Ed, *Thirty Tons A Day,* Viking, 1972

Voight, Charles Adolph, *Famous Gentleman Riders at Home and Abroad,* Hutchinson & Co, 1925

Watson, S.J, *Between The Flags,* Allen Figgis & Co, 1969

Whyte, J C, *History of the British Turf,* Henry Colburn, 1840

Williams, Guy St John, Hyland, Francis P M, *Jameson Irish Grand National,* The Organisation, 1995

Young, Tony Brett, *Great Sporting Fiascos,* Robson, 1993